AUG 1 0 2019

NO LONGER PROPERTY OF
SEATTLE PUBLIC LIBRARY

D0579186

THE BUCKET LIST

PLACES TO FIND
PEACE & QUIET

First published in the United States of America in 2019 by
Universe Publishing, a division of
Rizzoli International Publications, Inc.
300 Park Avenue South
New York, NY 10010
www.rizzoliusa.com

Copyright © 2018 Quarto Publishing plc

All rights reserved. No part of this publication may be reproduced,
stored in a retrieval system, or transmitted in any form or by
any means, electronic, mechanical, photocopying, recording, or
otherwise, without prior consent of the publishers.

2019 2020 2021 2022 / 10 9 8 7 6 5 4 3 2 1

ISBN: 978-0-7893-3388-9
        978-0-7893-3683-5 (Barnes & Noble edition)

Library of Congress Control Number: 2018945510

The Bright Press, an imprint of the Quarto Group
The Old Brewery
6 Blundell Street
London N7 9BH
United Kingdom
T 00 44 20 7700 6700
www.QuartoKnows.com

Publisher: Mark Searle
Associate Publisher: Emma Bastow
Creative Director: James Evans
Managing Editors: Isheeta Mustafi and Jacqui Sayers
Senior Editor: Caroline Elliker
Project Editor: Cara Frost-Sharratt
Cover and Design: Ginny Zeal
Picture Research: Lauren Azor

Printed and bound in China

THE BUCKET LIST

PLACES TO FIND
PEACE & QUIET

VICTORIA WARD

Perito Moreno Glacier, Santa Cruz Province, Argentina

CONTENTS

The entry numbers 1–1,000 in this book are colored according to activity categories as listed below. Throughout the book you will also find entries shaded in yellow—these are rare, off-the-beaten track locations, aptly named "hidden gems."

COLOR KEY

 Urban oases

 Mind, body, soul

The great outdoors

Luxury layovers

INTRODUCTION

For most people, finding those necessary moments of quiet in an increasingly busy world is a struggle. The unwelcome cacophony of sound—from the invasive ringing of cell phones to the never-ending thrum of traffic—accumulates around us, polluting our peace and disturbing any opportunity to truly switch off.

In 2011, The World Health Organization (WHO) recognized that excessive noise can seriously harm human health, causing physical and psychological effects ranging from stress, poor concentration, loss of productivity, heart disease, and cognitive impairment, as well as delayed reading and comprehension in children. The report found that while other forms of pollution are decreasing, noise pollution is increasing.

Is it a surprise then, that more people are craving an escape to find peace and quiet?

Travel is the solution for many people seeking calm from the frantic world around them—it can balance the mind and soothe the soul. We all have different environments that lift our spirits: for some it might be climbing mountains to deeply inhale fresh air; for others, the rolling hills of the countryside bring pleasure to the soul.

Great swathes of wilderness cover the globe, offering places to rediscover isolation and silence, and learn about your own strength and resolve. The raw beauty of wild landscapes and the wide-open blanket of stars above remind you to embrace your time on this planet.

There are few people who don't feel the weight of modern living lift when they step into nature's embrace. Tight schedules, constant distractions, worrying news reports, the ever-increasing time spent on screens all put up barriers to our primal need to engage with the earth. Leaving the surroundings of concrete and steel for a walk in the woods or a trip to the ocean can impact positively on our health.

However, while a wide stretch of powder-soft sand is a standard dream destination for leaving worries behind, cities also hold secret spaces where the volume of the urban chaos can be turned right down. Secluded courtyards and hidden gardens invite reflection and the chance to unwind. Small museums tucked down unassuming alleys transport you to other worlds. Libraries and quiet bookstores offer nooks and sofas for you to while away the day.

Getting lost in an unfamiliar city, where you can find a bench set back from the street and watch the people passing by, gives you a chance to slow down and see the tranquility that exists in the spaces between skyscrapers and shopping streets: leafy green oases hidden in the haze of the concrete jungle, rooftop gardens, and quiet corners of city parks.

Quiet isn't only about silence. Quiet is also about that satisfying sense of stillness you notice within you when you feel at peace. This book aims to provide you with inspiration and suggestions for places to visit to bring a little more of that peace into your life. You may not always have these places completely to yourself, but choose the right time of day and the right season, and you'll likely be sharing them with others who also appreciate quiet places.

Luang Prabang, Laos

NORTH AMERICA

The landscapes and cities of North America defy description. In the western United States, wind along the clifftops of the Pacific Coast Highway, pass through towering canyons, and find the quietest corners of massive national parks. In the heartlands, visit eerie ghost towns on remote prairies. Near Seattle, seek out the red rock that marks the quietest place in the USA. Even in the city, you can find places for contemplation: on New York's High Line rise above the urban bustle below.

The opportunities for peace in Canada are as vast as the country itself. Head west for remote islands, lush rain forests, and historic settlements. To the east lie cliffs, waterfalls, and glacial fjords. In the expanse between, snow-covered slopes guard the silent, turquoise waters of more than 32,000 lakes.

Garden of the Gods, Colorado, see page 33

1 MOUNT FREMONT LOOKOUT

Mount Rainier National Park has countless trails leading to astonishing places. One of the most impressive is the 3-mi (5-km) hike to Mount Fremont Lookout, a two-story elevated cabin built in 1934 for wildfire watchmen. The trail starts at the Sunrise Visitor Center and heads west through subalpine meadow and then on to rockier terrain. Keep your eyes open for marmots and chipmunks as you climb. Mount Fremont Lookout itself is unlikely to be open—but at 4,226 ft (1,288 m) above sea level, the watchtower's wraparound balcony provides unparalleled 360-degree views of Mount Rainier National Park. Bring your binoculars to spy mountain goats and black bears in Grand Park, and listen for the bugling calls of bull elk in early Fall. On a clear day, you may even spot the Space Needle in Seattle. Head out on a weekday morning out of season, planning to arrive before sunrise. Afterward, if you've got some mileage left, the Shadow Lake trail is a loop that offers views of the mountain's eastern flanks and glaciers.

SAN JUAN ISLANDS, WASHINGTON

2 SAN JUAN ISLANDS

Take a ferry from the Washington State Ferry terminal and explore the islands by bicycle. The rocky shorelines and quaint villages draw artists from all over.

SEATTLE, WASHINGTON

3 OPHELIA'S BOOKS

As with all the best bookstores, Ophelia's Books is full of cozy nooks and crannies for hunkering down and letting the hours drift by. There's a comfortable atmosphere in this popular place. The floorboards creak underfoot, while the wooden shelves and patchwork of carpets give the place a homey feel. There's even a little cat who can often be found washing his paws atop a pile of ancient books. Just one block north of the Fremont Bridge, Ophelia's Books specializes in rare books and special editions, which makes it perfect for finding those out-of-print and one-of-a-kind treasures.

SEATTLE, WASHINGTON

4 WATERFALL GARDEN PARK

A largely unknown city park featuring a man-made 22-ft (7-m) waterfall, as well as tables and chairs for you to take a moment's pause during a hectic day.

Olympic National Park

OLYMPIC NATIONAL PARK, WASHINGTON

5 ONE SQUARE INCH OF SILENCE

Part of ongoing research into noise control, a small red stone in the heart of the Hoh Rain Forest marks "the quietest place in the United States."

SEATTLE, WASHINGTON

6 ESPRESSO VIVACE

Just like the main store on Capitol Hill, this branch of Espresso Vivace in South Lake Union has a "quiet room" so you can tuck yourself away.

SEATTLE, WASHINGTON

7 INN AT THE MARKET

Elegant boutique hotel in Seattle's heart. The rooftop terrace lets you watch the busy market below without being caught in the crowd.

PORTLAND, OREGON

8 **THE TAO OF TEA**

This two-story teahouse in the Tower of Cosmic Reflections, within the Lan Su Chinese Garden, pairs the beauty of the garden with the elegance of the Chinese tea ceremony. The Tao of Tea is run by a Portland-based company that promotes the art and culture of tea, focusing on organic brews.

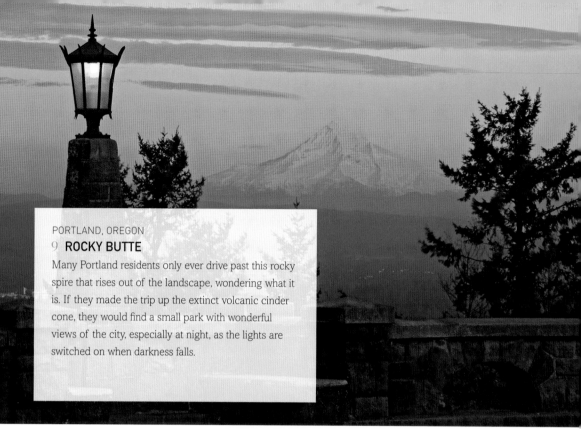

PORTLAND, OREGON
9 ROCKY BUTTE

Many Portland residents only ever drive past this rocky spire that rises out of the landscape, wondering what it is. If they made the trip up the extinct volcanic cinder cone, they would find a small park with wonderful views of the city, especially at night, as the lights are switched on when darkness falls.

PORTLAND, OREGON
10 SELLWOOD YOGA

A light-filled studio with yoga and mindfulness, including a candlelit yoga session of slow stretches to melt away tension.

PORTLAND, OREGON
11 NOBLE ROT

Enjoy citywide views from the fourth-floor restaurant, where the music is kept low and unobtrusive. Guests can also take a tour of the rooftop garden, where vegetables and herbs are grown and used to supply the restaurant's kitchen.

PORTLAND, OREGON
12 THE PORTLAND MUSEUM OF MODERN ART

The name references the large-scale art museums in cities around the world. There is a small exhibition space between a stairwell and the basement of an independent record company. This gallery is one woman's dream to showcase the art in her city.

BEND, OREGON
13 DUDLEY'S BOOKSHOP CAFÉ

Located in Downtown Bend, this cozy café has a new- and used-book selection to browse over coffee and cakes on the comfortable couch. Upstairs, a room can be reserved for more privacy or for book group discussions.

Goat Yoga

MONMOUTH, OREGON
14 GOAT YOGA

As the name suggests, Goat Yoga at Emerson Vineyards is yoga with goats added to the equation. As you stretch and flex, adorable, friendly goats wander freely around the group, enticing you to snuggle and pet them. The combination of being out in nature and bonding with animals—while also getting exercise—brings a sense of calm and joy.

DETROIT, OREGON
15 BREITENBUSH HOT SPRINGS

An off-the-grid health resort nestled in 154 acres (62 hectares) of ancient forest, built around a river in the foothills of the Cascade Range. The natural hot springs are channeled into stone-lined soaking ponds and tubs overlooking meadows and a flower garden, where guests at the wellness retreats can relax and soak up the tranquility.

CASCADE RANGE, OREGON
16 NORTH UMPQUA TRAIL

The North Umpqua mountain bike trail is an exhilarating 69-mi (111-km) ramble through the wilds of Oregon. It is a lonely, single-track trail that starts high on the Umpqua River, then plunges into deep forests of ferns, and along high mountain bluffs, with the mighty river constantly roaring below and the scent of fir trees heavy in the air; an adventure for all the senses.

RAINIER, OREGON
17 SLOTH CAPTIVE HUSBANDRY CENTER

If you want to learn about taking life slowly, why not make notes from the masters of the art? Sloths are famous for their laconic, leisurely pace. The center allows you to observe these creatures and learn about them in a captive environment aimed at conservation and education. Private visits can be arranged.

CASCADE LAKES, OREGON
18 MOONLIGHT CANOE TOUR

Wanderlust Tours canoe tours seek out the quiet of the shimmering waters of central Oregon's Cascades region by the light of the moon. Paddle beneath the blanket of stars on a clear sky, as your senses soak up the sights and sounds of the night and attune to the natural world around you. Afterward, return to shore for a welcome beer or hot chocolate.

Moonlight canoe tour

Mojave Desert

The Integratron

19 MOJAVE DESERT

Mojave is the driest desert in North America. Watch the wildflowers bloom from the Hole-in-the-Wall campground, or follow lava tubes into a subterranean world.

CALISTOGA, CALIFORNIA
20 CALISTOGA HOT SPRINGS SPA

Indulge in a traditional volcanic-ash mud bath. Invented by the indigenous Wappo people, it is a mix of the rich soil with warm spring waters.

MOJAVE DESERT, CALIFORNIA
21 DEATH VALLEY

Death Valley is North America's hottest spot. Don't miss the Titus Canyon drive, with its towering vertical walls rising 1,000 ft (305 m) above you.

LANDERS, CALIFORNIA
22 THE INTEGRATRON

Experience a singing-bowl "sound bath" inside a dome in the middle of the Mojave Desert. Described as "kindergarten naptime for grown ups."

AutoCamp

RUSSIAN RIVER, CALIFORNIA

23 AUTOCAMP

For retro cool in a rural setting, make a reservation in one of AutoCamp's modernized Airstream travel trailers. The Russian River site lies deep within a Californian redwood forest on a sleepy stretch of Sonoma's wine country. Here, you can get off the grid without roughing it: the trailers still feature the classic leather-and-walnut interior, with comfortable beds and walk-in showers—some even have baths. Take hikes in the misty redwoods by day, enjoy wine-tasting at the vineyards, and sample the harvest of coastal oysters in fall before toasting marshmallows in the communal fire pit.

ESCONDIDO, CALIFORNIA

24 GOLDEN DOOR

With instructions to leave your worries at the entrance, Golden Door offers a healing holiday 45 minutes north of San Diego that is medicine for your body, mind, and spirit. Choose from a range of spa experiences, as well as mindfulness and fitness classes.

25 ESALEN INSTITUTE

Steeped in the countercultural ethos of the 1960s, the Esalen Institute offers spiritual retreats, workshops, and digital detoxes with a side order of Californian Bohemianism. Fed by a natural hot spring, Esalen's famous thermal baths sit on a ledge above the North Pacific Ocean, overlooking the dramatic beauty of the coastline.

26 SINGLETHREAD FARM

Taste the seasonal bounty grown on SingleThread Farm at the destination restaurant in downtown Healdsburg. Five exclusive suites are available above the restaurant.

27 CARAVAN OUTPOST

If you plan a trip to the Bohemian city of Ojai, stay in a modernized Airstream caravan at the Caravan Outpost. As dusk sets in, step outside your trailer and recline on an oversized lounger to experience the valley's "Pink Moment," when the sky turns an incredible shade of pink, rose-tinting the city below.

28 LOST COAST

North California's "Lost Coast" is a 100-mi (161-km) stretch of sun-soaked coastline bypassed by the Pacific Coast Highway. There are few roads here, but plenty of trails to explore on foot with a backpack. Walk on wild beaches, spend the night in abandoned settlers' cabins, or hike out to the forgotten Punta Gorda Lighthouse.

Nepenthe

BIG SUR, CALIFORNIA
29 NEPENTHE

Perched high above the wild Pacific, the terrace at Nepenthe restaurant enjoys breathtaking views of the rugged stretch of Californian coastline that is known as Big Sur.

BODIE HILLS, CALIFORNIA
30 BODIE

Time stands still in this Californian ghost town. It is eerily frozen in a state of arrested decay after it was abandoned following the gold rush in the nineteenth century.

SAN FRANCISCO, CALIFORNIA
31 THE BATTERY

Exposed brickwork and hardwood floors are softened with luxurious rugs, original art, and vintage furniture at The Battery in the financial district. The courtyard deluxe room overlooks the garden, focusing your mind away from the hustle of the city on the other side of the wall. Guests have access to the private members' club.

SAN FRANCISCO, CALIFORNIA
32 HUA ZANG SI TEMPLE

Hua Zang Si is a nondenominational Buddhist temple. Inside the old Gothic church, fitted with Chinese doors, you can make an offering and receive a blessing before admiring the temple's holy treasures. The backyard is an oasis with a magnolia tree that is said to have once rained nectar for three days.

SAN FRANCISCO, CALIFORNIA
33 SAMOVAR TEA LOUNGE

This tea lounge is in Yerba Buena Gardens, a public park occupying two city blocks. Enjoy the selection of organic, single-origin teas from all over the world while learning about tea and food pairings. The clean architectural lines and large windows overlooking the gardens create a light and uncluttered ambience.

SAN FRANCISCO, CALIFORNIA
34 BARBRO OSHER SCULPTURE GARDEN

The highlight is James Turrell's *Three Gems* sculpture. Leafy foliage leads to a short tunnel that opens into a space carved out of a hill. Inside a black basalt dome, you view the sky through an oculus cut into the roof, as LED alter the experience. There is an entrance fee but you can see sculptures for free from the café.

SAN FRANCISCO, CALIFORNIA
35 HAUS COFFEE

Haus Coffee is a large, wood-paneled space that is popular with people looking for a quiet place to work or read. On a cold day, head directly for the black leather sofa by the fireplace; when it's warmer, head to a patio out back to catch some sunshine. The café also features rotating exhibitions by local artists so there's always something new to look at.

HIDDEN GEM

SAN FRANCISCO, CALIFORNIA
36 SAN FRANCISCO HISTORY CENTER

Hidden on the sixth floor of the city's main public library, the history center houses a treasure haul of books, photos, art, and ephemera from San Francisco's archives. Entrance is free: dig around and you will find event flyers, restaurant menus, and police records. It is a fascinating record of the lives of the citizens who give the city its character.

Yerba Buena Gardens, home of Samovar Tea Lounge

HIDDEN GEM
ACTON, CALIFORNIA
37 WOLF CONNECTION

For the indigenous Native American tribes who once lived on the land where Los Angeles now stands, wolves are a symbol of courage, strength, and loyalty. Wolf Connection is a wolf sanctuary in the Angeles National Forest that uses these qualities—plus the presence and natural balance of these deeply intuitive animals—to provide therapy and wellness programs. Visitors are taught the art of natural, peaceful, and healthful living alongside the science of human development. Wolf Connection offers monthly hikes with the wolves, overnight camps, and healing workshops with yoga and singing bowls.

LOS ANGELES, CALIFORNIA
38 VENICE CANAL HISTORIC DISTRICT

Walk across arching pedestrian bridges and admire the charming houses that are hidden within the beachside neighborhood that is known for its artistic and Bohemian spirit.

LOS ANGELES, CALIFORNIA
39 BRICKS AND SCONES

Family-run coffee shop with a no-talking rule. Settle at the corner desk by the window for a great street view while you work.

LOS ANGELES, CALIFORNIA
40 SELF-REALIZATION LAKE SHRINE

Lakeside gardens for meditation, reflection, and relaxation. Silence your phone, leave behind loud conversations, and bask in the peace and quiet.

LAS VEGAS, NEVADA
41 AKHOB

Hidden in the back of a luxury handbag store is the unexpected art installation *Akhob*, where visitors are silently bathed in color-changing light.

LAS VEGAS, NEVADA
42 HOTEL 32

Secret boutique residence at the top floor of the Monte Carlo Hotel, with views of the Strip and where guests are appointed personal concierges.

LAGUNA BEACH, CALIFORNIA
43 **THE PEARL LAGUNA**
Calming well-being retreat
focusing on yoga and nature,
nestled among the trees in
Laguna Canyon and just minutes
from idyllic Laguna Beach.

Brush Creek Ranch

GRANGEVILLE, IDAHO

+4 FRANK CHURCH– RIVER OF NO RETURN WILDERNESS

With almost 2.4 million acres (9.7 million hectares), the largest national forest wilderness in the United States, outside Alaska, has plenty of places to get lost. Discover rugged mountains, canyons, and whitewater rivers. No cars are allowed so pack well and prepare to be self-sufficient.

TWIN BRIDGES, MONTANA

+5 J BAR L

Stay on a solar-powered working cattle ranch in the remote Centennial Valley for a rustic-luxe adventure. Nature-loving travelers stay in restored homesteads and fishing cabins in the stillness of Big Sky country. Birdwatch, hike, and fish, but don't miss experiencing the peace of riding across the impossibly quiet prairie at night.

JOCKO VALLEY, MONTANA

+6 GARDEN OF ONE THOUSAND BUDDHAS

Nestled in a remote valley, the purpose of this Buddhist park is to counter global negativity. The garden contains 1,000 hand-cast Buddha statues set out in a design based on the eight-spoked dharma wheel, symbolizing the awakening of wisdom. People of all faiths cultivate inner peace.

SARATOGA, WYOMING

+7 THE LODGE & SPA AT BRUSH CREEK RANCH

A luxury Western resort featuring yurts and log cabin-suites set on 30,000 acres (12,000 hectares) in the Sierra Madre range. The resort was inspired by the region's history, so expect cowhide chairs, fur throws on king-size beds, and antler chandeliers above comfy leather couches. Step out, and the landscape is awe-inspiring.

YELLOWSTONE, WYOMING

+8 YELLOWSTONE NATIONAL PARK

Head to the less visited southwest corner of Yellowstone for pristine meadows, forests, and sparkling waterfalls that are unseen by most visitors. Pick up the trail at the Bechler Ranger Station and head to Distant Cascade Corner for the greatest concentration of waterfalls. You will have to head off the main trail, but the reward is worth it.

HIDDEN GEM

JOHNSON COUNTY, WYOMING

+9 HOLE-IN-THE-WALL

Hike into the wilds of Wyoming to the remote mountain hideout of Wild West train robbers, horse thieves, and cattle rustlers who include Jesse James and Butch Cassidy and the Sundance Kid. The hidden pass high in the canyons was the perfect place to look out for approaching lawmen while the outlaws pastured their rustled cattle in the fertile valley.

SOLITUDE, UTAH

50 THE YURT AT SOLITUDE MOUNTAIN RESORT

Follow your guide on a snowshoe adventure through a moon- and lantern-lit forest to an intimate dining experience in a traditional Mongolian yurt.

SALT LAKE CITY, UTAH

51 RUTH'S DINER

A converted historic railcar diner off the beaten track, with sweeping canyon views from the outdoor patio. This eatery is famous for its hearty breakfasts.

SALT LAKE CITY, UTAH

52 THE KURA DOOR

Japanese holistic spa drawing on ancient Eastern philosophies. Try the rejuvenating Japanese Ofuro Bath—a ritual treatment with detoxifying bath salts.

HIDDEN GEM

SALT LAKE CITY, UTAH

53 ENSIGN PEAK

This little park is the perfect place from which to view Salt Lake City. Take a picnic and watch the sun gently sink below the horizon.

Solitude Mountain Resort

Amangiri

CANYON POINT, UTAH
54 AMANGIRI

The sleek sandstone hideaway emerges organically out of the wild, wind-carved landscape of southern Utah. The heart of the desert, amid the mesas and canyons, might not be the place you would expect to find a sleek and stylish luxury hotel; however, Amangiri offers everything that you need for a fully pampered retreat. The James Bond–style swimming pool is lined with inviting white daybeds beneath shady parasols, or you can dip into the bubbling Jacuzzi beneath the starry night sky. The Amangiri draws on local Navajo healing traditions in its treatment menu.

SALT LAKE CITY, UTAH
55 THE GARDEN RESTAURANT

Enjoy spectacular views of Temple Square from the tenth-floor Garden Restaurant. A peaceful space with trailing greenery, Corinthian columns, and a retractable glass roof.

CANYONLANDS NATIONAL PARK, UTAH

56 THE MAZE

In the heart of Utah's high desert, Canyonlands
National Park covers almost 340,000 acres
(138,000 hectares). The Maze is one of the park's
least accessible districts, with difficult roads,
dead-end canyons, and virtually no marked trails.
Hiking requires self-sufficiency and preparation as
you'd be five hours from the ranger station.

SUNDANCE, UTAH
57 SUNDANCE MOUNTAIN RESORT

Actor and director Robert Redford's Sundance resort is a protected wilderness at the base of Mount Timpanogos. Stay in a rustic but comfortably furnished cottage tucked quietly and peacefully into the mountain for a period of pure escapism. Just five minutes from the resort is one of the world's premier trout fisheries: the Provo River offers year-round world-class fly-fishing.

SAN JUAN COUNTY, UTAH
58 MONUMENT VALLEY

Monument Valley's giant mesas and buttes were made famous by John Ford's western movies. For the Navajo people who live there, the land is considered to be the heart of the earth. Navajo Spirit Tours are led by local guides who grew up in the valley and understand the sacred rock formations and the meaning of each one.

BRIGHAM CITY, UTAH
59 BEAR RIVER MIGRATORY BIRD REFUGE

A wetland oasis for wildlife in northern Utah, where Bear River flows into the northeast arm of the Great Salt Lake. The whole area is a haven for waterbirds and wildlife, which are protected by the refuge here. A 12-mi (19-km) driving route offers excellent opportunities to observe the natural life, and there are plenty of places to pull up along the way for photos or contemplation.

LAKE POWELL, UTAH
60 HOT AIR BALLOON OVER LAKE POWELL

With 2,000 mi (3,219 km) of shoreline, Lake Powell in Utah is the second-largest man-made lake in America. See it at its best on a sunrise hot-air balloon flight, when the emerging sun sets the red rock cliffs, sandstone mesas, and rose-colored sandy beaches on fire, their reflections glowing a vibrant red in the perfectly still water.

The Brown Palace Hotel and Spa

DENVER, COLORADO
61 THE BROWN PALACE HOTEL AND SPA

The gorgeous Italian Renaissance atrium is the heart of The Brown and the perfect place to take afternoon tea. Accompanied by the gentle sound of a harp, you can admire the way the stained-glass ceiling—eight stories up—drapes its shimmery light over the Florentine arches and gold-filigreed balcony panels.

DENVER, COLORADO
62 THE ART

From the dazzling light installation at the entrance to the original works in every room, the art throughout this luxury boutique hotel has been curated to the highest standard. The fourth-floor terrace features a designer fire pit, while artists, including Tracey Emin and Ed Ruscha, have created site-specific pieces that can be found throughout the hotel.

DENVER, COLORADO
63 LITTLE OWL COFFEE

Small design-led café in the historic lower downtown district. White walls and soft wooden accents are flooded with light from floor-to-ceiling windows.

DENVER, COLORADO
64 ASPEN SHAKTI

Start your morning with a gondola ride up Aspen mountain to the sundeck for a mountaintop yoga class to rejuvenate body and soul.

GARDEN OF THE GODS NATIONAL PARK, COLORADO
65 GARDEN OF THE GODS
Hike the trails around dramatic 30-ft (91-m) towering sandstone rock formations set against a backdrop of snowcapped peaks and brilliant blue skies. You can learn about the geology of the region and the park's historic importance in Native American history in the visitors' center, or enjoy postcard-perfect views from the glass-enclosed café.

IDAHO SPRINGS, COLORADO
66 INDIAN HOT SPRINGS
Under a translucent dome, and draped in greenery, these indoor hot springs have private caves that are fed by natural hot spring water up to 104°F (40°C).

Garden of the Gods

Dunton Hot Springs

COLORADO ROCKIES, COLORADO

67 DUNTON HOT SPRINGS RESORT

A two-hour scenic trip through the mountains from Telluride airport brings you deep in the Colorado Rockies. This former ghost town has been restored and converted into a romantic getaway. The exquisitely furnished log cabins sit in a valley with a river flowing through it. Stay in the Well House, or Bjoerkmans for a view of the waterfall.

HINSDALE COUNTY, COLORADO

68 OLD CARSON GHOST TOWN

Promises of riches brought many to Colorado in the late 1800s, hoping to make their fortune by mining gold. Many of the towns that sprung up around the landscape were soon abandoned, fading into ghost towns. Old Carson's remote setting means it's not easy for tourists to find, helping the buildings maintain a good condition.

CUSTER COUNTY, COLORADO
69 WET MOUNTAIN VALLEY

The unspoiled valley nestled between the Sangre de Cristo and Wet Mountains seems stuck in a time warp. It is a landscape littered with the remains of old homesteads, barns, and one-room schoolhouses set against a backdrop of snowcapped mountain ranges towering over rolling plains. Stay on a family ranch and revel in the beauty and solitude of the great outdoors.

ROUTT COUNTY, COLORADO
70 STRAWBERRY PARK THERMAL POOLS

Take a midnight dip in the naturally warm mineral waters and ease your muscles while a spectacular star show takes place above you. The therapeutic thermal pools sit in a rustic mountain setting that is draped in snow in winter and perfect for swimming in summer. If you are feeling brave, you can plunge into the freezing river nearby beforehand, for a natural spa experience.

MANITOU SPRINGS, COLORADO
71 PIKES PEAK COG RAILWAY

Rise above it all on a 9-mi (14-km) trip in a historic train to the 14,000-ft (4,267-m) summit of Pikes Peak. The world's highest cog railway climbs slowly through forests of aspen and pine, and past cascading streams, to the incredible panoramas— and a welcome donut stand—at the top. Avoid peak times for the most peaceful trip up.

TELLURIDE, COLORADO
72 BRIDAL VEIL FALLS

Tucked away in the northern reaches of the Rocky Mountain National Park is the tallest free-falling waterfall in Colorado. Bike to the base of the falls and cool down in the mist before carrying on up to where a privately owned, historic power plant sits atop the falls. This is the gateway to the wildflower meadows and forests of the Bridal Veil basin.

73 DESERT BOTANICAL GARDEN

This 140-acre (57-hectare) garden celebrates
the Arizona desert's natural beauty, from the
towering cacti and brilliant wildflowers, to
strangely shaped succulents and unexpectedly
lush trees.

SEDONA, ARIZONA

74 MII AMO

This luxury spa's name means "One's Path" in the Yuman language. Choose a three-, four-, or seven-night "journey" based on Native American traditions.

PHOENIX, ARIZONA

75 SONGBIRD COFFEE & TEA HOUSE

Settle down in the porch swing when they open at 7a.m., or steal the couch in the quieter back room for some serious solitude.

YUMA, ARIZONA

76 THE WAYSIDE CHAPEL

The sign beside the dirt road invites passersby to "Pause, Rest, Worship." Follow the road into the crop field, and you'll come across one of the smallest churches in the United States.

GRAND CANYON, ARIZONA

77 YOGA ON THE EDGE

Take a sunset or sunrise class and gently stretch your body and awareness before the sweeping views of the Grand Canyon.

CHANDLER, ARIZONA

78 VIBETALITY

In the Germann Towne Center shopping mall you'll find this beautiful ecocenter for yoga practice, with a flotation tank therapy suite. Dark wood floors are paired with overflowing plant life to create a lush and soothing ambience.

Yoga on the Edge

79 TOWN OF SEDONA

Sedona has long attracted spiritual seekers who believe the area is full of vortexes that channel Earth's energetic power; a place where you can tap into the frequencies of the universe. It is considered to be North America's New Age capital, and so the town has more than its fair share of crystal shops, aura-reading psychics, and spiritual classes catering to the market. The real beauty of the place, however, lies outside of town, where the striking, rust-colored sandstone formations and soaring blue skies induce awe and inspire even the most skeptical of individuals.

Santa Fe City

SANTA FE, NEW MEXICO
80 SANTA FE CITY

Known as the "City Different," Santa Fe is rich in history, with Hispanic, Anglo, and Native American influences apparent in the architecture, food, and art. The city is a center for arts, where you can wander along centuries-old, shady lanes to the plaza, to peruse silver and turquoise designs of Native American jewelers.

SANTA FE, NEW MEXICO
81 RANCHO ALEGRE

Rancho Alegre is an extraordinary private home in the New Mexico desert that is available to rent. It was built in the adobe style at the beginning of the twenty-first century, with brown, mud-brick walls and high wood-and-stone ceilings. Inside is like a modern museum of priceless Native American and traditional cowboy treasures.

TAOS, NEW MEXICO
82 BLUE SKY RETREAT

Take one of Blue Sky Retreat's three-day silent programs in Taos. Built over a nineteenth-century farmhouse in the Carson National Forest, the center focuses on yoga, mindfulness, and meditation. It is a place to unwind and switch off, enjoying the peace and tranquility of the historic property and its surroundings.

ALBUQUERQUE, NEW MEXICO
83 SAN FELIPE DE NERI CHURCH

Built in 1793, the adobe church on the Old Town plaza is one of the city's oldest surviving buildings. It was constructed in the traditional colonial style, with Spanish overtones and eighteenth- and nineteenth-century decorative elements, including a wood-paneled interior, metal ceiling, and walls painted to resemble marble.

HIDDEN GEM

SANTA FE, NEW MEXICO
84 RA PAULETTE'S HAND-CARVED CAVES

New Mexico artist Ra Paulette carves subterranean sandstone caves into wonderlands of intricate detail, using only his hands and basic tools. Each cave is different, with fantastical elements and abstract designs. The Windows of the Earth cave is accessible on a tour and includes a twenty-minute singing bowls "sacred sound bath."

RIO ARRIBA COUNTY, NEW MEXICO
85 GHOST RANCH

The artist Georgia O'Keefe fell in love with Ghost Ranch the moment she saw it, and promptly bought it. She was attracted to the area close to Alburquerque by the sunlight, wide skies, and beautiful desert landscape, which inspired her art. Now, Ghost Ranch is part of a retreat center, including workshops that teach in O'Keefe's style.

SAN ANTONIO, TEXAS
86 HOTEL EMMA

San Antonio's eclectic Hotel Emma is built within the brick shell of a large nineteenth-century brewhouse. The giant cast-iron tanks and steel machinery are still on display inside. The rooms are modern with high ceilings and soft textiles, and the large and lush bathrooms have roomy rain showers. The Emma is a sophisticated urban retreat.

AUSTIN, TEXAS
87 ELIZABETH STREET CAFÉ

A local favorite, this Vietnamese café and French bakery offers guests the choice of a shady patio or sunny dining rooms. Behind the tall windows is a mix of French antiques, teahouse wallpaper, and Vietnamese and local art. Tucked off the main street, it is a popular spot in the evenings, so arrive early for coffee.

AUSTIN, TEXAS
88 HARRY RANSOM CENTER

Few visitors to the Harry Ransom Center head upstairs to the reading room, where treasures await, including copies of Shakespeare's First Folio.

Hotel Emma

Bat watching

AUSTIN, TEXAS
89 BAT WATCHING

At dusk, 1.5 million bats emerge from the Congress Avenue Bridge to blanket the sky. It's a spectacular sight that is best seen from a kayak.

AUSTIN, TEXAS
91 TRAVAASA TEXAS

Healing spa treatments and wellness workshops in a Zen-like setting. City slickers can take part in the on-site farming program to learn how to connect with nature.

AUSTIN, TEXAS
90 HOTEL SAN JOSÉ

Stylish understatement mixes with chilled-out charm at this mellow hangout off the main strip. Once a 1930s motel, the San José is a modernist affair featuring retro bungalows situated around a leafy courtyard and stylish rectangular pool. The quietest rooms are the Grand Suites at the back of the hotel near the garden.

MARFA, TEXAS
92 MARFA

Positioned in the high plains of the Chihuahuan Desert, one hour north of the Mexican border, the small town of Marfa is truly remote. It is also home to the baffling Marfa Lights, which have a dedicated viewing area outside town. The mysterious red, white, and blue lights that appear in the sky are said by some to be a paranormal phenomenon.

VARIOUS LOCATIONS, TEXAS
93 BLUEBONNET SEASON

The Texas Bluebonnet is the official flower of the Lone Star State. After winter rains, these pretty wildflowers come out in full force. They are best viewed on the scenic drive on the Willow City Loop, a narrow ranch road winding thirteen miles through some of the oldest and most unique geology in central Texas.

BIG BEND NATIONAL PARK, TEXAS
94 BIG BEND NATIONAL PARK

The night skies in Big Bend are as dark as coal. Beneath them, the sense of isolation is immense. One of the park's treasures is Gorman Falls. The climb down is challenging and the rocks smooth and slippery, but there are ropes to help. At the bottom, simply sit and enjoy the cascading water.

SHUBERT, NEBRASKA
95 INDIAN CAVE STATE PARK

Tucked along the Missouri River, on the eastern edge of Nebraska, Indian Cave State Park is a pristine area of wilderness just far enough off the beaten path to keep foot traffic low. A road winds through the entire park with places to stop, providing access to the scenery without the hike.

Lake Metigoshe State Park

BOTTINEAU, NORTH DAKOTA

96 LAKE METIGOSHE STATE PARK

The Chippewa people named the lake Metigoshe "Washegum," meaning "clear water lake surrounded by oaks." It is an idyllic spot nestled in the Turtle Mountains amid rolling hills and aspen forests. Those used to North Dakota's expansive prairie vistas will be surprised to find that woodlands and wetlands cover most of the park.

Berry Sweet Orchards

Louisiana Bayou

ETHEL, LOUISIANA
97 BERRY SWEET ORCHARDS
Pick your own blueberries in the beautiful Louisiana countryside at the state's first fully certified organic orchard, with over 1,500 blueberry bushes of different varieties.

MOREHOUSE, LOUISIANA
98 BASTROP
Rent a canoe from Bastrop in the north of Louisiana and take a leisurely paddle down a swampy bayou to explore the thriving paradise of cypress trees and wealth of Louisiana wildlife that inhabits the area.

DULUTH, MINNESOTA
99 BOUNDARY WATERS
The peaceful lakes and forests of Boundary Waters take you back to a time when nature was in charge. There are no roads and no towns in the area—just endless wilderness.

MINNEAPOLIS, MINNESOTA
100 ORFIELD LABORATORIES
The anechoic chamber at Orfield Laboratories absorbs 99.99 percent of sound, creating a silence so intense that visitors can start to see and hear hallucinations. Reservations must be made two weeks in advance.

DARROW, LOUISIANA
101 THE INN AT HOUMAS HOUSE
Experience famous Southern hospitality at this converted sugar plantation that features historic cottages that are surrounded by ancient oaks and lush gardens.

102 ATCHAFALAYA BASIN HOUSEBOAT

Covering more than 1 million acres (400,000 hectares), the Atchafalaya Basin is the largest swamp in the United States. Boaters have been exploring these wetlands that teem with far-flung bayous for hundreds of years. Enjoy the basin from the air-conditioned comfort of your own Louisiana houseboat, where you can sit on the porch overlooking the waters, as the swamp comes alive around you. These floating cabins have all the trappings of a rustic home and can be towed out to secluded spots where you can explore at your own pace—just keep an eye out for alligators.

NEW ORLEANS, LOUISIANA
103 GARDEN DISTRICT

The historic Garden District is a place of opulence and beauty, with well-preserved antebellum mansions, enchanting gardens, and oodles of Southern charm. A trip on the oldest continually operating streetcar in the world, the St. Charles Streetcar, will show you the main sights of this elegant area with a dash of added romance.

NEW ORLEANS, LOUISIANA
104 SONIAT HOUSE

A trio of typical Creole town houses at the quiet end of Chartres Street make up Soniat House. Each room has been furnished with art and antiques collected by the owners on trips abroad. The rocking chair on the private balcony of room twenty-eight is a restful spot to watch the chilled-out street scene below.

NEW ORLEANS, LOUISIANA
105 LAFAYETTE CEMETERY NO.1

Lafayette Cemetery No.1 has been immortalized in film, literature, and photography, and is a popular destination for visitors to the city. Lush greenery shades the pathways through the Gothic tombs and crypts. It is a little run-down, but that just adds to the unusual atmosphere in this part of the city.

NEW ORLEANS, LOUISIANA
106 CAFÉ BEIGNET NEW ORLEANS

The perfect time to enjoy the busy French Quarter is early in the morning, as sunlight gilds the plants spilling from the balconies above. Do as the locals do, and head to this well-known café to relax outdoors with a coffee and a beignet—a French-style square donut that is typically enjoyed here for breakfast.

HIDDEN GEM
NEW ORLEANS, LOUISIANA
107 SINGING OAK

Perched in the heart of the City Park, a giant oak provides shade from the sultry Louisiana summer heat. Take a seat on a bench under its expansive branches, and you will hear the enchanting symphony of wind chimes coming from above, placed there by local artist Jim Hart. It is an unexpected delight.

CHICAGO, ILLINOIS
108 GARFIELD PARK CONSERVATORY

Thousands of lush plant species are on display in this stunning conservatory, which occupies approximately two acres. In the tropical temperature beneath the glass exterior, you can truly escape the concrete jungle of Chicago and get back to nature, taking in the striking shades of green and exotic flowers of nature's art gallery.

CHICAGO, ILLINOIS
109 ART INSTITUTE OF CHICAGO

Truman Capote collected paperweights, calling them "some fragment of a dream." Chicago real-estate developer Arthur Rubloff agreed and, over his lifetime, collected almost 1,500 pieces, most of which he donated to the Art Institute. The mesmerizing patterns and beautiful colors make a pleasant diversion from the buzz of the city.

MISSISSIPPI RIVER, MISSISSIPPI

110 STEAMBOAT CRUISE

Travel up the Mississippi River in style on an iconic high-class steamboat. Glide past elegant antebellum plantations and ancient oak trees to the storybook landscapes that inspired author Mark Twain. Staterooms on the American Queen Steamboat Company's boats are opulent, and the decks ideal for lazily watching the river go by.

CHETEK, WISCONSIN

111 CANOE BAY

Cozy cottages sit in the middle of a forest on the edge of a cluster of lakes. Reserve the Rattenbury Cottage and enjoy the dramatic lake view from the cantilevered private deck or curl up in a well-worn leather chair by the fire with a book from the library. Canoe Bay is tailored toward couples.

CHICAGO, ILLINOIS

112 JOE AND RIKA MANSUETO LIBRARY

On first sight, there's something that seems rather essential missing at this Chicago library: books. Beneath the soaring elliptical glass ceiling, the 180-seat Grand Reading Room is part of a modern concept in book borrowing. All the books are stored underground and retrieved using an automated request system and robotic cranes, and you can enjoy sitting in peace beneath the vast glass-domed ceiling while you wait for delivery.

Joe and Rika Mansueto Library

113 NEVERSINK PIT

Experienced climbers have the advantage of being able to descend the staggering sixteen-story drop from the leafy surface to the stark bottom of this geological marvel in Jackson County, Alabama.

Lush ferns drip down the ledges at the entrance in spring, and ribbony waterfalls accompany you on the way down as you pass rare flora clinging to the limestone shelves. These are sensitive and endangered ecosystems that people are prohibited to touch. On a summer's night, the bioluminescent fungi *Armillaria mellea* decorate the depths and are easily mistaken for the enchanting luminosity of glowworms. The limestone sinkhole of Neversink Pit is 40 ft (23 m) wide at the top, opening out to a cave floor that spans more than double that area.

If you descend, take a moment at the bottom to enjoy the feeling of being in the very bowels of the earth. At 162 ft (49 m) above you, the sky seems a long way away. Venturing this deep underground, you feel like an explorer discovering something that few humans have seen before. Your only company down here is a colony of bats.

The Southeastern Cave Conservancy bought the sinkhole in the 1990s to preserve it for future generations. The group maintains the pit and has established two permanent rig areas at the mouth of the site, to discourage the use of trees to rig climbing ropes. While rappelling to the cave floor is the most incredible way of experiencing Neversink Pit, even for those without the climbing permit, it is still a unique place to visit. From the pit hole, shafts of daylight illuminate the drop, and you can see all the way to the bottom.

The region is well known for its scenic beauty and outdoor recreation, but many may not be aware of the hidden natural world that lies beneath the surface. The dissolving of layers of porous limestone belowground has been fundamental in the formation of the landscape in northern Alabama. Areas are marked by sinking streams, subterranean drainage, large springs, caves, and sinkholes like Neversink Pit. Along with adjacent states suffering the same issues, the area has become the caving capital of the country, with Jackson County having the most in the state. Neversink Pit is accessible via a fairly strenuous thirty-minute hike from a small parking area on an unnamed road.

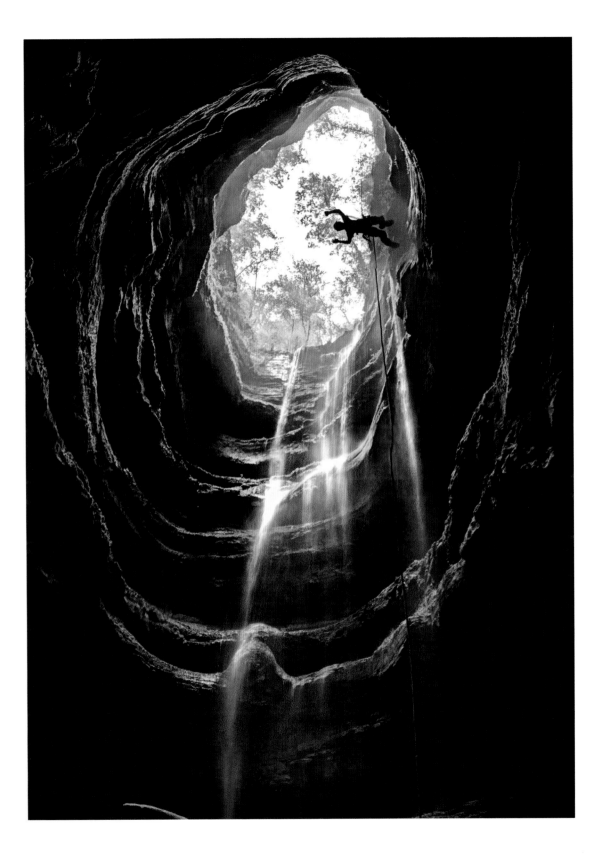

Rose Main Reading Room

NEW YORK CITY, NEW YORK
114 ROSE MAIN READING ROOM

The century-old Rose Main Reading Room in the New York Public Library is one of the city's most iconic locations. Light streams through the casement windows, illuminating the rows of weathered, dark wood tables and brass lamps where many well-known poets and authors have bent their heads to work.

NEW YORK CITY, NEW YORK
115 GROUNDED

A relaxed coffee shop on a quiet block with retro couches, wooden benches, and a well-stocked bookshelf; plenty of seating for quiet reflection.

NEW YORK CITY, NEW YORK
116 THE UNITED NATIONS MEDITATION ROOM

This is a room in the UN Headquarters dedicated to "silence in the outward sense and stillness in the inner sense."

NEW YORK CITY, NEW YORK
117 1 HOTEL BROOKLYN BRIDGE

The 1 Hotel overflows with reclaimed materials and naturally sourced furnishings. The industrial-chic styling is softened by indoor greenery, the natural palette giving the rooms a refreshingly calming vibe and sense of space. The highlight here is the tenth-floor plunge pool, with sweeping views looking out over the East River.

NEW YORK CITY, NEW YORK
118 NOGUCHI MUSEUM

In a former photoengraving plant in Queens, a light-filled space has been transformed into a celebration of artist Isamu Noguchi, who designed it to be an oasis amid the industrial setting.

HIDDEN GEM
NEW YORK CITY, NEW YORK
119 ELEVATED ACRE

A secluded one-acre meadow flanked by gardens above the bustling streets of the financial district. This space is little known, even by locals.

Noguchi Museum

Housing Works Bookstore Café

NEW YORK CITY, NEW YORK

120 NEW YORK SOCIETY LIBRARY

Head to the oldest library in New York City for a literary time-out from urban life. The first-floor reading room and exhibitions are open to the public, while members can check out books as well. The library is much loved and well used by writers, students, readers, and homeworkers, but the quiet ambience is respected by all.

NEW YORK CITY, NEW YORK

121 THE MET CLOISTERS

Four cloisters excavated from abbeys and monasteries in France and rebuilt in New York in the 1930s form the core of this museum specializing in European medieval architecture. The Cuxa Cloister and Garden is at the heart of the museum, its rose-pink marble columns supporting the shady walkway around the central fountain.

NEW YORK CITY, NEW YORK
122 HOUSING WORKS BOOKSTORE CAFÉ

There's an old-time elegance to this stylish bookstore, with its mahogany-paneled walls and the spiral staircase to the second floor. There are plenty of tables and seats for lingering, so you can take a break from the noise and business of downtown Manhattan. The place is entirely staffed by volunteers, and all profits go to charity.

HIDDEN GEM

NEW YORK CITY, NEW YORK
123 THE FRICK COLLECTION

The opulent eighteenth-century French-style mansion that was the home of steel magnate Henry Frick is open to the public to view his impressive art collection. It is small and seldom crowded, and you can get up close to the artworks here, or enjoy the peace and tranquility of the interior court and reflecting pool.

NEW YORK CITY, NEW YORK
124 SHIBUI SPA

Shibui's philosophy is one of balance between traditional and modern, nature and the city. Tucked away in the basement of Robert De Niro's The Greenwich Hotel, you'll be served hibiscus tea beside the lantern-lit swimming pool before being shown to a soaking bath scented with cherry blossom rice powder to melt away any tension.

NEW WINDSOR, NEW YORK
125 STORM KING ART CENTER

Large installations dominate the Storm King Art Center—an outdoor sculpture garden and art gallery an hour outside the city, in New Windsor. Set against a serene mountain backdrop, the sculptures seamlessly weave themselves into the rolling landscape, demonstrating the Storm King's philosophy of integrating art and nature.

NEW YORK CITY, NEW YORK

126 CONSERVATORY GARDEN

Central Park is a place to let the pressures of metropolitan demands loosen and unwind. At 843 acres it satisfies the needs of 1.65 million Manhattan Islanders to be near something living, growing, and green. At the northern end of the park, at 5th Avenue and 105th Street, lies the little-known Conservatory Garden, the only formal garden in Central Park. Six runner- and cyclist-free acres of beautiful seasonal plantings form three distinct areas. The French-style North Garden features a bronze casting of Walter Schott's *Three Dancing Maidens*. The Italianate central garden is bordered by walkways lined with fragrant crabapple trees. The real gem, however, is the South Garden. Inspired by Frances Hodgson Burnett's novel *The Secret Garden*, it is a feast of informally planted heirloom roses and peridot green grasses.

Wave Hill

NEW YORK CITY, NEW YORK
127 THE HIGH LINE

A disused elevated railway line, high above the city, has been repurposed into an urban oasis featuring wildflowers, greenery, and outdoor art—as well as some of the best views of Manhattan. Chelsea Thicket is an ideal resting spot, with a lawn and banks of seats.

HIDDEN GEM
NEW YORK CITY, NEW YORK
128 WAVE HILL

This city-owned garden in the Bronx has a different feel from New York's other botanical gardens. It is less manicured and more down-to-earth, featuring abundant wildflowers and shady pergolas, beds, and pots overflowing with flowers. Kick back in one of the chairs overlooking the Hudson and dream the day away.

NEW YORK CITY, NEW YORK
129 THE ALGONQUIN HOTEL LOBBY

Accented with Edwardian furniture in deep jewel tones, the low-lit hotel lobby feels like a throwback to an earlier era.

130 NEW YORK BOTANICAL GARDEN

The New York Botanical Garden's spectacularly verdant 250 acres (101 hectares) is a wonderland for everything that grows. It also contains one of the few remaining tracts of natural, uncut woodland in New York City. The garden offers a range of classes in soul-nourishing subjects such as horticultural therapy, herbal medicine, and floral design.

131 FORD FOUNDATION ATRIUM

Close to Times Square and hidden in the Ford Foundation foyer is a vast ten-story glass enclosure that is filled with tropical trees, ferns, and gardenias.

132 MEETING, SKYSPACE AT MoMA

This installation inside a former classroom is one of a series of "Skyspaces"—chambers with openings directly to the sky—by artist James Turrell.

Mount Mansfield, setting for Grafton Village

WINDHAM COUNTY, VERMONT
133 GRAFTON

Grafton Village was once a popular stagecoach stop for those traveling through the Green Mountains to New York. Deep in the Vermont forest, it is a picturesque village of bright red barns, steepled churches, and whiter-than-white houses. The backdrop of Mount Mansfield is spectacular when draped in the rich colors of autumn.

HIDDEN GEM
ST. JOHNSBURY, VERMONT
134 DOG CHAPEL

"Welcome all creeds, all breeds, no dogmas allowed," states the sign outside the small chapel celebrating the spiritual bond between dog and his man. The chapel is the pet project of folk artist Stephen Huneck, who was inspired to build the canine sanctuary on his mountaintop farm after a near-death experience.

CANTERBURY, NEW HAMPSHIRE
135 CHURCH IN THE WOODS

A series of visions led Reverend Steve Blackmer to establish a "church" in the wilderness to bring back the spirit of nature to religious practice. Set in 106 acres (43 hectares) of forest, this is a place where people of all beliefs can celebrate the natural world as the bearer of the sacred. People are welcome to meditate, to walk in the woods, or simply to sit quietly on a fallen tree.

NORTH CONWAY, NEW HAMPSHIRE
136 CONWAY SCENIC RAILROAD

Travel on the Crawford Notch route for a five-and-a-half-hour vintage-train journey through some of the most dramatic natural scenery on the eastern seaboard. The railroad was created over 140 years ago and was a feat for its time. You'll find a cozy pub in North Conway at the end of the round trip.

LINCOLN COUNTY, MAINE
137 BOOTHBAY HARBOR

This harbor is a quintessentially midcoast seaside getaway, and the shoreline is fringed with evergreen forests and rocky outcroppings. Whales, puffins, seals, lobsters, and lighthouse boats can be spotted from a leisurely cruise around the islands nearby. In town, the Blue Moon Café is a welcoming dockside café with a scenic patio and an ample menu.

VARIOUS LOCATIONS, MAINE
138 MAINE ISLANDS

The serrated Maine coast is rich in territory to explore. The sea looms large here, and it is from the sea that the jagged cliffs, peaceful harbors, and pebbly beaches of the state's numerous wilderness islands are best experienced. Coastal Kayaking Tours offers a three-day guided paddling tour along the 325-mi (523-km) Maine Island Trail.

139 LIGHTHOUSES

More than sixty-five lighthouses along 5,000 mi (8,000 km) of craggy coastline have earned Maine the nickname "the Lighthouse State." Built in the eighteenth century, some have museums on their grounds; others are now quaint inns or parts of large state parks; still others are inaccessible by land altogether. Cape Neddick's lighthouse and its keeper's house display picturesque beauty. From here, you can see the legendary Boone Island Light. Perched 6 mi (10 km) out at sea on a pile of rocks, Boon is New England's tallest lighthouse. Farther up the coast, Portland is home to the oldest lighthouse in the state: Portland Head Light. For a secluded overnight stay off the grid, try the Isle au Haut lighthouse, lit only by the glow of gaslights, candles, and kerosene lamps.

Clockwise from top: Cape Cod National Seashore; Martha's Vineyard; Public Garden; Buddhist Peace Pagoda

BARNSTABLE COUNTY, MASSACHUSETTS

140 CAPE COD NATIONAL SEASHORE

The hook-shape peninsula off the coast of Massachusetts is a site of quaint villages, lighthouses, seafood shacks, and unspoiled Atlantic shoreline. The Cape Cod National Seashore stretches for forty miles around the outer curve of the cape and is a bounty of unspoiled beaches, salt marshes, sand dunes, and well-preserved, forested trails. Head for Bound Brook—as remote a beach as you'll find on the Cape.

DUKES COUNTY, MASSACHUSETTS

141 MARTHA'S VINEYARD

New England's largest island has long attracted back-to-nature types. There are no chain restaurants here; instead you'll find green farms and welcoming independent inns.

LEVERETT, MASSACHUSETTS

142 NEW ENGLAND PEACE PAGODA

This is a Buddhist monument that was designed to inspire peace in its visitors. Rest upon a bench beside a pond filled with water lilies and contemplate the beauty of nature.

BOSTON, MASSACHUSETTS

143 PUBLIC GARDEN

The first public botanical garden in North America features meandering paths decorated by statues and fountains, plants, and trees, with a six-acre boating lake.

STOCKBRIDGE, MASSACHUSETTS

144 KRIPALU CENTER FOR YOGA & HEALTH

Book a self-guided retreat, and plan a week of as little or as much activity as you choose.

BOSTON, MASSACHUSETTS

145 THE COURTYARD RESTAURANT

Enjoy an elegant high tea in The Courtyard Restaurant, a hidden jewel overlooking the beautiful Italianate courtyard of the magnificent Boston Public Library.

BOSTON, MASSACHUSETTS

146 MAPPARIUM

Walk through the center of Earth in this three-story-tall globe made of brightly colored stained glass, bisected by a glass walkway. You will find the sphere at the Mary Baker Eddy Library.

147 BEINECKE RARE BOOK & MANUSCRIPT LIBRARY

The rarest manuscripts and books here are out of reach in an impressive six-story glass tower in the center of Yale's modernist library. In a peaceful courtyard, three abstract white marble sculptures represent the geometry of Earth, the sun, and the chance rolling of a die.

HIDDEN GEM
NEW HAVEN, CONNECTICUT

148 KASBAH GARDEN CAFÉ

Duck off the busy streets into a calm little courtyard for an authentic Moroccan mint tea. Nestled in a diminutive space between buildings, the Kasbah Garden Café serves Middle Eastern food in a beautiful and peaceful garden. The courtyard is decorated with flowering plants and birdcages—they provide aesthetic appeal as well as welcome shade from the sun and the city noise.

WASHINGTON, CONNECTICUT

149 GRACE MAYFLOWER INN & SPA

A feeling of calm sets in as soon as you set foot on this country resort's fifty-eight manicured acres, set within a nature reserve. Two hours' drive northeast of New York, the real gem here is the 20,000-sq-ft (1,858-m) spa. Enjoy treatments that feature meditation and wellness and are rooted in Eastern philosophies.

PROVIDENCE, RHODE ISLAND

150 PROVIDENCE ATHENAEUM

The "Ath" has literary history oozing out of its walls. It was a favorite haunt of horror aficionado HP Lovecraft, and Sarah Whitman broke off her engagement to Edgar Allen Poe here. Behind the neoclassical columns, the stacks hide plenty of hidden reading nooks, while the lower floor has individually lit, comfortable leather seats.

PROVIDENCE, RHODE ISLAND

151 SWAN POINT CEMETERY

Home to the final resting place of horror author HP Lovecraft, Swan Point Cemetery is anything but dark and foreboding. Locals use the largest green space in Providence as a public park, pedaling or jogging through the garden's serene spread of lawns and forests, azalea shrubs, and riverside walks.

NEWPORT, RHODE ISLAND

152 NEWPORT CLIFF WALK

You will see some of the most breathtaking coastal scenery in New England from this 3.5-mi (6-km) path along the eastern shore of Newport. The trail borders the back lawns of many of the seaside city's grand mansions, affording a chance to get a closer look at the elegant architectures. Guided tours of some of the homes are available.

Fallingwater

153 FALLINGWATER

Renowned American architect Frank Lloyd Wright designed this house as a holiday retreat for a private client. Built over a waterfall in the Pennsylvanian mountains, it exemplifies his philosophy of harmoniously uniting art and nature. Fallingwater and the surrounding Bear Run Nature Reserve is open to the public but you will need to book a tour in advance.

DELMARVA PENINSULA, MARYLAND

154 ASSATEAGUE ISLAND

Local folklore tells that the wild horses of Assateague Island are descended from the survivors of a shipwreck, though no records confirm the tale. Encountering their wild strength and beauty on the 37-mi (6-km) long uninhabited island commands respect and a sense of awe. It is advised to observe the feral horses from a safe distance.

BALTIMORE, MARYLAND

155 AMERICAN VISIONARY ART MUSEUM

While away an afternoon exploring the ways that the human spirit finds a voice through art. The colorful and often eccentric art displayed here is all by self-taught artists, resulting in some highly individualistic and creative pieces, each with its own written story attached. The sculpture garden features a 55-ft (17-m) tall, wind-powered whirligig.

HIDDEN GEM

WAYNE, PENNSYLVANIA

156 CHANTICLEER GARDEN

Chanticleer is one of the most relaxing gardens you'll visit and is just 30 minutes outside Philadelphia. With only 35 acres open to the public, it is a world away from larger, busier gardens in the country. The Teacup Garden is a secluded courtyard bursting with color; the perfect place to set up an artist's easel and let your creativity flow.

KENNETT SQUARE, PENNSYLVANIA
157 LONGWOOD GARDENS

Open almost continuously
since the eighteenth century,
this 1,000-acre (405-hectare)
oasis of gardens, woodlands,
and meadows provides
opportunity to wander
in thought.

TALBOT COUNTY, MARYLAND
158 ST. MICHAELS

This small town retains the look
and feel of a nineteenth-century
seaport. The Inn at Perry Cabin
by Belmond has airy rooms that
feel restful.

Top and Above: Longwood Gardens

WASHINGTON, DC
159 FRANCISCAN MONASTERY OF THE HOLY LAND IN AMERICA

Those participating in a week-long retreat in the monastery's secluded hermitage can also enjoy periods of reflection in the beautiful church or wander through the century-old contemplative garden with its rose beds and replicas of sacred shrines. Voluntary work in the vegetable garden is open to all.

WASHINGTON, DC
160 UNITED STATES NATIONAL ARBORETUM

Two miles (3 km) from the Capitol, this living museum sprawls across hundreds of acres. The twenty-two sandstone Corinthian pillars that were once part of the Capitol give the National Capitol Columns garden an otherworldly feel, while the bonsai collection is strangely meditative and features a tree dating back more than 400 years.

WASHINGTON, DC
161 THE MONUMENTS AT NIGHT

Strolling through the National Mall at night is a wonderful way to see some of Washington, DC's most famous memorials. Most monuments are beautifully illuminated, and in the moonlight, become even more impressive. Plan for about three hours' walking time, starting at the White House and ending at the Capitol.

WASHINGTON, DC
162 DUMBARTON OAKS

Set within sixteen acres of fairy-tale gardens, this mansion has free entrance and is home to a research library and collection of rare books. The historic gardens, designed by great American landscape architect Beatrix Farrand, are open to the public. The fountains, box hedges, and old shade trees are incorporated into principles of Italian, French, and English design.

Tidal Basin

163 **TIDAL BASIN**

For a tourist-free view of the Jefferson Memorial, head to the Tidal Basin to rent a paddle boat. As you enjoy a leisurely paddle, there will be nothing but water between you and the monument. Make the trip in March or April to experience thousands of cherry trees in full bloom along the banks.

BLUE RIDGE MOUNTAINS, VIRGINIA

164 **SKYLINE DRIVE**

The historic 105-mi (169-km) Skyline Drive winds its way along the spine of Virginia's Blue Ridge Mountains in the Shenandoah National Park. There are seventy-five scenic overlooks along the way, offering stunning views of the Shenandoah Valley in the west and rolling Piedmont to the east. Nestled at Skyline Drive's highest elevation, the Skyland Lodge has views that are phenomenal. Rustic cabins and more recently renovated rooms stretch along the crest and into the wooded area of the lodge, close to the Stony Man trail, which offers some of the best vistas in the park.

Skyline Drive

GEORGIA
170 COASTAL GEORGIA

Georgia's coast is wonderfully wild and unique. Fecund sea islands are lapped by salt tides and peppered with marshes, estuaries, and miles of flat beach. Roaring rivers descend from the northern mountains, marshlands teem with fiddler crabs and swaying cordgrass, and the low whisper of the Atlantic is never far away.

The seaside wilds of Georgia include fifteen barrier islands—four of these have become popular resort destinations, while the rest are accessible only by boat and are virtually unspoiled natural escapes. Each showcases the beauty of the coastline with its own distinct character and all are worth exploration.

Sapelo Island is a tangle of salt marsh and sand, and home to the Geechee people who have inhabited the coast here for more than 200 years. The Geechees have fought development of their island, and visitors must be part of an organized tour or guests of the residents.

Accessible by car, Jekyll Island is a more popular resort destination. However, it does have its own unspoiled secrets. Hidden down an unassuming palm-lined path is the visually arresting shore of Driftwood Beach, where whole trees, preserved in gray by the salt air, rest on their sides in a wild sculpture of twisted wood.

A third option is to rent the private Eagle Island. The rustic luxury lodge has spacious accommodation for up to ten people. It features a classic wraparound porch with a swinging bed, and an outdoor fireplace in front of a hot tub where you can watch the moon rising from the dock. Clearly, the accommodation has been designed to encourage enjoyment of the outdoors.

FLORIDA KEYS, FLORIDA
171 ISLAMORADA

Encompassing six islands in the Florida Keys, Islamorada is known as the Village of Islands. This little string of pearls (well, keys)—Plantation, Upper and Lower Matecumbe, Shell and Lignumvitae (lignum-vite-ee)—shimmers as one of the prettiest stretches of the Keys. It is world-renowned for its sport fishing, and there are ample opportunities to participate or otherwise enjoy the rich marine life around the islands. Wander through the Morada Way Art & Cultural District for a dose of inspiration when you are bored of the beach. Islamorada stretches across some 20 mi (32 km), from Mile Marker 90 to Mile Marker 74.

FLORIDA KEYS, FLORIDA
172 DRY TORTUGAS NATIONAL PARK

Reachable only by boat or seaplane, the Dry Tortugas are considered to be one of North America's most remote and least visited national parks. Your rewards for making the effort are snorkeling amid coral reefs, and an abandoned but beautifully preserved nineteenth-century fort to explore.

HIDDEN GEM
FLORIDA KEYS, FLORIDA
173 QUIET COVE KEY

Quiet Cove Key offers total seclusion on an exposed fossilized reef island, with hiking trails meandering through the mangrove trees and plenty of fishing and kayaking opportunities. There's no property on this island; instead guests stay on a 38-ft (12-m) houseboat that sleeps up to seven people. Camping on the island is also welcome.

FLORIDA
174 SANIBEL ISLAND

Off the west coast of Florida at Fort Myers, Sanibel Island's beautiful sandy beaches are the main draw for visitors here. Bowman's Beach is the island's most popular stretch for swimming, while Blind Pass Beach is a bit more off the beaten path and is a great place for shell spotters to collect conches and cockles, as well as the occasional shark's tooth.

EVERGLADES, FLORIDA
175 EVERGLADES NATIONAL PARK

Native American inhabitants called the Everglades the "River of Grass." It is an expansive area of wetlands and swamps, grasslands, and prairies that stretch across your entire field of vision. Explore the contented flow of the park by canoe along peaceful flatwaters and deep into lush subtropical mangrove forests full of rare wildlife.

Sanibel Island

MAUI, HAWAII

176 SUNSET YOGA

Take your yoga practice to paradise on the secluded beaches of Maui, Hawaii. Promoting mindful flow and connection to raw nature, Sunset Yoga's classes take place away from the bustling hotel buildings and luxury storefronts of the crowded coastline. By moving away from background interruptions, you can truly experience the stillness and serenity of the natural side of the island.

VOLCANOES NATIONAL PARK, HAWAII

177 TREE HOUSE IN A VOLCANO

Located near the Hawaii Volcanoes National Park, this tree house rental is half hidden in pristine, native Hawaiian rain forests with spectacular views from a deck.

HIDDEN GEM

WAIANAE, HAWAII

178 KAHUMANA ORGANIC FARM & CAFÉ

Tucked away in the rolling mountains of Waianae, this organic café and farm offers more than just good food. The community project is run by a nonprofit organization that helps homeless families get back on their feet. Visitors can enjoy the farm and relax in the gardens, supporting the project through the café.

Sunset Yoga

The Coffee Shack

HŌNAUNAU, HAWAII
179 THE COFFEE SHACK

This little restaurant in Kona offers fantastic views of Kealakekua Bay from the patio. The Kona bean is grown on the mountainside below the café.

MAUI, HAWAII
181 HALEAKALĀ

Wake early and climb to the volcano's summit to watch the night and stars fade away as the sun rises and lights up the sky.

KAPAAU, HAWAII
180 HAWAII ISLAND RETREAT

Tickled by the breeze from the ocean off Hawaii's north Kohala coast, this luxury ecoboutique hotel is set in 50 acres (20 hectares) of gardens, wild groves, and ancient trails. It is a place of intentional peacefulness, where you can feel hidden from the world. The hotel even generates its own solar and wind-turbine power.

OAHU, HAWAII

182 LANTERN FLOATING CEREMONY

As the sun sets, more than 6,000 candlelit lanterns bearing
remembrances and prayers illuminate the ocean at Ala Moana Beach
Park on Memorial Day. Despite the crowds, the calm, serene
movements of the lanterns on the water bring feelings of peace and
thoughtfulness as loved ones who have passed are remembered.

Lantern Floating Memorial

HONOLULU, HAWAII
183 LEARN HULA

Learn the spirit, grace, and history of the ancient form of hula, the well-known Hawaiian dance that preserves the stories, traditions, and culture of the islands. Traditional hula is usually accompanied by chanting and drumming, while modern hula is accompanied by contemporary music. The Royal Hawaiian Center in Honolulu offers free lessons.

KONA, HAWAII
184 HO'OPONOPONO'S HIGHER CONSCIOUSNESS WORKSHOP

"Ho'oponopono" means "to make right"; to correct wrongs with your ancestors and in your relationships. It is a spiritual practice based on forgiveness so that we can move forward. A company called Huna offers seminars and workshops on Kona to learn this ancient healing and spiritual shamanism of Hawaiian wisdom and connection to universal spirit.

HAWAII
185 NIIHAU

Tourism is severely restricted on the tiny untouched island of Niihau 17 mi (27 km) off the coast of Kauai. It is home to about 300 native Hawaiians who live a subsistence lifestyle and speak only the original Hawaiian language. Limited helicopter tours are organized to the island but offer no interaction with the islanders.

KAUAI, HAWAII
186 NA PALI COAST

Towering green spires, deep canyons, pristine beaches, and perilous cliffs dropping into the sea. The roadless expanse of the Na Pali coast is an adventurer's paradise. Hike the 11-mi (18-km) Kalalau Trail through valleys and around cliff faces to be rewarded with the postcard-perfect Kalalau Valley, or make the shorter trip to Hanakapai Falls.

187 EL MORRO FORT

Follow the charming cobblestone streets of Old San Juan northwest to the sea, to the sentry boxes of the Castillo San Felipe del Morro. Standing guard at the entrance to San Juan harbor to protect the island from pirates, privateers, and foreign states, the fort has seen off all sea-based attacks, falling only in 1598 when the Earl of Cumberland took it by land.

It is a steep climb to the entrance, but at the top, the refreshing ocean breeze cools you down. Explore the six levels of barracks, dungeons, alcoves, passageways, and secret staircases. Walk the ramparts or simply sit inside one of the domed *garitas*—sentry boxes—and watch the ships come and go. The views are spectacular in all directions. On the way back to town, rest awhile with the locals who fly kites on the fields at the foot of the fort.

Ice paddling in Alaska

SKWENTNA, ALASKA
188 WINTERLAKE LODGE
Situated on the western edge of the rugged Alaska Range, this remote and peaceful wilderness lodge provides relaxation and abundant opportunities for outdoor adventure—from bear watching to glacier trekking.

VALDEZ-CORDOVA, ALASKA
189 PAXSON
Nestled in the foothills of the mountains, Paxson is a wild, raw Alaskan town that is completely off the grid, with a population of just 50 people.

KING SALMON, ALASKA
190 ANIAKCHAK NATIONAL MONUMENT & PRESERVE
No roads lead to Aniakchak, one of the wildest and most isolated places in Alaska. Getting there involves days of trekking and rafting—perfect isolation.

Viewing the northern lights in Alaska

Mendenhall Ice Caves

ST. WRANGELL–ST. ELIAS NATIONAL PARK
AND PRESERVE, ALASKA

191 ULTIMA THULE LODGE

The only place to stay within the St. Wrangell–St.
Elias National Park and Preserve is 100 miles from
the nearest road. The lodge is nestled on a hillside
alive with flowers. When the sun sets, it gilds the
mountain peaks in pink. A fleet of small planes is
on hand to take you to the most remote and
isolated parts of the park, where guides will take
you to wild places that may never have been
explored. Perhaps you'll visit an abandoned gold
mine, or fly to the perfect fishing spot, then return
for a wood-fire sauna.

JUNEAU, ALASKA

192 MENDENHALL ICE CAVES

Breathtaking blue walls shimmer inside a partially
hollow glacier. To reach the caves, you must kayak
to the glacier and then ice climb over it.

HIDDEN GEM

KING ISLAND, ALASKA

193 UKIVOK

Located on the tiny King Island, this haunting
village was abandoned fifty years ago but still
clings precipitously to the side of a steep cliff.

TOFINO, BRITISH COLUMBIA
194 CLAYOQUOT WILDERNESS RESORT

A cluster of tents perched 4,500 ft (1,372 m) above sea level on Urus mountain provides the ultimate spot with a jaw-dropping view. Observation decks outside wooden-floored, white canvas explorer's tents allow wildlife-watching from a luxurious lookout. Enjoy a busy program of wilderness activities or hit the spa and do absolutely nothing but relax.

FIELD, BRITISH COLUMBIA
195 CATHEDRAL MOUNTAIN LODGE

Two hours west of Calgary, nestled deep in the Rockies, this cluster of traditional log cabins is set among sheltering trees, cloud-piercing peaks, and glacier-fed streams. From the deck of your cabin you can sit and spot wildlife, as you soak up the scent of pine and listen to the rushing sound of alpine waters.

HIDDEN GEM
HAIDA NATION, BRITISH COLUMBIA
196 HAIDA GWAII

This remote archipelago is the ancestral home of the Haida people. Few tourists take the trip out here: those who do are rewarded by traditional Haida hospitality and customs, and the serenity and cultural richness of their laid-back communities. Find abandoned villages to the south and rain forest-flanked beaches to the east.

CANADIAN ROCKIES, BRITISH COLUMBIA
197 KOOTENAY NATIONAL PARK

For a quieter alternative to the Rockies—which can often seem crowded in peak season—Kootenay is an untouched expanse of mountain peaks and lush, pine-forested lowlands; dramatic limestone gorges, and teal-hued lakes. Barely explored trails will attract serious hikers, while driving routes take you to surprise waterfalls and cedar groves.

BELLA BELLA, BRITISH COLUMBIA
198 KING PACIFIC LODGE

This five-star fishing lodge on the banks of Milbanke Sound is infused with the spirit of the Pacific Northwest. Here, you can enjoy world-class fishing amid the spectacular scenery of the rugged British Columbian coastline. Even if fishing isn't your thing, the humpback whales, sea lions, and eagles will keep you entertained.

Vancouver Island

199 VANCOUVER ISLAND

Vancouver Island is studded with colorful communities that have built up over the years from small fishing or logging villages. Take a dramatic drive over the central spine of snowcapped mountains to the wild west coast and the magical Pacific Rim National Park. Alternatively, head north to explore the quieter towns that are only accessible by boat or seaplane.

200 MIRAJ HAMMAM SPA

Travel to this spa near Granville Loop Park and you can relax on Jerusalem gold marble as old-world massage techniques combine with modern luxury to help you unwind and find your inner calm. After the treatments, you can enjoy deep rest on velvet beds and silk cushions. While relaxing, you will be served freshly prepared Arabian mint tea and sweet cakes.

201 STANLEY PARK

This semiwild city park sprawls over 1,000 acres (405 hectares) along the Vancouver coastline. Nestled between the pretty rose garden and the forest is the Shakespeare Garden. This quiet space pays homage to the English bard through the secluded arboretum of more than forty-five trees mentioned in his works, accompanied by their relevant quotes.

WHISTLER, BRITISH COLUMBIA
202 NITA LAKE LODGE
Tranquil spa and retreat beside
a stunning, glacier-fed lake. Book
the lake view studio suite for
a peaceful view from beside your
private fireplace.

WHISTLER, BRITISH COLUMBIA
203 WHISTLER PUBLIC LIBRARY
Settle down with a good book
against the backdrop of the
jagged mountaintops that circle
Whistler, one of the world's
premier skiing resorts.

WHISTLER, BRITISH COLUMBIA
204 LIFT COFFEE COMPANY
Take advantage of the
comfortable couches and chairs
on a sun-drenched patio at
this independent café near
the Whistler City gondola base.
It has a loyal following among
caffeine-loving locals.

Stanley Park

JASPER, ALBERTA

205 JASPER–PRINCE RUPERT TRAIN

If you want to see the scenery without putting in the legwork, take the train from Jasper to Prince Rupert, stopping off overnight in Prince George. On the first leg of the journey, you will climb to the highest point in the Rockies for sweeping views through panoramic windows of one of the most spectacular peaks in North America. Later, you will pass through corridors of fairy-tale landscapes of pine and fir trees, past abandoned settlements, and alongside vast mountain lakes. Bear sightings are common, and the driver will often slow down for the view.

BANFF, ALBERTA

206 WILLOW STREAM SPA

Breathe in the oxygen-rich mountain air at this award-winning spa surrounded by alpine rivers and glacial waters. Part of the Fairmont Banff Springs.

BANFF, ALBERTA

207 BANFF NATIONAL PARK

Canada's first national park boasts some of the country's finest unspoiled ecosystems. Don't miss the spectacular, turquoise glacial Moraine Lake and Lake Louise.

WHITEHORSE, YUKON

208 SOUTH CANOL ROAD

Hours can pass without seeing another car on this 140-mi (226-km) winding dirt road. If you want to break the journey over two days, stop on the way at the Quiet Lake campsites.

KLUANE, YUKON

209 KLUANE NATIONAL PARK AND RESERVE

Vast wilderness of glacial ice fields, forests of aspens and cottonwoods, and snowcapped peaks. Flightseeing trips are a popular way to see the highlights of this landscape.

HIDDEN GEM

HINTON, ALBERTA

210 WILLMORE WILDERNESS PARK

There are no marked trails here, just untouched wilderness at its best, where you can stay in hunters' wooden huts in dense forests.

Banff National Park

211 WOODBINE BEACH

Woodbine Beach has a decidedly laid-back atmosphere. It's a rugged stretch of beachfront where you can watch the kiteboarders and surfers, or join them. It can be busy in summer but it's not difficult to find a quiet spot—just keep walking eastward.

HIDDEN GEM

TORONTO, ONTARIO

212 KNOX COLLEGE

Vines spill from baskets above the benches that line the corridor running around the Quad at Knox College. The stunning arched ceilings curve down to ornate open-sided archways along the walls. These offer views out to the peaceful courtyard garden beyond, the fountain in the center, and the ivy-covered walls of the college exterior.

TORONTO, ONTARIO

213 HAMMAM SPA

The Hammam Spa in downtown Toronto is built on the ancient philosophy of traditional Turkish baths. The spa's signature service, Hammam Turkish Bath, is a one-hour treatment that starts in the steam room. It then moves to the candlelit Turkish suites, where you relax on a heated marble table as your body is deeply cleansed and purified.

TORONTO, ONTARIO

214 TORONTO SILENT FILM FESTIVAL

If you like going to the movies but find the explosions and thumping soundtracks of modern movies a bit too much, purchase a ticket for the Toronto Silent Film Festival, when the world's most famous silent films take over Toronto's independent movie theaters in April. Many screenings feature musicians playing along to the films.

TORONTO, ONTARIO

215 THE ISLAND CAFÉ

The shiny high-rises of Toronto seem a long way away as you look across the water from the Island Café's sunny patio. The family-owned café on idyllic Ward's Island supports local farmers and grows its own produce in the kitchen garden. Take a bike and explore the island before stopping here for refreshments.

NIAGARA, ONTARIO

216 NIAGARA-ON-THE-LAKE

Stretching north from Niagara Falls is a landscape of vineyards and orchards. Among these, you will discover the gorgeous nineteenth-century town of Niagara-on-the-Lake with its tree-lined streets, lush parks, and beautifully restored houses. Base yourself here to explore the wineries that take advantage of the Niagara Peninsula's unique humid microclimate to create award-winning wines.

Carbide Willson Ruins

OTTAWA, ONTARIO
217 CARBIDE WILLSON RUINS
Hidden within Gatineau Park on the edge of
Ottawa, the ruins of paranoid inventor Thomas
"Carbide" Willson's incredible secret workshop can
still be explored.

OTTAWA, ONTARIO
218 BLUMENSTUDIO
Blumenstudio in Westboro isn't your average
florist—it's also a café. Relax and sip your latte
while watching the experts create floral displays
with artistry and magic.

219 MADAWASKA RIVER

For the aboriginal people of Canada, the canoe was critical to almost every facet of life and was the principal means of transportation across the country. Flatwater canoeing is calm and restful and a great way to get in touch with nature. The gentle motions of the water lead your thoughts to wander as you float along the glass-like surface of the lakes. It's no wonder the pastime is still so popular here. The quieter waters of Golden Lake and Rice Lake on the Madawaska River are ideal spots to learn how to paddle.

OTTAWA, ONTARIO

220 THE STAFF ROOM

Pull a book in the false bookshelf at the back of Union 613 restaurant, and you will find yourself in a tucked-away twenty-seat speakeasy.

HIDDEN GEM

OTTAWA, ONTARIO

221 LA TERRASSE

Something of a secret within the Fairmont Château Laurier is La Terrasse restaurant. The patio boasts 180-degree views encompassing the Alexandra Bridge and Parliament Hill.

ALTON, ONTARIO

222 MILLCROFT INN & SPA

Countryside retreat and luxury spa focusing on the connection between the mind, body, and spirit, with a Tuscan dining room and selection of beautifully appointed guest rooms.

Pingualuit Crater

QUEBEC CITY, QUEBEC
223 **BASSE-VILLE**

Step back in time on the beautiful historic streets of Quebec City's Basse-Ville (Lower Town). This was the location of Quebec's original settlement on the banks of the St. Lawrence River. A funicular car takes visitors down to the ancient streets that are sprawled around the base of the steep cliff and perfect for exploring.

QUEBEC CITY, QUEBEC
224 **THE PLAINS OF ABRAHAM**

This city park becomes a winter playground once the snow falls, with cross-country ski trails for all levels, and historical snowshoe tours.

QUEBEC CITY, QUEBEC
225 **MORRIN CENTRE**

This 200-year-old prison in Old Quebec has been converted into the city's only English-language library. It is a lovely spot to enjoy the ambience of the past.

QUEBEC CITY, QUEBEC
226 **LE MONASTÈRE DES AUGUSTINES**

Silence and calm reside in the rooms of this wellness center, which offers a variety of holistic programs within a former cloistered monastery.

KATAVIK, QUEBEC
227 PINGUALUIT CRATER

The almost perfectly circular lake that fills the Pingualuit crater is said to be the purest freshwater lake on Earth. To reach it is a nine-day trek from Kangiqsujuaq village through the vast boreal landscape of the Ungava peninsula. On the way, you may spot Inuit people hunting and fox trapping, as well as roaming caribou.

Left and Above: Balnea Spa

BROMONT, QUEBEC
228 BALNEA SPA

Overlooking a breathtaking nature reserve and set within a sacred American Indian ritual site, Balnea Spa is a captivating sanctuary for complete relaxation. A jetty stretches out into the idyllic private Lake Gale, where guests can recline on loungers and dangle their feet into the tranquil waters following the Balnea thermal experience.

MONTREAL, QUEBEC

229 **AUBERGE DU VIEUX-PORT**

Open wide the casement windows of your room in this renovated mid-1800s warehouse to look out at the cobblestone streets of the old port below.

MONTREAL, QUEBEC

230 **CITY MUSEUMS**

A Montreal Museum Pass will grant access to forty-one sites across the city. The DHC/ART Foundation for Contemporary Art is a local secret.

MONTREAL, QUEBEC

231 **LACHINE CANAL**

Perfect for an afternoon bike ride, Lachine Canal was listed as the third most beautiful urban circuit in the world by *Time* magazine.

MONTREAL, QUEBEC

232 **SAINT HELEN'S ISLAND**

Take a bicycle to explore the pretty island with plenty of peaceful spots within the park to sit and watch the world go by.

Montreal Biosphere, Île Sainte-Hélène, Montreal

Saint Joseph's Oratory

HIDDEN GEM

MONTREAL, QUEBEC
233 GARDEN OF THE WAY OF THE CROSS

The outdoor Garden of the Way of the Cross is one of Montreal's best-kept secrets. Located in a wooded area near Saint Joseph's Oratory—the grand basilica on one of Mount Royal's peaks—the hidden garden is a calm and relaxing place to meditate in communion with nature. The green space features impressive sandstone sculptures of the Christian story of Jesus's Crucifixion and Resurrection, which can be followed on a pathway through trees and flowers to a reflecting pool and the Fountain of Redemption.

MONTREAL, QUEBEC
234 BOTA BOTA

A historic river ferry has been turned into a luxury floating spa with hot tubs and saunas, as well as beautiful, private relaxation rooms. Silence is encouraged throughout the spa so that guests can enjoy utter escapism and inner peace.

235 SHOBAC COTTAGES

Four minimalist cabins stare out across the wild Atlantic Coast of Nova Scotia, their backs to the mountains on a wild and beautiful peninsula. The cabins are elegant and simple, inspired by the frugal environment of living in a fishing boat. Each cabin has a large ocean-facing deck, while the entranceways look out to the dramatic rural landscape. Inside, the cottages have a deep sense of space and connection to the land.

Shobac is the project of celebrated architect Brian MacKay-Lyons. Behind the cottages on the mainland are a collection of other design-led vacation rentals, including a studio and a reconstructed nineteenth-century octagonal barn. Sheep roam freely, organic vegetables grow in the garden, sustainably farmed trout stock the ponds, and everything runs on solar power.

FOGO ISLAND, NEWFOUNDLAND
236 FOGO ISLAND INN

Every room of this ultramodern design hotel in the wilderness of Atlantic Canada has ocean views. Perched atop the jagged rocks of Newfoundland's northern coast, the hotel has a strong commitment to local fishing, boatbuilding, and artisan cultures. Soak in the massive bathtub, while listening to the ocean crashing into the rocky coastline below.

PORT SAUNDERS, NEWFOUNDLAND
237 THE VIKING TRAIL

The 489-mi (787-km) Viking Trail winds its way along the rugged coast of western Newfoundland. Ancient indigenous burial grounds, colorful fishing villages, the epic scenery of Gros Morne National Park, and 10,000-year-old icebergs are all on the route, which ends at L'Anse aux Meadows, the only known Viking settlement in North America.

GROS MORNE, NEWFOUNDLAND
238 GROS MORNE NATIONAL PARK

Sheer-sided fjords, glacial valleys, hidden sea caves, wild beaches, and mountains covered in alpine forests all wait to be explored in Gros Morne, which was designated a World Heritage Site in 1987. Hike the quiet trails for a chance to spot bears, moose, and reindeer. Geologists will literally have a field day here.

QUIRPON ISLAND, NEWFOUNDLAND
239 QUIRPON LIGHTHOUSE INN

With its own dedicated whale-watching hut, this converted 1922 lighthouse on deserted Quirpon Island could be the best place in Newfoundland for spotting orcas and humpback whales. They have even been known to come close enough to touch. It's also a prime location for iceberg spotting, as the Labrador Current carries the floating ice south.

Fogo Island Inn

AVALON PENINSULA, NEWFOUNDLAND
240 CAPE SPEAR

Rise in the morning to the first rays of sun that reach North America each day. With nothing between you and Europe but sea, Cape Spear is the easternmost point of land on the continent, and offers spectacular views of whales and icebergs. A boardwalk leads to the area's oldest remaining lighthouse, which is perched on a rugged cliff.

FORTEAU, LABRADOR
241 LABRADOR STRAITS MUSEUM

This small museum on Canada's remote eastern edge celebrates the region's rich local heritage. Through its exhibits and artifacts, a story is told about the lifestyle of the First Nation people who have lived along the coastline, the early European settlers, and the present identity of the communities that thrive here.

2+2 ENCUENTRO GUADALUPE

The stunning setting of this hotel is its star attribute. Individual, square, loft-style cabins rise above a boulder-strewn ridge overlooking the Guadalupe Valley in Mexico's wine country. The mountains beyond peek above a sea of cloud, and, as the sun rises, the red clay hills gild the infinity pool with a golden beige glow. At night, the stars are blindingly bright in the dark desert sky.

243 BIBLIOTECA VASCONCELOS

In one of the most polluted urban environments on Earth, the reading areas of the botanical gardens that have been integrated with this giant steel, concrete, and glass library offer visitors some much-needed respite from the sprawling cityscape that surrounds them. The garden houses more than 168 different species of trees, most of which are endemic to Mexico, while the library itself is of epic proportions—a light-filled space that is an antidote for body and soul.

244 DOSIS CAFÉ

This modern café has a distinctly North American vibe, owing to the proprietors' connections to San Francisco. They have created an open, industrial-chic space that is filled with natural light. There are communal and individual spaces, and even a hammock for complete relaxation. In the back room is a community space where visitors can practice yoga and meditation.

245 CONDESA DF

Step away from the urban chaos into the cool-edged calm of the Condesa DF hotel, where the ice-white modernism of the 1920s building is offset by bold floral prints, bright acrylic furniture, and an abundance of local color. Choose one of the rooms with a terrace to make the most of the serene and leafy tucked-away setting.

246 LIBRERÍA PORRÚA

The Chapultepec branch of this chain of Mexican bookstores stands out for its spectacular location and stunning views. It is nestled among the trees at the entrance of the Chapultepec forest, and the trees continue indoors so that it feels like the building is part of the forest. Visitors can enjoy views of the lake from any window.

247 MUSEO FRIDA KAHLO

When an accident left the Mexican artist Frida Kahlo housebound, she turned to her garden for inspiration. The grounds of her cobalt-blue walled house are filled with the bright flowers and native trees of the country she loved. Pots and beds overspill, and climbing vegetation bursts from walls and railings in the property grounds.

The Hidden Beach

HIDDEN GEM

MARIETA ISLANDS, MEXICO

248 **THE HIDDEN BEACH**

A gaping hole on the surface of this lush green island leads to a secret beach. There is sun, shade, and crystal clear water so pack a picnic, as you won't need to move from here all day.

Yäan Wellness

PUERTO ESCONDIDO, MEXICO

249 **HOTEL ESCONDIDO**

A peaceful and tranquil refuge on a virgin beach of sixteen *palapa* bungalows, made from wood and palm leaves, with private plunge pools.

NAICA, MEXICO

250 **CAVE OF THE CRYSTALS**

Crystals weighing up to fifty-five tons have been growing for 500,000 years in a cave that is 985 ft (300 m) beneath the earth's surface.

The Cape

CABO SAN LUCAS, MEXICO
251 THE CAPE

The Cape hotel in Cabo San Lucas possesses the only rooftop lounge in the city. Pull up a chair, sit back with a drink, and survey the Sea of Cortez and the El Arco sea arch from six stories up. Interwoven with the natural landscape, and complete with the soundtrack of crashing surf, this sleek and modern beach retreat mixes clean lines and glass with polished concrete and rich, dark wood. The villas have their own private plunge pools and personal butler service, while rooms on the second floor have comfortable swinging daybeds on the balconies.

TULUM, MEXICO
252 YÄAN WELLNESS

Follow the scent of the copal—a sacred resin burned to connect to the divine—to the therapy pools and garden treatment cabins.

TULUM, MEXICO
253 TEMAZCAL

Sweat it out at a fear-releasing temazcal, a sweat lodge ceremony. The powerful ancient Mayan ritual is designed to purify the mind.

TULUM, MEXICO
254 AMANSALA

Eat fresh, healthy food and join other like-minded individuals on a quiet patch of powdery white sand for twice-daily yoga sessions on Amansala's "Beach 'n' Bliss" yoga retreat. Once you have stretched and balanced, it's time to enjoy a relaxing massage with creamy, golden Mayan clay.

YUCATÁN, MEXICO
255 CHICHEN ITZA

Arrive early before the tour buses descend, and you will be able to take that selfie you're hoping for. The Hacienda Chichen ecolodge has its own secret entrance gate within its tranquil gardens, so you can even beat the souvenir sellers to the ruins in the morning.

MERIDA, MEXICO
256 CHABLÉ RESORT & SPA

Deep in the Yucatán jungle, the Chablé Resort is one of the few spas in the world that can boast its own underground cave pool. Choose your treatment from the Mayan-inspired spa menu or take a walk upon the firefly-lit meditation lawn as the sun sets.

VALLADOLID, MEXICO
257 COQUI COQUI RESIDENCE & SPA

An open-air staircase in a sleepy Yucatán town leads up to the frangipani-scented courtyard of this secluded one-room retreat above the site of its own perfumery. The aromas from below are inspired by the scents of the Yucatán Peninsula.

VALLADOLID, MEXICO
258 CENOTE ZACI

Cenotes are waterholes that form when a cave roof collapses, exposing the groundwater below. Many of these waterholes are hidden deep within the lush Mexican jungle. This unexpected one, however, is in the middle of the city, just a few blocks from the main square.

Cenote Zaci

ISLA HOLBOX, MEXICO
259 CASA LAS TORTUGAS

The Italian couple who fell in love with the raw
beauty of this unspoiled island on Mexico's
Riviera Maya have created an environmentally
conscious hotel on the beach, surrounded by lush
vegetation, colorful birds, and exotic fauna. Lodge
in a traditional Mayan bungalow and enjoy a
luxurious ecovacation.

CENTRAL & SOUTH AMERICA & THE CARIBBEAN

With the largest rain forest, the driest desert, and the highest waterfall on Earth, Central and South America don't have to try hard to impress. Add to that the blissed-out beaches and sultry volcanic shores of the Caribbean islands and you may have just dreamed up the ultimate escape-it-all itinerary.

The vast terrain between the Patagonian ice fields on Argentina's southern tip and the borders with North America play host to the swampy forests of the Orinoco Delta; the breathtaking beauty of the Andes; the silent sands of the Atacama Desert, and so much more. Then, far out to sea, Easter Island is the most remote inhabited place on Earth.

Torres del Paine National Park, see page 166

Caye Caulker

LIGHTHOUSE REEF, BELIZE
260 GREAT BLUE HOLE

There aren't many places in the world where you can skydive into a giant submarine sinkhole before boarding a diving boat to don your scuba gear and descend into its deep blue depths. The Great Blue Hole off the coast of Belize is, however, one of them. A ring of coral encircles the entrance to the sinkhole, and the deeper you go, the clearer the water becomes. If you are feeling brave, you can hide behind the stalactites and watch reef shark swim over and feed on chum bait that is laid by a fearless dive master.

CARIBBEAN SEA, BELIZE
261 CAYE CAULKER

With no cars, no fumes, and no worries, the unique atmosphere of Caye Caulker, which is off the coast of Belize, attracts laid-back travelers.

CARIBBEAN SEA, BELIZE
262 FRENCH LOUIE CAYE

This private island is surrounded by an exquisite coral reef. Arrange a night snorkel to see the rich, beautiful reefs bathed in moonlight—a truly memorable experience.

Cockscomb

STANN CREEK, BELIZE

263 COCKSCOMB BASIN WILDLIFE SANCTUARY

This sanctuary is the world's first jaguar reserve. It is also known for its spectacular waterfalls, mountain views, and diversity of tropical birds.

STANN CREEK, BELIZE

264 TURTLE INN

Think rustic with a lavish sprinkling of glamour, as brightly colored hammocks hang between slanted palm trees at Francis Ford Coppola's Indonesian-style beach retreat.

PLACENCIA PENINSULA, BELIZE

265 PLACENCIA

Perched right at the southern tip of 16 mi (26 km) of sandy beach, this former fishing village has a chilled ambience, as well as a selection of restaurants worthy of gourmands.

AMBERGRIS CAYE, BELIZE

266 EL SECRETO

Shed your shoes and go barefoot at this boutique hotel that can only be reached by boat. Stay in one of the sea villas that are just steps away from the warm water.

NICARAGUA
267 BAY ISLANDS UNDERWATER MUSEUM

Items representing the history of the area have been set into the warm waters of Roatán, making it a fascinating place to snorkel.

NICARAGUA
268 LITTLE CORN

One of Nicaragua's best-kept secrets, Little Corn Island may only be 1.5 sq m (2.5 sq km) in size, but it is bursting with character and color. The island is home to about 800 people: the small population maintain a friendly sense of community in their oasis of tranquillity where there is little to do but relax.

Little Corn

NICARAGUA
269 SURFING TURTLE LODGE

This beachfront hostel on a beautiful stretch of empty sand on Nicaragua's Pacific Coast has its own turtle hatchery. It releases the babies into the ocean between September and February, but you can visit at any time. You can camp, bunk in a dorm, or take a private room at this off-the-grid resort that is powered entirely by solar panels.

NICARAGUA
270 ISLETA EL ESPINO

The journey to Isleta El Espino gives you a hint of the upcoming experience as you pass uninhabited islands covered in lush, thick jungle, and spot local fishermen hauling in their day's catch. Accommodation-wise, there are only three rooms: a tree house, a bungalow, and a little house that can accommodate seven people.

HONDURAS
271 COPAN

These beautiful ruins at one of the greatest centers of the ancient Mayan civilization have the most impressive pre-Columbian art on view anywhere in the world.

HONDURAS
272 CAYOS COCHINOS

This is a marine reserve encompassing a group of islands and more than a dozen coral cays—a paradise of turquoise waters and deserted shores.

Isleta El Espino

MONTEVERDE, COSTA RICA

273 MONTEVERDE CLOUD FOREST BIOLOGICAL RESERVE

Monteverde's lush reserve is a misty oasis. Unfeasibly tall trees wrap around you in a sea of green, and you can spot hummingbirds and colorful quetzals feasting on ripe fruit just out of arm's reach. Set your alarm and arrive early when the trails are at their quietest.

PUNTARENAS PROVINCE, COSTA RICA

274 PLAYA ZANCUDO

This 6-mi (10-km) long sandy beach runs along the southern Pacific coast, its sparkling waters fringed by coconut palms and almond trees. Walk out onto the beach under the stars at low tide, and you will feel like you are the only person on Earth.

GUANACASTE PROVINCE, COSTA RICA

275 SANTA ROSA NATIONAL PARK

Santa Rosa National Park protects some of the last remaining tropical dry forest in the world. Only thirty visitors a day are permitted onto Nancite Beach, as it is a significant nesting sites for turtles.

BOQUETE, PANAMA

276 COFFEE ESTATE INN

Boquete is surrounded by coffee producers. The Coffee Estate Inn sits on the edge of a working coffee farm, nestled in orange groves, gardens, and forest. Bungalows all have views of Barú volcano, and Boquete valley below.

HIDDEN GEM

HORNITO, PANAMA

277 LOST & FOUND HOSTEL

The only way to reach this ecoretreat is to hike uphill through a cloud forest. But the view is worth the effort. Feed the monkeys, explore the forest, or visit local villages before retiring to the hammock.

CARIBBEAN COAST, PANAMA

278 SAN BLAS ISLANDS

The San Blas Islands are home to the Kuna people who maintain political autonomy from the mainland and control tourism on their own terms, preserving and sustaining this castaway idyll of white sand, warm sea, and few people.

PANAMA CITY, PANAMA

279 CASCO VIEJO

The old part of town feels like you have traveled to a completely different world with its mix of boutique colonial hotels and independent shops. Casa Sucre Coffeehouse serves Geisha coffee, one of the world's most expensive varieties.

BAHAMAS
280 JAWS BEACH

Towering sea grape trees provide shade at this isolated white sand beach that is usually completely deserted and always utterly beautiful.

CUBA
281 OLD HAVANA PERFUME MUSEUM

Beautiful perfume shop and museum located in an eighteenth-century mansion, evoking the feelings and fragrances of colonial Havana.

CUBA
282 CUBA LIBRO

Sip your cappuccino in the hammock at Cuba's only English-language bookstore and café. This Havana hangout brings locals and visitors together through great coffee, literature, and artworks.

CUBA
283 PRESIDIO MODELO

An abandoned prison complex that once held Fidel Castro now contains a museum and the haunting remains of the prison blocks.

Presidio Modelo

CUBA
284 WRECK DIVING

With its dazzling and well-preserved reefs, plunging sea walls, and swim-through caves, Cuba is a Caribbean destination apart for scuba divers. The Bay of Pigs is found in a rarely visited area on the south of the island, where you can dive and relax without being swamped by other people. Here, you will find the wreck of *El Jaruco*, deliberately sunk by locals in 1994 to provide an interesting dive site. The lack of currents at Maria la Gorda make for some relaxing dives, as you explore eighteenth- and nineteenth-century Spanish galleon and pirate wrecks in clear, still waters.

HIDDEN GEM
CUBA
285 CAMARA OBSCURA

Hidden on the rooftop of Gómez Villa, which is in the old town, the Camara Obscura provides a 360-degree panoramic view of Old Havana.

CUBA
286 BARACOA

The La Farola road cuts through 34 mi (55 km) of knife-sharp mountain peaks and fertile forests before arriving at the once-isolated and quirky eastern city of Baracoa.

Wreck diving, Cuba

Jamaican sunset

FALMOUTH, JAMAICA
287 LUMINOUS LAGOON

The Luminous Lagoon is one of the best places in the world to jump in and swim with the millions of bioluminescent microorganisms that shine in the shallow, warm water. They make the lagoon sparkle and glisten at night as they reflect the outlines of the fish and plants with their eerie glow.

ST. ANN'S, JAMAICA
288 STUSH IN THE BUSH

Enjoy an intimate, vegan culinary experience in this open-air dining room on an organic farm. You will be surrounded by the Jamaican jungle, with the sound of the ocean below, as you enjoy a meal that has been lovingly prepared by the husband-and-wife team who run the farm and restaurant.

CAP-HAÏTIEN, HAITI
289 CITADELLE LAFERRIÈRE

One of the largest fortresses in the Americas clings to the ridges of a Haitian mountainside. It is astonishingly huge and visitors have access to almost every part of the fortress, from the looming walls to the rambling ramparts and rooftop, with its fantastic views of tumbling peaks in every direction. Hire a guide in Milot to take you on the 7-mi (11-km) horseback trek in the local area.

HIDDEN GEM

LABADEE, HAITI
290 ÎLE RAT

Île Rat redefines the paradise island getaway. It is secluded and remote, and it takes less than ten minutes to walk around the fine white-gold beach ringing the lushly forested interior. Rent a boat taxi from Labadee and pay extra for the fisherman to rustle you up a fresh lobster lunch on the beach. Christopher Columbus is said to have used Île Rat as a lover's hideaway, and it's easy to see why.

JACMEL, HAITI
291 JACMEL

The old town center of Jacmel is full of mansions and coffee depots, wrought-iron balconies, and peeling facades. Beautiful beaches such as Ti Mouillage are nearby, as is the Bassin Bleu waterfall where only a few visitors are allowed each day. Stay at Hotel Florita, resplendent in old-world charm with a pool and plenty of Haitian art to admire.

DOMINICAN REPUBLIC
292 PLAYA LIMÓN

Take the scenic Highway 104 west through the mountains to the tourist-free hidden beach of Playa Limón. This is a 2-mi (3-km) long stretch of virgin Atlantic coast, which is lined with coconut trees leaning into the ocean. You are likely to have the spot to yourself; if not, the drive alone will justify the trip to this stunning stretch of coastline.

Plymouth ghost town

MONTSERRAT
293 FOXES BAY

After years of being strictly off-limits in the volcano exclusion zone, this beautiful and unspoiled piece of paradise is accessible once more.

MONTSERRAT
294 PLYMOUTH

On June 25, 1997, all residents of the largest settlement on Montserrat were evacuated following a series of volcanic eruptions. Montserrat Island Tours is one of the few tour operators that has gained permission to run excursions to the ghost town. It is a stark reminder of the fragility of the region and the power of nature.

ANTIGUA
295 SMILING HARRY'S

Enjoy a drink from this rustic beach shack at the mouth of a cove, which is famous for its Antiguan fare. Clamber over the rocks at the cliff-end of the beach for a natural mud bath.

BARBADOS
297 SANDY LANE

Backing on to a golden arc of sand, one of the Caribbean's most famous hotels oozes luxury and glamour and offers privacy to its paparazzi-shy guests.

BARBADOS
298 ANDROMEDA BOTANIC GARDENS

Located in the parish of St. Joseph, the lush vegetation and shaded pathways make a pleasant diversion from sea and sand. The garden is a profusion of tropical plants, with moss-covered walkways and bridges connecting the spaces, and manicured lawns and formal gardens complementing the mix.

ANTIGUA
296 JUMBY BAY SPA

Accessible only by boat, and with no cars in sight, Jumby Bay is an undisturbed island of powder soft beaches, winding cycle paths, and simple pleasures. The luxury rooms and villas spread across this private island are surrounded by lush landscapes and spectacular views out across the Caribbean Sea.

MUSTIQUE

299 MANDALAY

Blending ornate Balinese style with the natural charm of the Caribbean, this hilltop estate was built in 1989 for the late rock superstar David Bowie. It was designed around waterfalls pouring into koi-filled ponds; each of the five luxurious suites has its own private veranda from where you can enjoy gentle sea breezes. These porticos lead to the infinity pool overlooking the Atlantic. Guests also have access to the estate's catamaran.

Mandalay

HIDDEN GEM

DOMINICA

300 MACOUCHERIE DISTILLERY

You won't find the distillery for Dominica's only 100 percent homegrown rum in many tourist guidebooks. The tiny Macoucherie distillery dates back to 1760. It still uses a water-powered mill, antique machinery, and traditional methods to produce slightly more than enough rum for the island. Once local demand is met, small quantities go to neighboring Caribbean islands.

DOMINICA

301 JUNGLE BAY DOMINICA

Inside Jungle Bay's tree house hideaways, drenched in the tropical scents and sounds of the surrounding jungle, you are in your own private world. There is no need for television or other technology here; instead watch lazy lizards sunning themselves as the sea breeze caresses your skin while you sway gently on the porch hammock. It is almost impossible not to doze.

DOMINICA

302 MORNE TROIS PITONS NATIONAL PARK

Luxuriant tropical forest wraps itself around the volcanic features of the eponymous Morne Trois Pitons to create Dominica's wildest landscape. Here, you can relax on idyllic deserted shores fringed with coconut palms and cool off beside the 50-ft (15-m) Emerald Falls, before swimming deep into the Titou Gorge with its prehistoric ferns.

DOMINICA
303 WAITUKUBULI TRAIL

Few people have completed the full 71 miles (115 km) of the Caribbean's first long-distance walking trail. Running the length of Dominica, through virgin rain forest and over mountainous ridges to a boiling lake, the Waitukubuli Trail takes one week to hike. As you journey, you will travel along paths that were historically used by runaway slaves escaping the coastal plantations.

GRENADINES

304 PETIT ST. VINCENT

It is easy to forget that there are any other people on the island when you check in to Petit St. Vincent. One-bedroom cottages are discreetly tucked into the hillside, and two-bedroom beach villas nestle along the shoreline. The island is refreshingly free from telephones and television: a quaint flag system to communicate with staff replaces the former; wide-open ocean views replace the latter. With no wi-fi either, the outside world becomes practically nonexistent, leaving you to explore the 115-acre (47-hectare) volcanic island undisturbed. Guests also have access to the resort's private yacht, *Beauty*.

Diving in Petit St. Vincent

ANGUILLA

305 ZEMI BEACH HOUSE HOTEL & SPA

Zemi is set on the sugar-white sands of Shoal Bay. Reserve the beachfront suite for a private slice of sandy shore and your own personal plunge pool.

SAINT LUCIA

306 RAINFOREST SPA AT SUGAR BEACH

Look out across the waterfall as you are gently massaged and moisturized in one of the spa's tree house–style luxury treatment rooms.

BONAIRE ISLAND

307 NO NAME BEACH

Take a water taxi to No Name Beach on the tiny uninhabited island of Klein Bonaire and step ashore to enjoy pure isolation.

HIDDEN GEM
CURAÇAO

308 KLEIN CURAÇAO

This ghost island is abandoned and uninhabited except for a growing turtle colony. The only signs of its former glory are a lighthouse, shipwrecks, and abandoned homes.

TRINIDAD & TOBAGO
309 LITTLE TOBAGO

A birdwatcher's paradise, where bridled terns, brown boobies, and red-billed tropicbirds live in the quiet coves and cliffs of the tiny salt-sprayed island. Don't forget your binoculars.

TRINIDAD & TOBAGO
310 ASA WRIGHT NATURE CENTER

Rise at dawn to watch hummingbirds sipping sugar solution from the birdfeeders on the veranda. The Asa Wright Nature Center comprises nearly 1,500 acres of mainly forested land in the Arima and Aripo Valleys of the Northern Range in Trinidad and Tobago.

Hummingbird, Trinidad & Tobago

Mastic Trail

CAYMAN ISLANDS
311 MASTIC TRAIL

Not many tourists undertake this challenging hike
on Grand Cayman but those who do are greatly
rewarded. As the last surviving untouched forest on
the island, the swathe of vegetation is a far cry
from the wide golden beaches nearby. You will see
indigenous flora and fauna as you are led along the
trail by an expert guide. Alternatively, you can
guide yourself; expect to be walking for around
three hours and wear sturdy footwear.

HIDDEN GEM
CAYMAN ISLANDS
312 TEMPLE BETH SHALOM

A small and charming Jewish temple surrounded
by lush vegetation and lovely gardens in the
grounds of Mango Manor bed-and-breakfast.

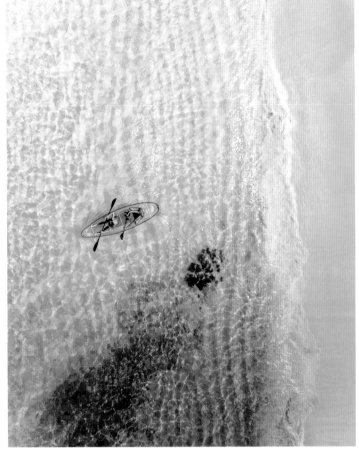

Turks and Caicos Islands

TURKS AND CAICOS ISLANDS

313 TURKS AND CAICOS ISLANDS

Hiding at the southern tip of the Bahamian archipelago, this sparsely populated string of low-sand cays possesses some of the most spectacular coral reefs in the world. You will find jungle-wrapped ruins, laid-back beach bars, and colonial towns where the pace of modern life has been abandoned in favor of a more relaxed approach to passing the day.

CAYMAN ISLANDS

314 STARFISH POINT

An undeveloped stretch of beach, freckled with starfish of all different colors and sizes that gather in the shallows of the shoreline. The pristine sands and surroundings are straight out of a lifestyle magazine. Arrive by boat, drop anchor, and let the day and your thoughts drift away on the beautiful, crystal clear currents.

BERMUDA

315 PINK SAND BEACHES

The south shore between Horseshoe Bay Beach and Warwick Long Bay has Bermuda's best pink sand beaches. It is prohibited to collect the sand as a souvenir.

VENEZUELA
316 ORINOCO RIVER

The great Orinoco River runs from the rain forests of deepest Colombia and through Venezuela, to spill out of a vast, jungled delta into the Atlantic. It is one of the largest river systems in the world, far less known and less frequently visited than its mighty sibling the Amazon, but just as rich an experience for those who do make the effort.

A cruise on the Orinoco River starts at the harbor town of Ciudad Bolivar. or the small port of San Jose de Buja near Maturin. You will be taken deep into the delta to lodge in simple riverside cabañas such as those at the Orinoco Eco Camp. These are on a nature reserve inside virgin jungle. You will then be led by indigenous Warao guides through the most isolated parts of the delta to watch the wetland's wildlife. As you move silently, you are accompanied only by the sounds of the paddle pulling through the water as it gently laps against the wooden hull of the boat.

These swampy forests at the ocean's edge are home to jaguar, puma, ocelot, and various monkey species. Birdwatchers can hope to spot macaws, parrots, toucans, egrets, falcons, and hummingbirds, among others. And of course, the marine life is abundant too, including dolphins, cayman, turtles, piranha, and catfish. Guides will lead you on treks into the jungle, to learn about the medicinal plants, sweet fruits, and exquisite orchids, or to explore caves with prehistoric petroglyphs.

Watch the sun set back at the cabaña, before the Orinoco waves lull you to sleep.

IWOKRAMA FOREST, GUYANA

317 IWOKRAMA RIVER LODGE

Nestled on the banks of the majestic Essequibo River, in the heart of one of the last untouched tropical forests in the world, Iwokrama River Lodge and Research Center is an ecotourism gem. While the research center attracts scientists studying the rich biodiversity of the region, the Lodge is an exclusive destination for amateur naturalists who are interested in learning about rain forest conservation and the importance of protecting this fragile environment.

Guests take up temporary residence in one of eight two-person thatched-roof cabins that stand on stilts overlooking the Essequibo. The cabins are basic but spacious, with everything powered by solar panels. Hammocks sway enticingly on the wraparound veranda, offering the perfect place to watch the sun rise and set over the still water as you listen to the shrieks of monkeys and calls of the forest birds. When the rain begins to pour, the cabin is the perfect refuge to reflect upon the incredible sights of the day.

For guests who want to balance relaxation with activity, there is an excellent trail system that starts directly from the Lodge. A nearby network of canopied walkways allows an impressive perspective over Guyana's lush, forested interior. From the treetop bridges a world of wildlife comes to life, which would be invisible from the forest floor, and you will see monkeys more agile, and birds more colorful, than you had ever imagined.

Iwokrama is one of the best places in the world to spot the elusive jaguar in the wild. Expert guides lead small expeditions in the early morning, or at dusk, through the rain forest passage, on the lookout for the mysterious beasts. The big cats are notoriously good at hiding, but many have been lucky to see jaguars in their native habitat.

Another impressive trail takes visitors on a two-hour climb to the summit of Turtle Mountain, from where you can soak in the view from an unparalleled vantage point of horizon-to-horizon old-growth rain forest. From up here, you might be lucky to spot macaws and toucans, red howler monkeys, or the harpy eagle. The creek at the foot of the mountain serves as a watering spot for tapirs and agouti. On your return, the open-air restaurant is the perfect place to watch the wildlife on the river from a more sedate spot, while enjoying traditional Guyanese cuisine.

BOGOTÁ, COLOMBIA
318 BOGOTÁ GRAFFITI TOUR
A tour of the urban art scene started by a street artist and a graffiti writer who wanted to promote Bogotá's exciting local artists to visitors.

BOGOTÁ, COLOMBIA
319 COLOMBIAN COFFEE TOUR
Visit small family farms as you learn about Colombia's coffee-growing culture and taste some of the world's smoothest coffee.

BOGOTÁ, COLOMBIA
320 CAFÉ CULTOR
A shipping container has been converted into a cool café, complete with a pretty rooftop terrace. It is the perfect spot for enjoying sunny afternoons in the capital, away from the hustle and bustle.

MEDELLÍN, COLOMBIA
321 CAFÉ VELVET
Natural sunlight hits a wall of cascading greenery at the back of this warm and inviting place that is popular with locals looking for a quiet spot to work.

Café Velvet

Biblioteca de España

MEDELLÍN, COLOMBIA
322 BIBLIOTECA DE ESPAÑA

This ultramodern library rises like a volcano from the mountaintop. Its progressive design transports visitors away from the violence that has affected so many from the nearby community since the 1980s.

On a clear day, the views from the patio areas are amazing. Ride the Metrocable above the rooftops and back down to the main city. The library is closed on the weekends, so you may get a gondola to yourself and be tempted to ride the line out over the mountains and forests on the edge of Medellín to beautiful Arvi Park.

MEDELLÍN, COLOMBIA
323 MUSEO CASA DE LA MEMORIA

The views over the city park and surrounding hills alone make this museum commemorating armed conflict a worthwhile trip. But do spend time inside exploring the many fascinating exhibits.

HIDDEN GEM
BOYACÁ, COLOMBIA
324 VILLA DE LEYVA

High in the Andes, the sixteenth-century cobbled streets and whitewashed buildings of this picturesque town, have been preserved almost in their entirety. Restaurante Savia, in an old colonial house with a large back garden, specializes in vegetarian fare and using local, artisanal produce.

CARIBBEAN COAST, COLOMBIA
325 CARTAGENA

Here you can wander without aim or schedule, savoring the architectural details of Cartagena's narrow streets. The Convento de la Popa sits atop the city's highest hill. Follow its brick path for expansive views over the city and discover a crumbling courtyard draped with bougainvillea.

ANTIOQUIA, COLOMBIA
326 LA CUEVA DEL ESPLENDOR

Water rushes furiously through the hole in the cave's ceiling, kicking up a cloud of mist within the Cave of Splendor. Journey on horseback from Jardín, then stay awhile and absorb nature's power, before making the return ride through the raw beauty of the Colombian hills.

SIERRA NEVADA, COLOMBIA
327 CIUDAD PERDIDA

Deep in the Sierra Nevada de Santa Marta mountains is an ancient city that remains accessible only on foot through remote jungle. The trek can be made over three to six days, and much of this time will be spent blissfully alone, with just nature and calling wildlife for company.

Villa de Leyva

META, COLOMBIA
328 CAÑO CRISTALES

For a brief period every year, the Caño Cristales river blossoms in a vibrant explosion of color when the plant that lines the riverbed turns a brilliant red. The natural phenomena that is the rainbow river is found in a remote park, where visitor numbers are severely restricted so it's never crowded.

SAN ANTONIO DEL TEQUENDAMA, COLOMBIA
329 TEQUENDAMA FALLS MUSEUM

This lush mountain mansion-turned-nature museum stands majestically above the spectacular 151-ft (46-m) Tequendama Falls. Once an elegant hotel that fell to rack and ruin, the building was reopened in 2013, its beautiful grounds and viewing terrace welcoming the public once more.

BANOS, ECUADOR

330 SWING AT THE END OF THE WORLD

Deep in the Ecuadorian wilderness, a long, lone swing hangs from a tree high over the steep sides of a canyon. This is the Swing at the End of the World at the Casa del Arbol volcano monitoring station. It will suit those seeking that exhilarating feeling of freedom, as they literally fly out over the expansive landscape below.

QUITO, ECUADOR
331 BASÍLICA DEL VOTO NACIONAL

Instead of gargoyles, this massive Gothic church on a hill in the Old Town is home to a host of stone turtles and iguanas celebrating Ecuador's rich natural history. For a little extra distance from the crowds, you can climb the basilica's towers for a 384-ft (117-m) high panoramic view of the city's historic spires, tiles, and towers.

HIDDEN GEM
QUITO, ECUADOR
332 CONVENTO DE SAN DIEGO

Climb the narrow stairs to the bell tower and walk along the rooftop overlooking the city, or sit in the quiet seventeenth-century convent's courtyard.

QUITO, ECUADOR
333 CASA GANGOTENA

Standing proudly on the site of an Incan temple in the center of Quito, this former mansion-turned-boutique hotel gives a colonial twist to 1920s elegance. Some rooms overlook the hotel's internal courtyard, where a splash of tropical intensity breaks the white stucco-columned classicism of the design aesthetic.

QUITO, ECUADOR
334 BARRIO SAN MARCOS

Meandering through the streets of one of the oldest parishes in Quito is like visiting an open-air museum of architecture.

GUAYAQUIL, ECUADOR
335 SEMINARIO PARK

This is a pretty park in the center of the city that is populated with dozens of land iguanas that hang out in the sunshine of the ornate gardens. You can get close to them as they laze on tree limbs, sunbathe at the edge of a pond, and saunter across the street. These laid-back lizards are so used to seeing people that they will even pose for a selfie.

MASHPI, ECUADOR

336 MASHPI LODGE

Enjoy the view of the cloud-shrouded rain forest from your Philippe Starck–designed bathtub at the ecofriendly Mashpi Lodge, situated deep in the foothills of the Andes. Tempered glass walls throughout mean that the jungle is ever present, while the open-air viewing platform is the perfect place to watch butterflies and hummingbirds at play in their natural habitat.

MINDO, ECUADOR

337 MINDO NAMBILLO CLOUD FOREST RESERVE

The Mindo Nambillo Cloud Forest Reserve is one of the most diverse natural landscapes of Ecuador. A chorus of frogs, insects, birds, and animals accompanies the thunderous roar of waterfalls. Hummingbirds as tiny as your finger flit between orchids that burst with color while butterflies as large as your hand play in the blooms above.

COCA, ECUADOR

338 AMAZON RIVER

The Amazon River is a wild, untamed realm at the very heart of the Ecuadorian rain forest. Discover the mystery and spirit of this multicolored prism of life aboard Anakonda Amazon Cruise's luxury eighteen-suite vessel. From hammocks on the expansive observation deck, you can watch pink river dolphins play, and spot otters and turtles.

SANTA CRUZ ISLAND, ECUADOR

339 LAS GRIETAS

A wild swimmer's dream, these long fractures in
the earth's surface were formed from cooling
volcanic lava and are filled with emerald-green
water and brightly colored fish. Float on your back
and look up at the dramatic sheer-sided canyon
walls of dark volcanic rock towering hundreds of
feet above you. *Las Grietas* means "the cracks."

SANTA MARIANITA, ECUADOR

340 PUNTA LA BARCA

The owners of this bamboo house that watches
over deserted Pacific beaches welcome slow
travelers who wish to get to know the gentle
pace of life in the quiet fishing village of Santa
Marianita. Long-stay guests and international
digital nomads are welcome.

341 PIKAIA LODGE

You don't have to be an evolutionary biologist to appreciate the sheer spectacle of the place that inspired Charles Darwin's theory of natural selection. The Galápagos Islands provide a home for an all-star cast of plants, birds, and animals, many of which are found nowhere else on the planet. Tourism is carefully controlled: Visitors are permitted to enter only small pockets of the national park and only with registered tour guides, making solitude hard to find. However, guests at the 14-room, eco-friendly Pikaia Lodge, balancing on the cone of an extinct volcano on the edge of Santa Cruz Island, have access to a private yacht. An expert guide knows exactly when and where to make the best landings to avoid the crowds.

URQUILLOS, PERU
342 EXPLORA VALLE SAGRADO

View Peru's spectacular Sacred Valley through a picture window at the Explora Valle Sagrado, the perfect base for becoming better acquainted with the whole area.

ANDES, PERU
343 MACHU PICCHU

The mysterious architectural site high in the Andes is breathtaking beyond belief. Up to 2,500 people visit the ancient ruins every day, but you can avoid the crowds by staying at the Belmond Sanctuary Lodge—the only hotel at the entrance to the park. For the most spectacular view, purchase one of 200 tickets to make the morning climb up Huayna Picchu mountain, which flanks the ruins. At the top, make sure you enter the Temple of the Moon, which is tucked away in a cave on the mountainside.

HIDDEN GEM
MOYOBAMBA, PERU
344 WAQANKI CENTER

A large botanical garden within a cloud forest containing almost 400 species of orchids, as well as a hummingbird sanctuary. There are two small lodges for visitor accommodation.

CHOQUEQUIRAO, PERU
345 CHOQUEQUIRAO
Sit and watch woolly clouds unravel around Andean peaks.
Choquequirao is three times larger than Macchu Picchu
but receives less than 1 percent of the visitors so you can
be sure of seclusion.

MADRE DE DIOS, PERU
346 MANU NATIONAL PARK
This unspoiled area of the
Amazon rain forest is an
unexplored paradise that is
home to isolated tribes. Book a
place on a riverboat cruise and
meander along the mighty river.

URUBAMBA, PERU
347 MORAY
Stunning Incan ruins in a remote
area of the sacred valley. Enjoy a
sense of peace and almost total
isolation, since this treasure is
rarely mentioned in guidebooks,
and welcomes only the most
intrepid travelers and locals.

AREQUIPA, PERU
348 COLCA CANYON
Colca Canyon is the second-
deepest canyon in the world,
and also one of the best places
for spotting the endangered
Andean condor—it is a truly
humbling experience to watch
these majestic birds in flight.

ICA PROVINCE, PERU

349 HUACACHINA

The day is almost done and the sun is about to set. From your position high on top of a giant wind-sculpted sand dune, the colors of the desert landscape shift through a spectrum of golden yellows and rusty reds. Up here, you are alone with just your thoughts and the dramatic sweeping view for company. Miles and miles of undulating hills of sand stretch into the distance in all directions. However, 656 ft (200 m) below you, at the base of the dune, there is an unexpected oasis; a tranquil lagoon fringed with exotic palm trees, flourishing foliage, and a scattering of elegant buildings.

There are only ninety-six permanent residents in Huacachina, most of whom make their living through tourism: renting out dune buggies and sandboards and running the handful of hotels and guesthouses around the lagoon. There is really not a lot to do here but poke around the few quaint shops, browse a little in the library, and spend a few days idling around the lagoon and climbing the sand dunes.

The lagoon is said to have healing properties and was a popular bathing spot in the 1940s for wealthy Peruvians. Legend has it that the rolling waves of sand were created by the flowing cloak of an Incan princess while she was fleeing a hunter.

Huacachina is on the backpacker trail, but it isn't difficult to avoid the party hostels and choose a more remote spot to stay.

Autor 2

350 **AUTOR 2**

This stylish guesthouse in the center of Miraflores, in downtown Lima, has just six charming, bespoke rooms, with private balconies, a peaceful internal courtyard, and a Jacuzzi on the roof terrace.

351 **LIBRERÍA EL VIRREY**

Idle away some time in serene solitude as you escape the chaos of Peru's capital city. Literature reigns in this oasis of peace and knowledge, but there are other activities when it's time to put your book away. Take a seat at the chessboard and invite a passerby to play, or sit and stroke the bookshop's cat while you enjoy a coffee in the café.

352 **PRIVATE TOURS**

The hidden courtyards and ramshackle rooftops above the city of Lima are often accessible only to those in the know. Hiring a guide to explore the crumbling houses and secret gardens opens up a wealth of historical art and architecture. High-end tour company Aracari can organize a local guide, and tailor a tour to your specific interests.

Paragliding in Lima

LIMA, PERU

353 PARAGLIDE OVER THE CITY

Lima's cliff-top location and strong winds make it the ideal location for urban paragliding. Aeroxtreme offers one-day courses that will take you high above the city for some incredible vistas.

CUSCO, PERU

354 SAN BLAS

This corner of Cusco feels a lot quieter than the rest of the tourist-drenched city. Take a seat on a well-worn bench outside the ancient church and enjoy some time reflecting.

CUSCO, PERU

355 PALACIO NAZARENAS

Each of this intimate urban retreat's fifty-five spacious suites are oxygen-enriched and come with their own personal butler. Hidden in a tranquil and historic square behind the city's main plaza, the Palacio Nazarenas spa is built upon ancient Incan walls and set around sun-filled courtyards. It is also the location of Cusco's only heated, outdoor swimming pool.

356 LENÇÓIS MARANHENSES NATIONAL PARK

Named for the Portuguese word for "bedsheets"—
lençóis—this national park of tall, white sand dunes just
outside the Amazon basin, stretches for 43 mi (70 km)
along the coast and 31 mi (50 km) inland. Between
January and June, rainstorms usher in thousands of
crystal-clear lagoons, which reach their peak in July. Stay
in the village of Atins, a clutch of laid-back beach bars,
restaurant shacks, warm waters, and swaying palm trees,
all tickled by the sea breeze.

Atlantic Forest

ATLANTIC COAST, BRAZIL
357 ATLANTIC FOREST

The Brazilian Atlantic rain forest is one of the most endangered forests in the world, but if you visit, you will have the opportunity to see some of its incredible natural treasures. The forest contains an incredible 40 percent of Earth's 20,000 plant species.

BAHIA, BRAZIL
358 FUMAÇA WATERFALL

Hike the isolated trails of the gorgeous Chapada Diamantina mountains to the base of Brazil's highest waterfall before climbing to the top to take in the awesome view. A three-day hike from Lençois sees you camping in open caves and the shells of old churches before traveling deeper into the remote valley.

Uxua Casa Hotel & Spa

TRANCOSO, BRAZIL
359 UXUA CASA HOTEL & SPA
Choose the two-bedroom Gulab Mahal suite with its own private garden and open-air bathrooms at this stylish retreat in the historic town of Trancoso.

ALTO PARAÍSO DE GOIÁS, BRAZIL
360 VALE DA LUA
Ancient river and lava flow has smoothed the rocks of Moon Valley to create an otherworldly lunar landscape of pits and hollows. The valley is on private property but is open to visitors, although you will need a local guide to find it, as it is a long way off the beaten path.

PARANA, BRAZIL
361 IGUAÇU FALLS
These mighty waterfalls lie on the border of Brazil and Argentina. The 275 waterfalls are a magnificent display of nature, set within a lush, subtropical rain forest. The largest waterfall here is almost twice as tall as Niagara, so the scale is truly epic. Stay at the Belmond Hotel das Cataratas within the park to experience the falls when the tours have left.

RIO DE JANEIRO, BRAZIL
362 TIJUCA NATIONAL PARK

Tijuca National Park, one of the largest urban rain forests on the planet, is filled with well-marked trails through a terrain of beautiful trees, waterfalls, and mountain peaks. Find the Vista Chinesa gazebo that looks down upon Rio's lagoon and its seemingly endless beaches.

RIO DE JANEIRO, BRAZIL
363 LARGO DO BOTICÁRIO

The faded grandeur of this all-but-abandoned colonial-era city square only adds to its charm. The bright reds and yellows of the peeling paintwork are matched in vibrancy by the encroaching rain forest vegetation. Its location means that few tourists add it to their itineraries, which is a real shame—but means having the square virtually to yourself. At number 32 is a small art gallery.

RIO DE JANEIRO, BRAZIL
364 CAFÉ SECRETO

In a city famed for its carnival atmosphere, Café Secreto is a little slice of peace amid the nonstop partying. Hidden down a charming, artistic alleyway off the bustling Largo do Machado, this little coffee shop often goes largely unnoticed by those not in the know.

RIO DE JANEIRO, BRAZIL
365 PURO

The large glass windows and clean lines of this unfussy restaurant next to the botanical gardens highlight the area's lush greenery. Reserve a table on the third-floor terrace of the unassuming house for fresh air and the best views of the magnificent gardens below.

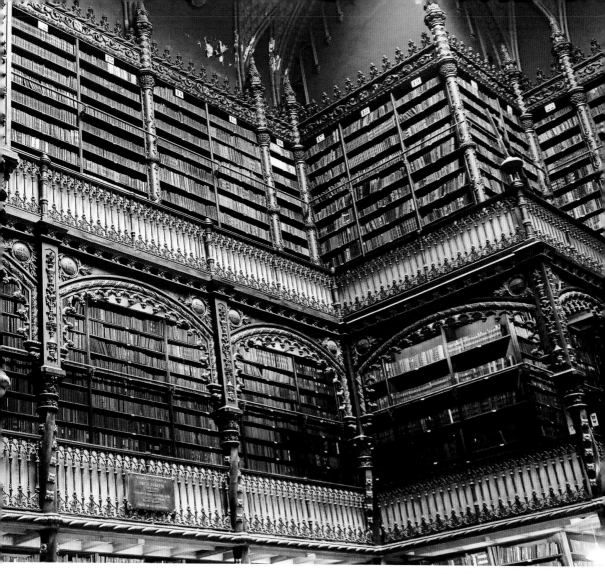

Royal Portuguese Reading Room

RIO DE JANEIRO, BRAZIL

366 CASA MARQUES

Each room in this cool, converted mansion in the Bohemian neighborhood of Santa Teresa has been stylishly decorated with original art and artisanal furnishings. The views from the rooftop pool span across Rio to Sugarloaf Mountain and Guanabara Bay and are truly impressive.

RIO DE JANEIRO, BRAZIL

367 ROYAL PORTUGUESE READING ROOM

This dazzling Gothic ode to literature only receives an average of 150 visitors a day, making it the ideal spot to quietly take in some architectural genius and culture. The beautiful stained-glass dome bathes the reading room in natural light.

SALVADOR, BRAZIL
368 VILLA BAHIA

This sustainably run boutique hotel is in a pair of restored Portuguese-style colonial houses. As well as gorgeous rooms and peaceful courtyards, there is a panoramic terrace and a plunge pool.

SÃO PAULO, BRAZIL
369 SKYE BAR
Perched atop the luxurious Hotel Unique, the Skye bar has a sweeping view over Ibirapuera Park and the entire São Paulo skyline.

SALVADOR, BRAZIL
370 PALACETE DAS ARTES
This small palace was once home to one of the wealthiest families in Salvador before it was donated to the state and converted into a museum. Its tranquil grounds are pleasantly shaded by mango trees and host a few sculptures cast by the French artist Rodin. The peaceful tropical garden also contains an open-air café with large, comfortable couches for lounging. The museum itself is a modern space that hosts rotating contemporary art exhibitions, while the halls of the opulent palace can be explored for their architectural interest.

SÃO PAULO, BRAZIL
371 THE CRYPT AT THE CATHEDRAL OF SÃO PAULO
Explore the vast hall of Gothic columns and arches, and marble sculptures, of the huge crypt beneath the metropolitan Cathedral of São Paulo.

SALVADOR, BRAZIL
372 PORTO DOS LIVROS
Take a break from the chaotic city and browse the shelves in this unique new-and-used bookstore with a small English-language section.

SALVADOR, BRAZIL
373 PARAISO TROPICAL
This is an award-winning organic restaurant in a rustic-looking house off the tourist trail in a residential district. Choose a garden table for alfresco lunch.

SALVADOR, BRAZIL
374 CAFÉ TERRASSE
Take a seat in this hidden café on the rooftop of a French-language institute and enjoy an amazing view of the ocean and the Bay of All Saints.

Train cemetery

HIDDEN GEM

UYUNI, BOLIVIA

375 TRAIN CEMETERY

On the deserted outskirts of a small town perched high in the Andean plain, dozens of abandoned steam trains lie decaying, buffeted for decades by corrosive salt winds. These haunting relics are best enjoyed in the evening, when the tours have departed and you have the rusting giants to yourself.

UYUNI, BOLIVIA

376 ISLA DEL SOL

Revered in Incan mythology as the sun's birthplace, this sacred island in Lake Titicaca is one of Bolivia's most serene spaces. The archaeological marvels are sprawled across the small island and are best explored at a peaceful pace, the better to soak up their sense of mysticism.

UYUNI, BOLIVIA

377 HOTEL LA CÚPULA

COPACABANA, BOLIVIA

Scattered up the hillside above Lake Titicaca are the beautiful white-domed rooms of Hotel La Cúpula. In the garden, tiny hummingbirds dance around the deck chairs and hammocks that overlook the lake, giving an unbeatable vantage point for a spectacular sunset.

UYUNI, BOLIVIA
378 CAFÉ GOURMET MIRADOR

SUCRE, BOLIVIA

For the best view of Sucre, make the steep climb up to the patio loungers at Café Gourmet Mirador. Refresh yourself with a juice and gaze across the rooftop sea of white and terracotta to the mountains surrounding Bolivia's most beautiful city.

UYUNI, BOLIVIA
379 SALAR DE UYUNI

As dawn breaks over the seemingly endless sea of salt, the rising sun illuminates a surreal landscape of pristine white that spreads endlessly from horizon to horizon. This savagely beautiful, otherworldly terrain is one of the most remarkable vistas on Earth.

TIWANAKU, BOLIVIA
380 TIWANAKU

Dive into the myths and mysteries of the lost civilization of Tiwanaku at these ancient village ruins, which may even be the oldest city in the world. Wander about and puzzle over humanity's great progress through time as you peruse the architectural wonders of the enigmatic culture.

RÍO DE LA PLATA, URUGUAY
381 COLONIA DEL SACRAMENTO

Colonia is an irresistibly picturesque town on the bank of the Río de la Plata estuary, on the east coast of South America. The town's historic district sits on a small peninsula jutting into the river, holding a charming clutch of colonial-era, narrow, cobbled streets, tree-lined squares, and shaded riverside cafés. Major renovation occurred in the 1960s and in 1995 it was declared a UNESCO World Heritage Site.

PATAGONIA, CHILE

382 TORRES DEL PAINE NATIONAL PARK

Avoid the crowds that flock to this jewel in southern Chile's crown by taking the longer O trail over three to six days, rather than the shorter, more accessible W trail. You will never forget the moment when you first set eyes on the awe-inspiring mass of the Southern Patagonian Ice Field.

HIDDEN GEM

PANGUIPULLI, CHILE

383 TERMAS GEOMÉTRICAS

This Japanese-style labyrinth of hot springs and wooden walkways hidden in a Chilean forest canyon makes a quiet, if hard-to-find, rest stop.

Torres del Paine National Park

PATAGONIA, CHILE
384 PATAGONIAN FJORDS

Slow-cruise the coastline by no-frills cargo ferry, visiting tiny authentic fishing villages and looking out for colonies of native Magellanic penguins or migrating humpback whales. Receding glaciers have created a lacework of deep fjords, rugged peaks, and channels through colossal, ice-blue glaciers. Set your alarm and rise early to watch dawn break across this spectacular landscape.

PAPUDO, CHILE
385 PUNTA PITE

A twisting cliffside coastal pathway carved from stone. Staircases and passageways lead to hidden viewing platforms and secluded pebble beaches.

CHILOÉ, CHILE
387 CHURCHES OF CHILOÉ

Declared a UNESCO World Heritage Site in 2000, sixteen of the island of Chiloé's many churches are made entirely in native timber.

PUCÓN, CHILE
386 HACIENDA HOTEL VIRA VIRA

Hide away from it all in a bucolic riverside villa suite. From your bed, you will enjoy panoramic views of verdant meadows, volcano peaks, and doe-eyed cows. From the star-soaked outdoor hot tub, you can listen to the sounds of the surrounding nature reserve. Rise early for yoga practice or try your hand at fly-fishing from your own private patio.

Hacienda Hotel Vira Vira

388 ATACAMA DESERT

At night the desiccated air, gasping altitude, and lack of cloud cover in the world's driest desert create a canvas peppered with stars and planets. The Milky Way, Saturn, and Jupiter are routinely visible and, on the clearest nights, so are the distant dwarf galaxies known as the Magellanic Clouds. Guests at the Explora Atacama can use a 16-mm Meade telescope, clear and sharp enough that constellations burst from the heavens.

JUAN FERNÁNDEZ ISLANDS, CHILE
389 ROBINSON CRUSOE ISLAND
Follow the trails that take you to the island's lookouts. Once you arrive, you will understand the absolute feeling of isolation on this treasure island.

PUERTO VARAS, CHILE
390 CHILEAN LAKES
When Chileans want to escape urbanity, they head to the ancient forests and clear lakes hidden in the snowcapped mountains of the Lake District.

PANGUIPULLI, CHILE
391 MONTAÑA MÁGICA LODGE
Each cozy room is named after a local bird species in this mountain-shaped hotel that is covered in lush jungle vegetation.

AYSÉN, CHILE
392 AYSÉN
The least populated of Chile's fifteen regions has ample opportunity for solitude and reflection, with one sole road connecting the region's end-of-the-world towns.

Aysén

EASTER ISLAND, CHILE
393 EASTER ISLAND

From the top of Mount Terevaka, you can see the
unbroken waters of the South Pacific for 360
degrees around you, reminding you—should you
have impossibly forgotten—that you are standing
on one of the most remote places on Earth. Easter
Island is shrouded in legend and famed for its
Moai, which are the stone statues representing the
ancestors of the indigenous Polynesian inhabitants.
Hike the island's rugged coastline to discover sandy
coves and pitch-black lava tunnels opening out
onto the dramatic cliff face above crashing waves.

CHILE CHICO, CHILE
394 MARBLE CAVES

Take a boat trip through the intricate network
of marble caves carved over many thousands of
years by the waves of a brilliant blue glacial lake.

HIDDEN GEM
WELLINGTON ISLAND, CHILE
395 VILLA PUERTO EDÉN

This tiny village can only be reached by boat. Once
ashore, there are no roads, and electricity is only
available for a few hours each day.

Easter Island

SANTIAGO, CHILE
396 GALERÍA TAJAMAR

Off any tourist's map, Galería Tajamar is a prime example of the hidden treasures that await the curious traveler within Santiago. The small outdoor exhibition space is hidden deep within a large complex of postmodernist buildings. Its glass walls allow the artworks to be enjoyed at all hours.

SANTIAGO, CHILE
397 JARDIN CASTILLO HIDALGO

Found at the top of the Cerro Santa Lucía is a prettily landscaped garden with unforgettable views of the capital. Take your time on the climb, since the hill has plenty of lookouts and green spaces tucked away on its slopes, so you can pause for a breather.

SANTIAGO, CHILE
398 CERRO SAN CRISTÓBAL

Take the funicular between the sections of this huge hill at Santiago's center. On its peak, you will discover the benches of an outdoor church, and a little farther down its slopes, the Tupahue public swimming pool is beautifully landscaped and meticulously maintained.

VALPARAÍSO, CHILE
399 VALPARAÍSO

This colorful coastal city was the frequent inspiration for Chilean poet Pablo Neruda. The sprawling hills it is built upon can be traversed using the iconic one-hundred-year-old funiculars that are emblematic of the city. Take a camera and shoot the prolific street art as you travel slowly up and down.

VALPARAÍSO, CHILE
400 LA SEBASTIANA

Sunshine pours into the upper rooms of Chilean poet Pablo Neruda's Valparaíso home, which sits on top of a hill with heart-stopping views over the harbor. Spend the afternoon discovering mosaic pathways in the garden. These lead to benches that are hidden below a tangle of greenery.

VALPARAÍSO, CHILE
401 CAFE CON CUENTO

While the area around this quirky bookstore seems a little run down, Café con Cuento is a cute store with a small café that's popular for the tea time tradition of eating "once"—a selection of sweet and salty foods taken with tea. A small book exchange is maintained alongside those for sale.

Street art in Valparaíso

TIERRA DEL FUEGO, ARGENTINA
402 RÍO GRANDE
Several large estancias run luxury fishing lodges on the Río Grande, which is arguably the best river on the planet for fishing sea trout.

TIERRA DEL FUEGO, ARGENTINA
403 USHUAIA
Boats head from here—a town at the end of the world on South America's southernmost point—to an even more remote locale: Antarctica.

SANTA CRUZ PROVINCE, ARGENTINA
404 PERITO MORENO GLACIER

The Perito Moreno Glacier is one of the largest glaciers in the Southern Patagonian Ice Field. It is a jagged mass of dramatic ice scars and towering ridges, beaming white and marbled, copper-sulfate blue, surrounded by Patagonian forests and mountains. You can see it from dry land, but to experience it up close and personal, and away from the crowds, take the three-hour trek on the glacier. This way you can explore the ever-evolving formations of crevasses, caves, and lagoons that create a landscape unlike anything else on the planet.

GUALEGUAYCHÚ, ARGENTINA
405 ESTANCIA SANTA MARIA

This Argentine estancia on the pampas of Entre Ríos gives guests the chance to experience life on a traditional working cattle ranch—working, eating, and sleeping like a real vaquero.

MENDOZA, ARGENTINA
406 VINEYARD TOUR

Rent a bike and ride through the vineyards amid spectacular Andean scenery. Stay at Finca Adalgisa's leafy lodge, and you will be surrounded by Malbec vines and olive trees.

CAFAYATE, ARGENTINA
407 HOSTAL RUSTY-K

Eat grapes straight from the overhead vines in the beautiful backyard garden of this hostel in Argentina's second center for wine production.

Ushuaia

Alvear Palace Hotel

BUENOS AIRES, ARGENTINA
+08 EL ATENEO GRAND SPLENDID

For a tiny reading room with a giant atmosphere, curl up in one of the boxes of this converted theater in downtown Buenos Aires, which now houses a bookshop and café. It is often voted among the world's most beautiful bookshops.

BUENOS AIRES, ARGENTINA
+09 RECOLETA CEMETERY

Arguably the most beautiful place in the world to rest in peace. In this city of the dead, life is surprisingly abundant. Birds sing, wild cats stretch and slink to shady spots, and plants grow cheerfully around the marble mausoleums.

HIDDEN GEM

BUENOS AIRES, ARGENTINA

+10 DECATA

Duck off the main street and through an archway covered in lush vines to discover an unexpected quiet courtyard in the heart of the city. Decata's tables spill out of the doors to fill the cobbled and transformed coalyard, creating a pocket of calm in the busy city.

BUENOS AIRES, ARGENTINA

+11 ALVEAR PALACE HOTEL

The Alvear afternoon tea attracts an elegant crowd and is served in the beautiful, flower-filled orangery of the landmark Alvear Palace Hotel. Exuding Belle Epoque splendor, the Alvear sits in the exclusive Recoleta neighborhood, near its elegant boulevards and leafy parks.

BUENOS AIRES, ARGENTINA

+12 LIBROS DEL PASAJE

Slip into the sunroom of this charming bookstore and café, settle down at a table, and choose a book from the dark wooden bookshelves. The shelves hold mostly Spanish-language books, but there is also a small selection of English-language titles.

BUENOS AIRES, ARGENTINA

+13 BE JARDÍN ESCONDIDO

When movie director Francis Ford Coppola is in town, this lush, green oasis in one of Buenos Aires's most vibrant neighborhoods is his personal retreat. When he isn't around, you can rent his hidden paradise and enjoy the garden for yourself.

EUROPE

From the wild, windswept coast and rugged poetry of the Scottish Highlands, to the bleak, lonely isolation of the Siberian steppes, this is a continent of scenic beauty, epic history, and dazzling cultural diversity. Whether you're cruising the Turkish coast in a traditional gulet or exploring the rambling ramparts of fairy-tale castles in Austria, it's hard not to get swept up in the sheer romance of Europe.

Head north to effortlessly chic Scandinavia, where the Norwegian fjords carve their way dramatically through snow-capped mountains. And then there are the azure waters, sandy-white coves, and wide-open skies of the Mediterranean coastline. Even Europe's headline-stealing cities all have their quieter sides.

Madonna della Corona, see page 254

GALWAY, IRELAND
414 LOUGH CORRIB

This large lake is renowned for its world-class brown trout and salmon fishing. Angling on Lough Corrib is free, and there are plenty of boats and guides for hire around the shoreline. Row out to wooded Inchagoill island with its spectacular mountain views, secluded beaches, and the tiny twelfth-century Church of the Saints.

COUNTY KERRY, IRELAND

+15 SKELLIG RING

While the scenic Ring of Kerry throngs with tourists, no tour buses take the Skellig Ring, a little-traveled loop through Ireland's wildest countryside. Pull over at Coomanaspic for one of the best views in Ireland. From here, you can see the remote island of Skellig Michael, where *Star Wars: The Last Jedi* was partly filmed.

WATERFORD, IRELAND

+16 CLIFF HOUSE HOTEL

Clinging to a cliff above Ardmore Bay, this stylish five-star hideaway is a great base for walking on the rugged beaches below. Each room has a private balcony or terrace overlooking the Irish Sea, and is adorned with Irish artworks. Glass-walled showers capture superb sea views across the bay.

ARAN ISLANDS, IRELAND

+17 TEAMPULL BHEANÁIN

The beautiful and isolated Aran Islands have attracted and inspired many Irish artists and poets over the years. The unique, weather-battered landscape is home to the ancient ruins of Teampull Bheanáin, an eleventh-century Celtic church that sits on a ridge above the sea, its roofless silhouette a striking sight against the skyline.

DUBLIN, IRELAND

+18 MARSH'S LIBRARY

The Long Library at Trinity College is well known to tourists, but few know the oldest public library in Ireland: Marsh's Library. Tucked through a Gothic archway behind St. Patrick's Cathedral, stepping inside feels like going back to the 1700s. Don't miss the alcoves at the back where readers were locked in to prevent theft.

HIDDEN GEM

DUBLIN, IRELAND

+19 THE CAKE CAFÉ

A literal hidden gem—access is through a stationery shop, along a leafy path, and into a petite courtyard near trendy Camden Street. Inside you will discover an aura of peace and quiet. The mismatched tablecloths and brightly colored flowers give the place an almost sunny, tropical feel, whatever the weather decides to do outside.

Edinburgh, Royal Mile

EDINBURGH, SCOTLAND

+20 DR. NEIL'S GARDEN

Known as "Edinburgh's Secret Garden," Dr. Neil's Garden is a place of artistic and spiritual inspiration—for meditation and contemplation—that is just a stone's throw from the city. In this serene space, accessible through the tearoom of Duddingston Kirk, you will find secluded corners with wrought-iron benches for watching the clouds float over the loch.

EDINBURGH, SCOTLAND

+21 HIDDEN GARDENS OF THE ROYAL MILE TOUR

Take Greenyonder's guided walking tour to discover the little-known secret gardens and green nooks and crannies that are hidden behind the historic buildings of Edinburgh's Old Town. This relaxing tour is the perfect way to pass a couple of hours, away from the bustle of the capital city.

EDINBURGH, SCOTLAND

+22 ST. BERNARD'S WELL

The Greek goddess of health—Hygeia—presides over this natural spring, which was discovered in 1760 and was believed by locals to have healing properties. The circular Roman temple at the site is only open occasionally, but the peaceful wooded location makes for a pleasant place to sit awhile and ponder.

National Portrait Gallery

EDINBURGH, SCOTLAND
+23 NATIONAL PORTRAIT GALLERY

A quiet haven in which to admire great art. Seek out Café Portrait, a serene place to surround yourself with light and art.

EDINBURGH, SCOTLAND
+24 WELL CAFÉ

A welcoming café in a Nicolson Square Methodist church. It's light and bright inside, with an outdoor space to sit in the sun and people watch.

EDINBURGH, SCOTLAND
+25 THE TOWER AT NATIONAL MUSEUMS SCOTLAND

There's a fantastic skyline view from this seventh-floor rooftop garden. It was planted to tell the story of the Scottish landscape from the coast to the Highlands.

ISLE OF ARRAN, SCOTLAND

+26 **GOAT FELL**

The ascent up the highest peak on the Isle of
Arran is physically demanding, but you will be
accompanied by the sweet scent of heather,
and there is the opportunity to spot buzzards
and golden eagles. This, plus the incredible view
from the top, make the arduous trek worthwhile.
The round-trip from Brodick Castle will take you
up to six hours.

VARIOUS LOCATIONS, SCOTLAND

+27 **MOUNTAIN BOTHIES**

The Mountain Bothies Association maintains about
one hundred wilderness shelters in the most
remote parts of Scotland, for the benefit of all who
love wild and lonely places. The shelters—often
just four walls and a roof—are unlocked for anyone
to use and are at least several hours' walk from
a main road. In the furthest reaches of northwest
Scotland, Kervaig bothy has a private beach.

HOLY ISLE, SCOTLAND

429 CENTRE FOR WORLD PEACE AND HEALTH

The ancient spiritual heritage of Holy Isle dates to the sixth century. Now, a retreat program runs at the center throughout the summer, focusing on yoga, mindfulness, and spirituality. Visitors abide by the five golden rules, and everyone is invited to join in a daily meditation schedule.

SCOTTISH HIGHLANDS

428 MELLON UDRIGLE

With the sort of fine white sand and turquoise water usually found on tropical islands, the wild and remote beach at Mellon Udrigle is an unexpected paradise amid the soaring peaks and promontories of the Highlands. In wet, windy weather, the beach takes on a bleak atmosphere that might be straight out of a Brontë novel.

ARGYLL, SCOTLAND

430 ECOYOGA

Stress will seep away the moment you arrive at EcoYoga's tranquil riverside retreat. Here, the emphasis is on sustainable ecoliving, rustic and wholesome pleasures, vegetarian feasting, and of course, yoga. At the end of the day's practice, take a wild river swim before scrubbing, soaking, and sinking into the outdoor bathtub that overlooks a waterfall.

HIDDEN GEM

ISLE OF MULL, SCOTLAND

431 LIP NA CLOICHE GARDEN AND NURSERY

With a population of less than 3,000, and excellent hiking trails, you can walk for miles on Mull without meeting a single soul. Head inland to Lip na Cloiche, a small, densely planted garden open to the public. Here, you can enjoy stunning views of Loch Tuath and the Isle of Ulva, with its restaurant, The Boathouse.

MALLAIG, SCOTLAND

+32 MALLAIG TO EDINBURGH TRAIN

Six and a half hours of stunning Highland scenery. Look out for the twenty-one-arch Glenfinnan Viaduct made famous in the Harry Potter films.

SCOTTISH HIGHLANDS

+33 RANNOCH MOOR

Explore a vast untamed wilderness of blanket bog, lakes, rivers, and rocky hills. Lower level walks start at the remote Rannoch station.

ISLE OF SKYE, SCOTLAND

+34 THE CROFTER'S HOUSE

This is a peaceful nineteenth-century crofter's cottage for rent. Chic minimalism with a touch of Scandinavian style creates a cozy rural hideaway. Sit quietly in the window seat to spot otters and deer outside.

ISLE OF SKYE, SCOTLAND

+35 THE CUILLIN

The Cuillin is the most challenging and dramatic mountain range in Britain. You will find easier walks in the shadow of the ridge.

ISLE OF SKYE, SCOTLAND

+36 BLUE SHED CAFÉ

Enjoy coffee and homemade cake in the middle of nowhere. As the name suggests, the building itself is a large shed—albeit a lovingly renovated and decorated one— and the café overlooks the Cuillin mountain range. The owners are extremely knowledgeable about the local area so stock up on information while you enjoy lunch.

Mallaig to Edinburgh train

Loch Lomond, southern Scotland

ISLE OF IONA, SCOTLAND

437 ST. COLUMBA'S BAY

Follow the saint's footsteps to a picturesque beach with beautiful pebbles. Look out for slivers of greenstone known locally as "Columba's Tears."

VARIOUS LOCATIONS, SCOTLAND

438 SCOTLAND'S LOCHS

Scotland's countryside is a walker's paradise. The glens and dales, highlands, and islands seem to come straight out of fairy tales. The sparkling jewels in the countryside's crown, however, are the lochs. Numbering more than 30,000, they come in all shapes and sizes, from the famous Loch Ness to the little Loch Ard. After a long day hiking, find some "you time" at the five-star Loch Ness Lodge spa hotel, on the banks of Loch Ness. The lodge has seven individually designed rooms, all inspired by nature. Dores beach at the rear of Dores Inn offers a very peaceful lookout over Loch Ness.

+39 TRELLYN WOODLAND CAMPING

In the entire sixteen acres of Trellyn Woodland Camping, there are just five fields, three yurts, and a couple of geodomes. All are nestled in their own secluded and shady glade. This welcome consideration of privacy leaves you to enjoy the idyllic woodland setting, with accompanying birdsong, at your own pace.

For those seeking more luxury than the standard camping experience, the yurts offer raised rug-covered wooden floors, handmade furniture, and sumptuous beds draped with cushions and sheepskins. A woodburning stove provides your evening warmth, with a basket of wood already cut and waiting upon your arrival. For the utmost privacy, request the Starlight Sailor yurt at the end of the track. This yurt is named after a story book illustrated by a local artist, a copy of which is left for you to enjoy.

The two domes are impressive structures built to have as little impact on the environment as possible. They have been constructed out of rejected timber from an oak kitchen manufacturer. Many of the fitted items inside are recycled from reclaimed materials and household waste by-products, such as plastic bottles, which have been used creatively within. With the campsite being close to the sea and away from large towns, there is virtually no light pollution here. Through the panoramic window above the bed in the Star Dome, you may even see the Milky Way on a cloudless night as you drift off to sleep. Trellyn's owner is happy to provide you with star charts if you ask.

If you opt to camp, each field is like a little pocket of peace carved out of the woodland, providing you with everything you need to cater for yourself. The two Valley fields are perfect sun traps, separated from each other with a planted willow maze. For those who find the sound of a babbling brook to be soporific, ask for the Valley 1 field. Valley 2 is a little closer to the sea, while the Meadow fields are the closest to the campsite's private access to the beach and to the path to the village. If you're really getting in to the spirit of the wild, the owner runs three-hour bushcraft courses.

There's something about Trellyn that is truly magical—from the dappled yellow light through the trees to the beautiful Abercastle harbor beach that is just a couple of minutes' walk from the site—and will have you wishing you were staying longer.

Abercastle harbor beach

440 SECRET SUNRISE AT STONEHENGE

Completed more than 3,500 years ago, the monument of Stonehenge is generally accepted to be a prehistoric temple aligned with the movements of the sun. The two-ton bluestones were brought more than 150 mi (241 km) from the Preseli Hills, while the twenty-five-ton sarsen stones were likely from a quarry almost 20 mi (32 km) north in the Marlborough Downs. Visitors swarm, but if you get up early and approach Stonehenge from the west, a quiet dirt road on the left leads to a public footpath that gets you almost as close as the official entry ticket allows.

Glastonbury Tor

WILTSHIRE, ENGLAND
++1 GLASTONBURY TOR

Legend has it that King Arthur visited Glastonbury Tor, a hill topped by the remains of a fourteenth-century church tower. The tor is a beautiful place to walk, unwind, and relax, with breathtaking views across the English countryside. For pagans, this place is considered one of the most spiritual sites in the country.

HIDDEN GEM
CORNWALL, ENGLAND
++2 PENTIRE STEPS

For a truly calendar-worthy Cornish beach, follow the path from Pentire Farm House to the coast, then scramble down the cliffs to Pentire Steps beach. Still something of a secret, the golden sands and aqua sea, backed by dark imposing cliffs, are a photographer's dream. This secluded site is close to the popular Bedruthan Steps.

CORNWALL, ENGLAND
443 THE BEACH AT BUDE HOTEL
There's a young and contemporary vibe at this modern boutique hotel on the beach. The pastel-tinted New England–style rooms—with their pale wood furnishings, white duvets, and seashell-print cushions—are flooded with North Cornwall light. Request deluxe room 11, with its private sea-facing terrace and bathtub with a window view.

GLOUCESTERSHIRE, ENGLAND
444 CALCOT SPA
Borrow a pair of boots and explore the rolling rural Cotswolds landscape surrounding the fourteenth-century weathered stone farmhouse and farm buildings of Calcot Spa. There are many cozy nooks dotted around with squashy sofas to curl up on after a long hike, while the indulgent spa is impossible to resist.

DEVON, ENGLAND
445 MARISCO TAVERN, LUNDY ISLAND
A two-hour ferry from the English mainland, followed by a steep climb, will bring you to the Marisco Tavern—the only pub on Lundy island, and the only place with electric lighting after the generators shut down for the night. All gadgets are banned; there is no music and no ringing of slot machines.

NORTHUMBERLAND, ENGLAND
446 KIELDER FOREST
The exact location of the UK's most tranquil spot —according to acoustic engineering professor Trevor Cox in his book *Sonic Wonderland: A Scientific Odyssey*—is a secret. However, he reveals that it is deep within Kielder Forest in northeast England. The forest also has the darkest night skies in England making it perfect for stargazing.

LONDON, ENGLAND

447 **BARBICAN CONSERVATORY**

Hidden inside the brutalist concrete architecture of the Barbican Centre in central London is one of the city's most surprising secrets. The Conservatory is a hothouse of more than 2,000 species of tropical plants and trees. Here, you can hide away from the hustle of England's capital in a tranquil environment full of life and color. Following paths through the plants, you may stumble upon the little bridge over a pond, from which you can watch fat carp and lazy terrapins lounging below. Or take a relaxing stroll to find a peaceful corner in which to sit and appreciate the surrounding vegetation before climbing the wooden steps to the arid house, which bristles with the spikes of cacti and succulents of all shapes and sizes.

The Conservatory wraps around the huge flytower of the theater beneath it, the concrete structure morphing into the jungle-like foliage. The whole place gives the impression of a futuristic landscape from a science-fiction film, where the wilderness has taken over in the absence of human intervention. While you're here, take afternoon tea in the shadow of fig trees. The traditional menu of finger sandwiches, scones, and prosecco is inspired by the herbs, fruits, and spices found in the Conservatory. Booking ahead is essential.

The Barbican is one of London's most important cultural destinations. It is a complex of buildings that houses art galleries, performing arts spaces, and libraries. It is home to the London Symphony Orchestra and base for the Royal Shakespeare Company. At the heart of the development is St. Giles's Cripplegate church, one of the few remaining medieval churches in the City of London. The light and peaceful interior provides another calm spot in the city, and a break from the brutalist architecture of the Barbican.

Also within the Barbican Centre is one of London's newest public gardens. Beech Gardens is located on a roof area amid the walls of coarse concrete, looming towers, and tiled walkways. The planting ensures different flowers bloom month by month, treating you to delicate white cyclamen, lavender-blue flowers of scabious, and red crocuses. The garden is a secluded space rarely populated by anyone other than residents. The Conservatory is London's largest glasshouse after Kew Gardens. It is free to enter, or you can book a private tour with the gardeners to learn about its history.

The British Museum

LONDON, ENGLAND
+48 THE BRITISH MUSEUM
Enjoy stunning natural light in the museum's modern forecourt. The Enlightenment Gallery is often one of the quieter spots in the museum.

LONDON, ENGLAND
+49 CHUAN BODY + SOUL
A central spa that focuses on balance and restoration. It's found within the five-star luxury Langham Hotel close to London's Oxford Street.

The Ivy Chelsea Garden

LONDON, ENGLAND

450 ESPA SPA AT CORINTHIA

Whether you're resting in a heated marble recliner, or draped on a daybed beside the pool, this beautifully styled spa is an invitation to completely unwind. Black marble teamed with gold-and-cream paneling creates a sumptuous setting in which to enjoy the many relaxation spaces, including a fabulous glass-walled sauna. Highlights include the sleep pods—personal chill-out areas scattered with cushions and cashmere blankets to snooze between treatments. The Residential Mindful Sleep package focuses on being more present in the moment, with breathing techniques, massage, and Yoga Nidra meditation.

LONDON, ENGLAND

452 BOUNDARY

Design-led rooftop restaurant in Shoreditch for art lovers. The heated orangery is filled with citrus trees. A fire pit provides warmth in winter.

LONDON, ENGLAND

451 THE IVY CHELSEA GARDEN

Dine among beautiful blossoms and verdant foliage in this cross between a French brasserie and an English country garden.

LONDON, ENGLAND

453 FLOATWORKS

Natural flotation tank therapy elevates mood and lifts anxiety. The benefits are said to be similar to those of yoga, meditation, and mindfulness.

Southern Iceland

SOUTHERN REGION, ICELAND
454 VATNAJÖKULL NATIONAL PARK

Covering 13 percent of Iceland, this national park contains the largest glacier in the world outside of the Arctics. White ice descends into black volcanic sands for a dramatic mix of hot springs and frozen lakes. Head west where primitive roads are the ideal places for solitude.

SOUTHERN REGION, ICELAND
455 SELJAVALLALAUG

Avoid the most popular of Iceland's famous natural thermal baths and seek out others off the beaten track to enjoy in peace. Deserted Seljavallalaug was built into the mountainside in a narrow valley in 1923 and is fed by natural hot springs. The pool is free to use—if you manage to stumble across it!

SOUTHERN REGION, ICELAND
456 VÍK Í MÝRDAL

While Iceland might be best known for thermal baths, towering volcanoes, and lunar landscapes, it also has some stunning beaches, such as the black sand Reynisfjara. Folklore tells that the rocky sea stacks were once trolls that pulled ships to danger, until the sun rose and turned them to stone.

Icelandic vistas

REYKJAVIK, ICELAND
+57 STOFAN CAFÉ

The laid-back café in a historic brick building is split into little living areas, where vintage décor gives a cozy and snug feel to the place. The plump couches, resting on worn wooden floors, are exactly where you want to be when the temperature drops outside. The word *stofan* means "living room" in Icelandic.

TROLL PENINSULA, ICELAND
+58 DEPLAR FARM

Situated on the unspoiled wilderness of the Troll Peninsula, former sheep farm Deplar Farm has thirteen cozy suites, a stylish spa, and stunning views. It is a remote luxury getaway for an Icelandic adventure. Request the Nordic-style Flóki room, with its two-person hammock and three window-walls so you can enjoy the mountain panorama beyond.

459 AURORA SPOTTING

Halfway between mainland Norway and the North Pole, lie the Svalbard islands. This is raw, untouched Arctic wilderness at its wildest. It is also considered to be one of the best places to view the aurora borealis—or northern lights— during the "polar night" when there is practically no daylight. Tours operate out of Longyearbyen.

WESTERN NORWAY, NORWAY

+60 HJORUNDFJORD

Western Norway's deep blue fjords that cut through the snowcapped mountains are a popular draw. However, avoid the main tourist hubs such as Ålesund, Geiranger, and Trollstigen. A grown-up's swing overhangs Hjorundfjord in the garden of the Christian Gaard pub in Trandal, a roadless settlement accessible by boat.

ÅLESUND, NORWAY

+61 MOLJA LIGHTHOUSE

At the end of a jetty, five minutes from the main building, is room 47 of Hotel Brosundet: the 150-year-old Molja Lighthouse. Downstairs is a compact bathroom, while upstairs a snug bedroom looks west toward the Atlantic. In stormy weather, the sea sends spray high into the air, and waves lash the lighthouse walls.

ØSTFOLD, NORWAY

+62 VESTERØY

The Norwegian archipelago of Hvaler boasts the most number of sunny days per year to be found anywhere in the country. Part of Hvaler, this private island is totally off-the-grid, with no running water or Internet, making it perfect for a two-person getaway. The sweet, romantic cabin has everything you need and is drenched in Scandinavian charm.

DOVRE, NORWAY

+63 VIEWPOINT SNØHETTA

In the remote Dovrefjell Sunndalsfjella National Park, architects have built a secluded observation pavilion designed to resemble a stone eroded by wind and water. The park is said to be one of the last places in Europe to see wild mountain reindeer. A fireplace keeps visitors warm in winter.

OSLO, NORWAY

+64 OLD AKER CHURCH

Absorb the hushed sense of calm and scent of ancient stonework in the oldest building in Oslo, and one of the oldest in Eastern Norway. Local legend has it that the Old Aker Church is built upon four pillars of gold above an ancient Viking silver mine. The mine is said to be full of treasure that's guarded by a dragon.

COPENHAGEN, DENMARK

465 CENTRAL HOTEL AND CAFÉ

In the garret of a former shoemaker, on top of a small café, is a hotel with only one room. It is oozing with charm, its Scandinavian interior design embodying the Danish concept of *hygge*. The tiny café downstairs has only five chairs and is popular with locals for its delicious coffee. You'll find it near the south end of the Sankt Jorgen lake.

FAROE ISLANDS, DENMARK

466 FAROE ISLANDS

This is a collection of eighteen islands adrift in the Atlantic whose remoteness lends a unique air to the landscape and the self-sufficient Nordic people. This land is a wild, untamed, natural beauty, with diminutive grass-roofed wooden churches, networks of footpaths crossing the treeless moorlands, and gleaming pastures with isolated cottages and tiny communities.

BORRE, DENMARK

467 MØENS KLINT

The trails along the clifftop at Møens Klint weave through an ancient woodland of twisting trees. At the bottom of a long wooden staircase lies a land lost in time, the towering chalk-white cliffs striking against a vivid sea. It has been exposed by the sea, and you can find seventy-million-year-old fossils along the narrow shoreline. It has been designated one of the best stargazing sites in Europe.

COPENHAGEN, DENMARK

468 PALUDAN BOG & CAFÉ

This café is all about the books. Paludan is a secondhand bookshop-cum-coffee-shop in the city center behind Copenhagen University. You are encouraged to choose books and take your time to browse them over a cup of tea and a plate of warming food, all while enjoying the atmosphere of coziness and conviviality.

COPENHAGEN, DENMARK

469 FREETOWN CHRISTIANIA

Visit the hippie commune of Freetown Christiania, a green, car-free zone packed with art galleries and organic cafés. Christiania is an autonomous, peaceful district in the middle of Copenhagen, built upon a former military barracks. Walk the small alleys, admire the quaint colorful houses, and relax on the wooden platform on the waterfront.

COPENHAGEN, DENMARK

470 TIVOLI GARDENS

Opened in 1843, the pleasure gardens that inspired Hans Christian Andersen's fairy tale, "The Nightingale," have maintained their nostalgic grandeur and make a beautiful escape from the city. The striking, landscaped parterre are ideal for a quiet spot in the sun. At night, you can explore the enchanted gardens, which are draped with sparkling colored lights.

Treehotel

NORRBOTTEN, SWEDEN
+71 TREEHOTEL

Indulge your inner child and stay in a tree house. You'll need to scramble up ladders and follow treetop walkways to reach the six uniquely designed dens hanging in the branches of the Treehotel's forest. Rooms include the Mirrorcube, with its rustic chic interiors and private terrace, the spacious and modern Dragonfly, and the well-camouflaged Bird's Nest. Or you can climb a metal beam up to the UFO. Whichever you choose, enjoy the gentle sway of your room in the wind, knowing you are tucked away safely inside.

NORRBOTTEN, SWEDEN
+72 ICEHOTEL 365

The world's first permanent ice-and-snow hotel. With names such as Dreamscape, each room features stunning ice sculptures designed by different artists.

SIGTUNA, SWEDEN
+73 MARIAKYRKAN

This ancient brick church, built in the 1200s, is the oldest building still in use in Sweden's oldest town, Sigtuna. The historic town is one hour from Stockholm.

VÄSTERÅS, SWEDEN
+74 UTTER INN

Sleep in an aquarium in this floating, underwater hotel. Guests are provided with an inflatable boat for transport and are then left alone until supper is delivered.

Mariakyrkan

VÄSTMANLAND, SWEDEN
+75 SALA SILVERMINE SUITE

Spend the night dreaming in the deepest bedroom in the world, in the bowels of a mine. Down here, you will feel like you are a million miles from anybody else.

STOCKHOLM, SWEDEN
+76 FOTOGRAFISKA

A popular photography museum with a lovely café upstairs. Fotografiska also offers courses and workshops in photography for beginners and professionals.

STOCKHOLM, SWEDEN
+77 BARISTA

Indulge in the Swedish concept of *fika*. Take time out for a latte and a cinnamon bun in this small café inside the independent theater Viktoria.

Utsjoki

UTSJOKI, FINLAND
+78 **UTSJOKI**

If you're looking for remote, the northernmost municipality in Finland might be for you. At 280 mi (450 km) above the Arctic Circle, Utsjoki is far from the usual tourist trail. You can snowmobile and dogsled across unending expanses of pristine snow. The river Teno is well known as the best salmon-fishing river in northern Europe.

HELSINKI, FINLAND
+79 **CLARION HOTEL**

Sixteen stories up, this hotel has a glass-bottomed rooftop swimming pool offering far-reaching views across Helsinki. There are separate saunas for men and women, which are located on the West Harbor, and these enjoy the same view.

HELSINKI, FINLAND
+80 **SAUNASAARI SAUNA ISLAND**

A trip to Finland wouldn't be complete without a visit to a traditional Finnish sauna. Often places for silent reflection, saunas are an integral part of Finnish culture. Fifteen minutes by boat from Helsinki's market square, Saunasaari is a whole island of saunas. For views of Helsinki, try the smoke sauna.

Hotel Kakslauttanen

LAPLAND, FINLAND
+81 KAKSLAUTTANEN ARCTIC RESORT
While the log cabins with their private saunas might sound a tempting option in this Finnish Arctic resort, it is the glass igloos that really steal the show. Warm and cozy behind thermal glass, you can recline on the bed and admire the forest of snow-covered trees, or catch a glimpse of the northern lights in the night sky.

HELSINKI, FINLAND
+82 ANDANTE
Raw food and fresh flowers are in perfect harmony. Sit and enjoy a leisurely brunch amid the heady scent and bloom of the delightful floral displays.

HELSINKI, FINLAND
+83 LÖYLY HELSINKI
This spa is a beautiful wooden-clad building on the waterfront, with a terrace where you can jump straight from the smoke sauna into the sea.

Utsjoki

TALLINN, ESTONIA
484 **TALLINN OLD TOWN**

Winding cobblestone streets carry you under
Gothic spires and past grand merchant houses
in this beautifully preserved medieval city of
enchanting Hanseatic architecture. Find the
Danish King's Garden—one of the Old
Town's most peaceful and secluded corners,
with beautiful views across the red rooftops.
The town is a UNESCO World Heritage Site.

KLAIPEDA COUNTY, LITHUANIA
485 ORVIDAS

On the outskirts of the town of Salantai is an unusual sculpture garden filled with religious and traditional statues that sums up one Lithuanian artist's rebellion against Soviet-era oppression. Vilius Orvidas collected sculptures that would have been destroyed by the government, adding his own works, with an emphasis on folktale themes.

VILNIUS, LITHUANIA
486 LITTERA KNYGYNAS

With its dark wooden interior and low lighting, this small bookstore on the campus of Vilnius University has the feel of a personal library in a private residence. The highlight is the vaulted ceiling with its painted frescoes depicting caricatures of professors and students, and their studies of medicine, astronomy, botany, and art.

COURLAND, LATVIA
487 CAPE KOLKA

Once a high-security military base, the Cape Kolka peninsula is now a hauntingly desolate— yet beautiful—stretch of coastline, with tiny villages where it feels as if time has stood still. Situated close to the entrance for the Gulf of Riga, the cape is part of the rugged expanse of the Slitere National Park, which is home to wild deer, elk, buzzards, and beavers.

RIGA, LATVIA
488 ISTABA GALLERY

This tiny restaurant with a laid-back Bohemian atmosphere has no menu. Instead you tell the chef what flavors and ingredients you love, and he prepares a selection of dishes based on your preferences. While you wait for your food, the little art shop and gallery downstairs showcases work by local artists that make brilliant Latvian souvenirs.

Krakow Old Town

KRAKOW, POLAND

489 PLANTY

Take a walk through Planty, a ring of greenery where the city's defensive walls once stood filled with trees, flowers, gardens, benches, and historic monuments. Benches beneath the trees lining the lawns on the west side of the park running down to the castle are quieter than those in the northern gardens. Then take a walk through the historic market square in Krakow's Old Town, which is the perfect place for people watching.

WALBRZYCH, POLAND

490 TOTENBURG MAUSOLEUM

This mysterious mausoleum in the middle of the forest has a sinister history as a memorial to the Silesian people of the area who fought alongside the Nazis in World War I. The square, fortress-like building was also possibly used for Nazi SS initiation ceremonies. Desolate and abandoned, it is a haunting place to reflect on a tragic moment in human history.

Stilo Lighthouse

OSETNIK, POLAND
491 STILO LIGHTHOUSE

Climb the Stilo lighthouse in Osetnik for a wonderful view over this coastal region of Poland. The observation deck at the top of the striking red, white, and black edifice is 246 ft (75 m) above sea level, giving visitors an uninterrupted view of the Baltic seashore and sand dunes that blend seamlessly into the surrounding forest.

KRAKOW, POLAND
492 MASSOLIT BOOKS & CAFÉ

Sit in the back room of the café or find a nook in the maze of books within this independent bookstore in Krakow's Old Town, and you'll be left to browse at leisure. For an interesting take on the Polish literary scene, grab a copy of the Polish-English bilingual literary zine *Widma*.

BRATISLAVA, SLOVAKIA
493 LITERÁRNA ČAJOVŇA

A charming little teahouse in Bratislava serving high-quality teas from around the world. Admire the artworks on the walls by young Slovakian artists before taking a table in the smaller backroom library. Tuck yourself away from the world to read, enjoying the delicious aroma of scented tea and Arabic vegetarian food.

SLOVAK CARPATHIANS, SLOVAKIA
494 CARPATHIAN WOODEN CHURCHES

Driving through the Carpathian Mountain region, you can find nine wooden churches that make up this UNESCO World Heritage Site—more than fifty others spread out across the sleepy meadows and mountainsides. You may need to ask around in a nearby village to find who has the key to let you in.

BUDAPEST, HUNGARY
495 OMOROVICZA BOUTIQUE & SPA
Modern spa using minerals from local thermal waters. Lie on heated waterbeds while therapists cleanse, scrub, and massage away your worries.

BUDAPEST, HUNGARY
496 ISTVÁNTELEK TRAIN YARD
This abandoned train yard, known as The Red Star Train Graveyard, is littered with decaying locomotives over a vast area outside Budapest.

BUDAPEST, HUNGARY
497 MADAL CAFÉ
Budapest is a burgeoning hotspot for independent coffee shops. If you like spiritual enlightenment with your coffee, Madal Café is the place to head. The owners teach meditation and are followers of the Indian guru Sri Chinmoy. Inspired by his philosophy, they have decorated the café with quotes and sayings from his teachings, as well as photos of the man himself. With its harmonious décor and distinctly Zen vibe, the Madal is their attempt to establish a little peace and quiet in the whirl of the city. The name is apparently Sri Chinmoy's childhood nickname.

KOMÁROM-ESZTERGOM, HUNGARY
498 BOKOD
This little floating village is a favorite with photographers and winter fishing enthusiasts. The cabins and cottages are suspended on stilts over Lake Bokodi. The best views are from the east side of the lake.

SZENTENDRE, HUNGARY
499 MICRO WONDER MUSEUM
This fascinating museum contains a collection of intricate sculptures so small they could fit on a pin. Look through microscopes and you can see tableaux including the Great Pyramids, a miniature chess set and a chariot rider.

Madal Café

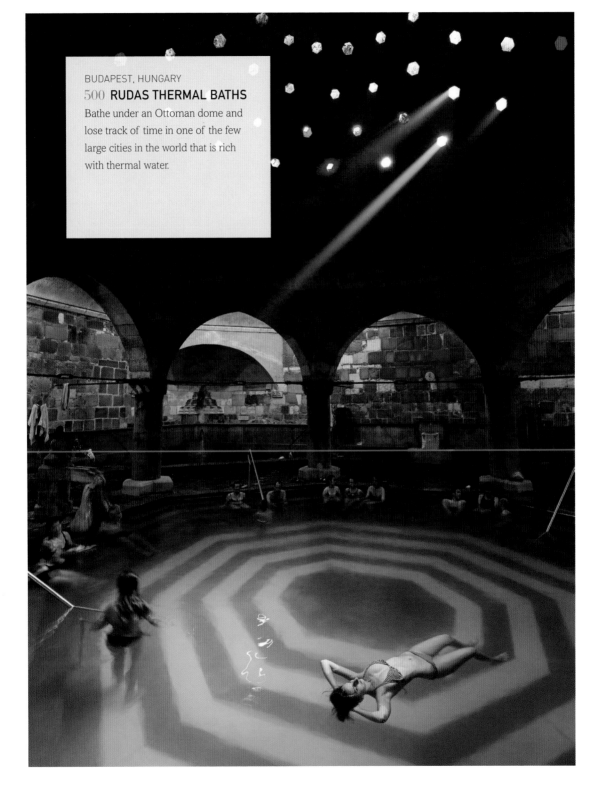

BUDAPEST, HUNGARY

500 RUDAS THERMAL BATHS

Bathe under an Ottoman dome and lose track of time in one of the few large cities in the world that is rich with thermal water.

Dox Center for Contemporary Art

PRAGUE, CZECH REPUBLIC

501 DOX CENTER FOR CONTEMPORARY ART

High above a contemporary art museum in Prague is lodged a 138-ft (42-m) long wooden and steel airship known as *Gulliver*. Inside, there is a beautiful space entirely dedicated to reading and literature that is flooded with natural light. The shape represents the optimistic ideals of an era of unprecedented technological advances. The center itself is a refurbished factory site and includes a design boutique, library, and café alongside the exhibition spaces.

PRAGUE, CZECH REPUBLIC

502 GRAND CAFÉ ORIENT

Located on the first floor of the House of the Black Madonna, —a historic building in the Old Town housing the Czech Cubism Museum—this café has an artistic retro feel. The space enjoys fantastic views.

BLANSKO, CZECH REPUBLIC

503 **MACOCHA ABYSS**

A boat trip along the subterranean Punkva river carries you quietly through echoing caves and cathedrals of stalactites and stalagmites to the bottom of the largest sinkhole of its type in Central Europe. Lush green vegetation covers the towering walls of the abyss, leading 476 ft (14.5 m) down to the dark blue pool. There are also two observation decks from which to admire the abyss from above.

PRAGUE, CZECH REPUBLIC

504 **AUGUSTINE HOTEL**

For an incredible 360-degree panorama of the city from the comfort of your bedroom, reserve the tower suite in the former astrological tower of this five-star, thirteenth-century monastery-turned-hotel. The hotel combines history with sharp design, modern furnishings, and artworks. The monastery gardens are a peaceful place to sit.

HIDDEN GEM

PRAGUE, CZECH REPUBLIC

505 **HIDDEN BAROQUE GARDEN CAFÉ**

Just a few steps away from busy Wenceslas Square is a small house nestled between two bigger buildings on Vodičkova Street. Pass through the home décor shop inside, and along the passage through the house, to find an unexpected hidden café in a baroque garden. Many locals have no idea that it's there.

SOUTH BOHEMIA, CZECH REPUBLIC

506 **ČESKY KRUMLOV**

A maze of twisting cobblestone alleys built on the bends of the Vltava river below a thirteenth-century castle makes Česky Krumlov one of the most picturesque towns in Europe. It is small enough to explore the Renaissance and baroque architecture in one day, then hike in the surrounding woods and fields the next.

EAST TYROL, AUSTRIA
507 AUSTRIAN ALPS

Exhilaratingly clean air, spectacular sights, hiking trails, mountain lakes, and glacial valleys all await the visitor to the Austrian Alps. East Tyrol remains untouched by the package vacation trade, making it one of the best regions in the country to see the glorious alpine scenery. Try one of the wooden cabins at Ufogel.

PATERGASSEN, AUSTRIA
508 ALMDORF SEINERZEIT

Book into Honeymoon Cottage at the Almdorf Seinerzeit in the Austrian Alps, and you could be alone in the branches in your private tree house, with only a king-size bed, the fresh mountain air, and the stars for company. If you feel the urge to climb down from your treetop enclave, you can enjoy local organic food in a typical Austrian setting.

STYRIA, AUSTRIA
509 GÖSTING CASTLE

A thirty-minute uphill hike (twenty minutes if you set a steady pace) brings you to the eerie ruins of the medieval Gösting Castle, which served as a defensive outpost above the city of Graz. A lightning bolt destroyed much of the castle in the early eighteenth century, and the building was abandoned. However, now you can explore the chapel and the keep freely.

SALZBURG, AUSTRIA
510 SIVANANDA YOGA RETREATS

Take your yoga practice out of the studio and into the mountains on an alpine yoga vacation. Participate in the daily yoga and meditation schedule at the retreat house, swim in the mountain lakes, and sit in stillness on the green meadows, all against the backdrop of the wild Kaiser mountain range.

SALZBURG, AUSTRIA
511 EISRIESENWELT

More than 26 mi (42 km) of icy passageways burrow into the mountainside leading to the largest accessible ice cave in the world. As you climb wooden steps and descend into pitch-black passages, the light from your headlamp casts otherworldly shadows across chambers of blue ice and sparkling white frost.

Palmenhaus

VIENNA, AUSTRIA
512 PALMENHAUS

This is a light and spacious restaurant in a converted nineteenth-century greenhouse where palm trees were once overwintered. Dine at dusk to enjoy the setting sun.

VIENNA, AUSTRIA
513 KAFFEEFABRIK

A welcoming coffee bar that boasts its own organic roasting house, this small coffee shop makes you feel welcome as soon as you step inside.

VIENNA, AUSTRIA
514 PEACE MUSEUM VIENNA

This small museum celebrates those dedicated to creating world peace. The *Windows for Peace* exhibition outside displays photos and biographies of international peace heroes.

VIENNA, AUSTRIA
515 AUSTRIAN NATIONAL LIBRARY

This is a historical baroque library with a magnificently decorated central hall. Keep your eye out for library staff slipping through secret passageways hidden behind bookcases.

SALZBURG, AUSTRIA
516 CITY CYCLING

Salzburg is one of the most cyclist-friendly cities in Austria. The network of safe, wide cycling paths crossing the city stretches for more than 112 mi (180 km), taking you through tree-lined lanes, green parks, and picturesque neighborhoods. The city's most popular cycling path meanders along the banks of the Salzach river, with its wide esplanades on either side, allowing you a leisurely ride in the fresh alpine air. South of the river you can pick up car-free Hellbrunner Allee and ride all the way to the ornate gardens of Hellbrunn Palace with its "trick" fountains.

HIDDEN GEM

SALZBURG, AUSTRIA

517 ST. PETER'S ABBEY

This is an eerily beautiful monastery in catacombs hewn into the mountainside. A sense of serenity accompanies you as you climb into the mountain surrounded by tombs.

SALZBURG, AUSTRIA

518 HOHENSALZBURG CASTLE

Roam the ramparts of this dramatic 900-year-old clifftop fortress, the biggest fully preserved castle in Europe and possibly the most beautiful, too.

St. Peter's Abbey

LUCERNE, SWITZERLAND

519 HOTEL VILLA HONEGG

Zigzag along the single-track road leading from the turquoise waters of Lake Lucerne, up Mount Bürgenstock, and you will discover an opulent, blue-shuttered art nouveau villa well-situated on a sunny meadow.

Choose a corner suite for a 180-degree view over the valley beyond, where you can watch red kites and alpine swifts fly as you listen to the sound of cowbells jangling. Is anything more quintessentially Swiss than this? Opulent luxury flows throughout, with polished wood flooring and palatial marble bathrooms with gilded mirrors and huge tubs. Here, the luxurious rooms are dressed in a palette of creams, toffees, and golds, with sumptuous leather armchairs to sink into after a day's hiking.

Upstairs, the wellness area features a hammam and Finnish sauna, while the heated rooftop infinity pool boasts an incredible view out across Lake Lucerne. Music is played underwater in the indoor pool.

The villa's chef picks fresh herbs from the hotel's garden, inspired by the plants that grow on the hillside below the hotel. The fish is caught from Lake Lucerne, and meat is sourced from the butcher across the valley. An international influence flows through the dishes. From the restaurant's terrace, you can enjoy the relaxing panorama of peaks, or in colder months, the fireplace in the lounge will warm your toes.

Nearby Lucerne is a picture-perfect Swiss city with a well-preserved medieval center of covered bridges, and sunny plazas lined with candy-colored houses. It has a rich musical reputation that made it popular with Wagner.

The Matterhorn

VORARLBERG, SWITZERLAND
520 KARTAUSE ITTINGEN

Navigate the garden's thyme maze; stroll through the ancient cloisters; join in a group meditation; or gather your thoughts in the silent room, where time and space dissolve, at this unique retreat and seminar center in a former charterhouse monastery. It is the perfect place to experience nature in peace and tranquillity, the quiet atmosphere inspiring creativity and insight. The forest on the doorstep is great for running and hiking, or you can take a bike out to the lake. While modern, the rooms retain a monastic simplicity.

VALAIS, SWITZERLAND
521 ZERMATT

Zermatt is a pretty ski resort with magnificent views of the Matterhorn mountain. Experienced off-run skiers can head on a hut-to-hut tour, ending at the remote Monte Rosa Hut.

Geneva Museum of Art and History

VALAIS, SWITZERLAND
522 WHITEPOD

Stay in a geodesic dome high in the Swiss Alps. The exclusive ecocamp only takes thirty guests and has its own private ski run.

GENEVA, SWITZERLAND
523 MUSEUM OF ART AND HISTORY

Enjoy coffee in the center patio with the beautiful building of the Museum of Art and History surrounding you.

BERN, SWITZERLAND
524 BERN

Wander the charming streets of the picture-perfect UNESCO World Heritage–listed old town. Rent a guided audio tour from the tourist office.

JUNGFRAU REGION, SWITZERLAND
525 HOTEL OBERSTEINBERG

Stay in pared-back Hotel Obersteinberg amid the beautiful mountains and meadows of Mürren—no electricity, no hot water; just candles and peace.

BERLIN, GERMANY

526 FIELD STATION IN TEUFELSBERG

Built on a mountain made from the rubble of 400,000 buildings destroyed in World War II, this abandoned National Security Agency listening station has become something of an open-air street art museum. Located in the Grunewald forest on the western edge of Berlin, the US spy station was used by the Allies to intercept satellite signals, radio waves, and other transmissions. These were then analyzed, in order to learn what was happening in Russian-controlled East Germany in the 1960s.

The previous tenant of the site encouraged street artists to enter and decorate the place, and now hundreds of huge paintings can be admired on the walls of the old buildings. There is a small entrance fee, and this allows you to join a tour to explore the cold-war relic, climbing up into some of the tall buildings and the derelict radar domes.

Filmmaker David Lynch once tried to buy the site to convert it into a "happiness college," but his proposals were rejected. Current proposals exist to build a café, beer garden, and art gallery on the site. In many ways, it seems more appropriate to leave it be, as it is slowly and steadily dismantled and reclaimed by nature. The eerie feel to your adventure can be enhanced by arriving on foot through the mysterious Grunewald forest. The strange structure can be spotted through the treetops as a beacon for miles around.

Father Carpenter Coffee Brewers

BERLIN, GERMANY
527 FATHER CARPENTER COFFEE BREWERS

Hidden in a quiet courtyard in the heart of the Mitte district, in front of a pretty fountain, is this pearl of a coffee shop. There are plenty of tables in the quiet courtyard where the noises of the trendy district beyond the buildings won't penetrate your peaceful ambience. And the coffee here is sublime.

BERLIN, GERMANY
528 LUISENSTRASSE

See the infamous Berlin Wall, away from the tourists, by heading along the northern edge of the St. Hedwig Cemetery. It is known as a "wild wall."

BERLIN, GERMANY
529 GEORG KOLBE MUSEUM

This beautiful art museum is hidden in a tiny street close to one of the city's main thoroughfares, yet it retains a wonderful sense of seclusion. The sculptor Georg Kolbe's studio, with floor-to-ceiling windows letting in light, is now a museum featuring a sculpture garden of his works and a pretty garden café.

BERLIN, GERMANY
530 BERLINER UNTERWELTEN

Subterranean museum touring Berlin's most important wartime underground structures, such as bunkers, abandoned railway stations, air-raid shelters, and people-smuggling tunnels.

MUNICH, GERMANY
531 NATURBAD MARIA EINSIEDEL

This ecological swimming pool is set in an idyllic location within Munich's Isar canal. Natural microorganisms keep the water clean.

532 HOUSE OF SMALL WONDER

This little café is a small wonder indeed: a little oasis of greenery that calms the spirit as soon as you set foot inside. A twisting staircase, framed and hung with potted plants, leads to an airy atrium-style café flooded with light. Enjoy the eclectic interior, created from salvaged wood and vintage decoration.

GABLENZ, GERMANY
533 RAKOTZBRÜCKE

A spectacular arched bridge in a large rhododendron park that creates a perfect circular reflection in the water below, which calms and focuses the mind.

BERCHTESGADEN ALPS, GERMANY
534 STÖHRHAUS

This is a remote mountain hut belonging to the German Alpine Club. The accommodation is a great starting point for long alpine hikes.

BADEN-WÜRTTEMBERG, GERMANY
535 THE BLACK FOREST

It's the Germany depicted in fairy tales and on cookie tins. Explore higgledy-piggledy villages or strike off on your own into the forest.

SCHLESWIG-HOLSTEIN, GERMANY
536 HOTEL VILLAGE, KAMPEN SYLT

This thatched-roof hotel is set within a beautiful garden. Near the beach, the hotel offers luxury boutique accommodation in a warm and welcoming environment.

BAVARIA, GERMANY
537 LANSERHOF TEGERNSEE

This is a super swanky digestive health spa set in impressive surroundings. Personalized programs of fasting and detoxing mix old-school approaches with contemporary healing techniques.

BAVARIA, GERMANY
538 OBERSEE LAKE

Nestled between the slopes of the mount Watzmann massif, Lake Obersee in
Berchtesgaden National Park can only be reached by crossing the spectacular lake
Köenigssee by boat and then completing the hike through the forest to the Lake's edge.
The conclusion of the trek is marked by an abandoned fisherman's hut at the end of
a wooden walkway. This stretches into the crystal clear waters of the lake that begs you
to take a photo before you jump in for a brisk swim. You can carry on around the rocky
basin to the end of the valley for the impressive Rothbach waterfall.

Obersee Lake

STUTTGART, GERMANY

539 STUTTGART CITY LIBRARY

Noah's Ark, the Confucian theory of concentric order, and Stanley Kubrick's film *2001: A Space Odyssey* are all said to have inspired this building's stunning conceptual design. Inside, the result is a five-story funnel-shape reading room furnished in calming pale gray, with secluded reading areas nestled around the periphery of each floor.

BRANDENBURG, GERMANY

540 BEELITZ-HEILSTÄTTEN

Shrouded in mystery, this eerie, abandoned hospital complex is home to more than sixty buildings in various stages of decay or preservation. It started life as a tuberculosis sanatorium and was taken over as a military hospital during World War I. The 75-ft (23-m) high treetop walk around the site offers impressive views of the ruins.

HAMBURG, GERMANY

541 ENTENWERDER 1

Rent a bike in the city and ride through Entenwerder Park and over the old bridge to the colorful café built on a floating pontoon. Here, you can enjoy an iced coffee on the waters of the Elbe, surrounded by flowers and butterflies while watching the ships glide in and out of the pretty harbor.

HIDDEN GEM

DRESDEN, GERMANY

542 KUNSTHOFPASSAGE

Various Dresden artists have transformed a series of courtyards in the Neustadt district into an art experiment. Each courtyard has its own theme and charm. In the *Courtyard of Elements*, falling rain turns a system of drainpipes affixed to an eye-catching turquoise wall into a musical instrument. Other installations include the *Courtyard of Lights*.

FRANKFURT, GERMANY

543 CHINESE GARDEN

Frankfurt is one of Germany's greenest cities. Of the total urban area, 52 percent comprises open spaces and water. The GreenBelt encircles the heart of the city with orchards, woodlands, and meadows. Within the city, the tiny Chinese Garden has a meditative feel to its ornamental bridges, pagodas, and calming carp ponds.

FRANKFURT, GERMANY

544 THE PURE

North of Frankfurt train station, a former textile factory is your invitation to relax in a creative home away from home. The Pure is a minimalist fantasy with a futuristic interior of light, white, leather, and marble. The harmony and clean lines help to keep your mind free from clutter. On the patio, beanbags, fountains, and bamboo create a Zen-like space to relax when the weather is warm.

545 RIJKSMUSEUM RESEARCH LIBRARY

While you can't borrow from the Rijksmuseum Research Library's catalog without the appropriate authorization, you can request and study the prints, drawings, photographs, and documents in the restored nineteenth-century-style reading room. The research library is one of the largest art history libraries in the world and is situated inside the Rijksmuseum.

HIDDEN GEM

AMSTERDAM, NETHERLANDS
546 BEGIJNHOF

You would never guess that behind the unassuming arched wooden door of Spuiplein restaurant lies one of the most unexpectedly peaceful places in Amsterdam. On the other side of the door, an enclosed medieval courtyard with a central green garden is completely out of earshot of the nearby city traffic. The Begijnhof was built in the fourteenth century as a sanctuary for a religious sisterhood of single women.

AMSTERDAM, NETHERLANDS
547 THE KATTENKABINET

Owning a cat has been scientifically proven to decrease stress levels. For those who can't keep one themselves for whatever reason, a visit to Amsterdam's Kattenkabinet ("Cat Cabinet") museum on the Herengracht Canal will have the same effect. This is a small but serious museum that is dedicated entirely to the feline form. The museum comes complete with live specimens freely roaming the rooms.

LISSE, NETHERLANDS
548 TULIP FIELDS, KEUKENHOF GARDENS

By the time the tulip-growing season is in full swing, the fields outside Amsterdam are a swath of colorful blossoms. The most popular place to see this spectacle is Keukenhof Gardens. After visiting the gardens, a lazy bike ride through the surrounding flower fields will get you away from the crowds.

SOUTH HOLLAND, NETHERLANDS
549 BOOK MOUNTAIN IN SPIJKENISSE

From the town's market square, you can see the books inside Spijkenisse's new pyramid-shape library through the glass facade, earning the building the nickname Book Mountain. Inside, a spiral of pathways, staircases, and terraces leads visitors up through five floors of flowerpot bookshelves to the café and reading space.

GELDERLAND, NETHERLANDS
550 KRÖLLER-MÜLLER MUSEUM

Tucked away in the forest of provincial Holland, in one of the most beautiful nature reserves of the Netherlands, is the second-largest collection of artworks by legendary Dutch painter Vincent van Gogh. This beautiful gallery is far from the tourist trail and also features one of the largest sculpture gardens in Europe.

BRUGES, BELGIUM
551 THE BRIDGES OF BRUGES

This Belgian city is so charming you could imagine it has been lifted straight from the pages of a fairy tale. Its compact size makes it easy to explore the cobbled lanes and picturesque canals on foot, crossing medieval stone bridges to find historic market squares linked by narrow byways beneath soaring spires and towers. Soak up local folklore about the water sprites that live beneath the bridges along the waterways at Minnewater, or pick a bench to people watch on the Rozenhoedkaai.

Besides pretty bridges the city is the perfect destination for a romantic escapade. At the center of the canal system, the Lover's Bridge spans the Lake of Love. Legend has it that if you kiss your partner upon this bridge, your love will be eternal. However, if you have come here alone, don't worry; it's still a great place to enjoy the scenery.

Another beautiful bridge can be found nestled between the regal Gruuthuse Palace and the quaint Arentshof park. The Bonifacius Bridge has a built-in bench, making for the perfect seat to watch the boats and swans float by. When the sun starts to set, saunter along the quiet quayside at Gouden-Handrei or Sint-Annarei. They're less crowded than popular Rozenhoedkaai but equally picturesque. Come in the early morning, and you will feel like you're the only person in this magnificent medieval world.

The city is home to groups of whitewashed almshouses, some of which were built around tranquil gardens that are open to those members of the public who respect their peaceful ambience. Many also have their own tiny chapels that you can take a peek inside. Visit the almshouses at De Meulenaere and Sint-Jozef to find a pretty garden of low box hedges, tall trees, rose beds, geraniums, and euphorbia.

Pop in to the museum at Princely Beguinage Ten Wijngaarde, where daffodils bloom in the peaceful convent garden in springtime. Once the home of emancipated lay women who lived pious lives, today it is inhabited by eight sisters of the Order of Saint Benedict who welcome you to their historic household and museum, where you can get an idea of what day-to-day life was like in seventeenth-century Bruges. The city receives a lot of day-trippers—who miss out on the floodlit spectacle at night—so stay a few days in the middle of the week to see Bruges at its best.

552 INCLES VALLEY

This pretty valley in the Eastern Pyrenees is unspoiled by modern buildings and traffic-heavy roads. The valley is relatively flat, which makes for an easy hike through spring flowers that ends in a spectacular lake. To go farther, hike up to Fontargent Pass and climb to Juclá Lake mountain refuge, where you can stay overnight.

ESCALDES-ENGORDANY, ANDORRA
553 CALDEA

Large spa complex fed by mountainous hot springs. At its heart is a large lagoon that is kept at a constant 89.6°F (32°C).

MONTE-CARLO, MONACO
554 THERMES MARINS

Stylish and luxury spa in glamorous surroundings offering cryotherapy treatments—brief exposure to extreme cold temperatures designed to boost energy, prevent illness, and enhance physical recovery. Massage, relaxation treatments, and aqua fitness are all on offer, as well as four-day packages.

ESCH-SUR-SÛRE, LUXEMBOURG

555 ESCH-SUR-SÛRE CASTLE

The little village of Esch-sur-Sûre lies within the curve of a gently meandering river. The enchanting castle ruins above are illuminated beautifully at night.

MONTE-CARLO, MONACO

556 JARDIN EXOTIQUE DE MONACO

On a hilltop high above the harbor, the Jardin Exotique offers visitors to Monte-Carlo a brief respite from the glamour of the city. This long, well-kept garden hangs on a cliff overlooking the azure waters of the Mediterranean and its crowd of luxury yachts below. It also offers a guided cave tour.

ENSCHERANGE, LUXEMBOURG

557 CAMPING AT VAL D'OR

This tiny country of 998 sq mi (2,585 sq km) rarely features on anyone's bucket list. However, tucked away in the valley of the Clerve river is the beautiful Val d'Or campsite. You can pitch right beside the river that runs through this enchanting oasis of greenery, or cross the wooden footbridge to find a more secluded spot.

558 LE PIC DU MIDI OBSERVATORY

Astronomers have been making the arduous climb to
Pic du Midi since 1870 for its prime observing
conditions of a magnificently dark night's sky.
Nowadays, visitors can take a fifteen-minute cable-car
ride from the town of La Mongie up through the clouds
to the observatory and museum at the top.

From almost 10,000 ft (3,048 m) above sea level,
visitors to the complex of buildings and domes
sprawling across the peak are privy to a breathtaking,
eagle's-eye view of the surrounding Pyrenees. Gazing
down from the extensive panoramic terraces, you are
offered a spellbinding view of a world of ice and snow.
It is from up here that NASA scientists mapped the
surface of the moon for the Apollo landings.

Stargazing packages offer an overnight stay in the
small, modern scientists' rooms of the observatory.
Guests will have the night's skies explained by an
astronomer and enjoy a private tour of the telescopes.
When you switch off the lights in your room, the
snowy peaks shimmer in the moonlight below. On a
clear night, you can see the glow of Barcelona in the
far distance.

The restaurant serves superb traditional cuisine
made with local produce and gives you the chance to
watch the sun set over the mountain peaks with a glass
of champagne in hand. At the end of their stay,
experienced skiers can ski back down through pristine
powder to the Pyrenean ski resort of Le Tourmalet.

Clockwise from top: Shakespeare &
Company; Jardin de la Vallée Suisse;
Bibliothèque Historique

PARIS, FRANCE
559 SHAKESPEARE & COMPANY

In exchange for working in the shop and writing a one-page autobiography, volunteers—known as tumbleweeds—can stay in the bookstore.

PARIS, FRANCE
560 JARDIN DE LA VALLÉE SUISSE

Secret garden hidden in plain sight close to one of Paris's busiest thoroughfares and popular tourist attraction, the Champs-Élysées.

PARIS, FRANCE
561 HÔTEL PARTICULIER MONTMATRE

Parisian art-house opulence in a serene secret-garden setting. Choose the Végétale room to feel like you're sleeping in a light-dappled forest glade in the center of Montmartre.

PARIS, FRANCE
562 BIBLIOTHÈQUE HISTORIQUE

Naturally calm and contemplative places, libraries offer respite from the chaotic outside world. Browse the historical collections in the warm, welcoming reading room.

PARIS, FRANCE
563 LE TIGRE YOGA CLUB

Despite its name, Le Tigre Yoga Club offers a lot more than yoga classes. Choose from various holistic therapies and practices at the different locations throughout the city.

PARIS, FRANCE
564 HOTEL SOUBISE

Benches beckon the weary in the cloisters of this eighteenth-century rococo mansion, found through an archway at Rue des Archives in Le Marais. Keep exploring to find a serene garden.

HIDDEN GEM

PARIS, FRANCE
565 JARDIN NATUREL PIERRE-EMMANUEL

The shops and boulevards fade into the distance when you step into the stillness of the Jardin Naturel. The peaceful, secluded setting adjoins Paris's grand Père Lachaise cemetery and echoes its tranquillity without the morbidity. Although this organic garden is quite large for a neighborhood park, its concealed location keeps the tourists away, and you're likely only to pass a few locals out for a stroll. The garden is part of the city's biodiversity initiative; the focus on the wild flora of Ile-de-France attracting wildlife among the wild oaks and heavily scented chamomile.

PROVENCE, FRANCE

566 THE LAVENDER FIELDS

The lavender in Provence blooms from June until harvest in August. During this time, the countryside is a sea of purple and blue hues, the air thick with their scent. Head to the roads above Sault before mid-July to avoid the peak time for tourists. Private distillery tours are worth seeking out.

PROVENCE, FRANCE

567 DOMAINE DE RONSARD

Retreat to this flower-festooned hideaway near Saint-Rémy-de-Provence in the South of France for a true Provençal experience. Throughout the sprawling garden, roses scale the walls, spilling out of borders and climbing trellises. From the heated pool you can smell thyme and rosemary, as well as the region's famous lavender fields.

HIDDEN GEM

BRITTANY, FRANCE

568 BELLE-ÎLE

The island of Belle-Île lies forty-five minutes from the mainland and is a well-kept secret from most visitors to France. Stop for crepes and a peaceful bayside view from the outdoor terrace of La Mere Michele in Sauzon. Explorers of the northwest coast will find a savage beauty of rock pools, sea-sprayed cliffs, and deep ravines.

HAUTE-LOIRE, FRANCE

569 SAINT-MICHEL D'AIGUILHE

After climbing more than 250 steps up a craggy volcanic rock, visitors can take a well-deserved rest in this beautiful tenth-century mountaintop chapel, one of the most breathtaking in southern France. In this peaceful place of contemplation, you can enjoy spectacular views of the surrounding villages before making the slow descent.

BURGUNDY, FRANCE

570 CANAL BOATING ON CANAL DU NIVERNAIS

Experience French life flowing at a gentler pace on the canals of Burgundy. As you float down the 110-mi (177-km) of Canal du Nivernais from Auxerre to Clamecy, you'll have grebes, mallards, and swans for company—but few people, other than lock-keepers and fellow barge-dwellers.

GASCONY, FRANCE

571 LITTLE FRENCH RETREAT

Little French Retreat offers authentic and intimate retreat experiences for small groups, from a beautiful country home in the rural historic village of Montesquieu. Yoga is taken outdoors in the tranquil surroundings, encouraging guests to slow down and focus on well-being. Nourishing home-cooked food is provided during your stay.

The lavender fields, Provence

ALENTEJO, PORTUGAL

572 **CASA NO TEMPO**

One hour south of Lisbon, in the unspoiled countryside of Portugal's Alentejo region, stands the white low-rise retreat of Casa No Tempo. Once you arrive, you can forget about your to-do lists, appointments, and chores and simply take a step back from it all.

 This beautifully minimalist property came about when two brothers, charged by their grandfather with renovating a tumbledown family farm, enlisted the help of renowned Portuguese architect Manuel Aires Mateus. The task was to transform the crumbling ruin into an understated oasis where history, design, and nature coexist. The result is a modern retreat that fits elegantly into the surrounding countryside.

Azores paragliding

AZORES, PORTUGAL
573 AZORES PARAGLIDING
Paragliding over this volcanic Atlantic archipelago gives you a bird's-eye view of a remote and tranquil destination, where the land is a patchwork of protected areas and marine reserves. From above, you will see springs, pastures, and blue lakes ringed by laurel forests and cedar woods.

MADEIRA, PORTUGAL
574 FAJA DOS PADRES
Escape the tourist cruise ships of Funchal to hike the wild interior of the volcanic island of Madeira. Ask locals for directions to the cable-car station that will take you to the cove of Faja dos Padres—a historic vineyard with a private beach, where you can stay in a converted worker's cottage.

ALENTAJO, PORTUGAL
575 CABANAS NO RIO
Two converted fisherman's huts combine luxury with escapism. The name translates to "cabins on the river," which says all it needs to.

LISBON, PORTUGAL
576 MIRADOURO DA NOSSA SENHORA DO MONTE
On a leafy hillside in the Grace neighborhood, you can find Lisbon's highest lookout point. It is a peaceful place, shaded by lush pine trees. Next to it, you'll find an accessible viewpoint, leaving you free to enjoy the sunset minus the crowds.

LISBON, PORTUGAL
577 CASA DO ALENTEJO
You don't need to have a reservation at its restaurant to be able to wander around this former palace that preserves the region's culture.

LISBON, PORTUGAL
578 LIVRARIA DO SIMAO
A tiny bookshop with barely room for two people to peruse the shelves. Despite its diminuitive size, the Livraria boasts an impressive collection of 4,000 used books.

LISBON, PORTUGAL
579 CAFÉ DA GARAGEM
There are huge windows here from which to admire Lisbon's landscape. The café above the Garagem Theatre opens in time for the afternoon sun to shine in.

HIDDEN GEM

MADRID, SPAIN

580 SAN ANTONIO DE LA FLORIDA CHAPEL

The frescoed ceiling is one of the few places where you can see Goya's work in its original setting.

MADRID, SPAIN

581 BARCELÓ EMPERATRIZ

Ultra-stylish hotel with a beautiful roof-terrace pool. The interior décor is sumptuous and designed to befit a nineteenth-century empress.

MADRID, SPAIN

582 SIESTA & GO

Rent a bed by the minute at this city center "nap bar." It also features armchairs and quiet workspaces so you can read or take a break.

BARCELONA, SPAIN

583 MONESTIR DE PEDRALBES

Religious art in the beautiful, Gothic Monestir de Pedralbes. The chapel is decorated with a magnificent mural series dating back to 1343.

Monestir de Pedralbes

Olokuti

584 OLOKUTI GRACIA

The shelves in Olokuti Gracia are stacked with ecofriendly, organic
Fairtrade products, books, and craft materials. However, if you bypass
the store's eclectic wares and head through to the back of the shop,
you will find yourself in a tiny hidden courtyard. Pause and catch your
breath over a cup of tea in a tree-shaded garden that is peppered with
informally placed tables and plants. There is a self-service machine
where you can choose from the coffees and teas on sale in the shop,
as well as juices and soft drinks. Olokuti Gracia in the Gracia
neighborhood also offers a program of workshops and talks.

585 LIBRERÍA ANTICUARIA COMELLAS

This is an impressive rare book
collection in a modernist
mansion. Located in a historic
district, the shop has the
atmosphere of ancient libraries.

CASTILE AND LEÓN, SPAIN

586 CAMINO DE SANTIAGO

Few pilgrims choose the difficult ascents and descents along the isolated footpaths of the Dragonte route, opting instead for easier courses on the famous Camino de Santiago. Those who do follow this section are richly rewarded with stunning mountain views. Plus, this is the only part of the 500-mi (805-km) long route where you are likely to find yourself truly alone.

LANZAROTE, SPAIN

588 BREATHING SPACE RETREAT

Experience the transformational effects of "conscious breathing" on the magical island of Lanzarote. These one-on-one or group retreats combine breathwork sessions with beach walks and ocean swimming. This is about taking time out to improve the relationship you have with yourself and to find the clarity to move forward in a safe, supportive environment.

ALICANTE, SPAIN

587 VIVOOD LANDSCAPE HOTEL

The Vivood was designed to blend into its rural setting so that guests can escape the stresses of life by immersing themselves in nature. Each cabin is raised above the ground so as not to disrupt the existing vegetation, while providing spectacular views across the valley below. Choose a Pool Suite with a private Jacuzzi.

IBIZA, SPAIN

589 CAN TONI D'EN COVAS

Set in a wildflower-strewn plot, there are no neighbors at this remote eighteenth-century farmhouse. Step from the master bedroom to the poolside or find a secluded spot to sunbathe in the beautiful garden. Nearby Benirrás beach is known for its spectacular sunsets—catch at least one while you're there.

TUDELA, SPAIN

590 HOTEL AIRE DE BARDENAS

Spend a night under the moonlit sky in an award-winning Bubble Room. The transparent ceilings of these spherical tents allow you to watch fiery sunsets before the stars come out. Or wake early to see the sun rising over the lunar-like landscape of the UNESCO Biosphere Reserve and National Park.

HIDDEN GEM

GALICIA, SPAIN

591 LAS ISLAS CÍES

Known locally as the Galician Caribbean, this archipelago of three islands limits visitors to just 2,200 per day. There are no hotels here—only a basic campsite and a couple of simple restaurants. Swim in the refreshing Atlantic waves, relax on the powdery soft beaches, or wander aimlessly along the Ruta Monte Faro.

SARDINIA, ITALY
592 CAGLIARI

Sardinia is a captivating island, its mountainous interior fringed with dazzling beaches nestled in bays along a wild coast. The lush interior is largely untouched by tourism, so you can hike between hillside hamlets such as Orgosolo, or explore the medieval quarter in Cagliari, then head up to its ramparts for magnificent views.

UMBRIA, ITALY
593 EREMITO

Surrounded by 7,400 acres (3,000 hectares) of rolling, forest-carpeted Umbrian hills, the Eremito provides the ultimate in digital detoxing. As well as no Internet or television to distract you, the hotel offers a "silent" dinner experience, heightening your awareness of your other senses as you feast on the day's harvest.

HIDDEN GEM
TUSCANY, ITALY
594 HOTEL MONTEVERDI

An unpaved road climbs up to the hilltop hamlet where you will find the Monteverdi blending seamlessly into the cobbled medieval streets built around the twelfth-century chapel. The turquoise infinity pool overlooks the lavender fields of the Val d'Oria, while the spa treatments are infused with the herbs and flowers grown on the hillside.

TUSCANY, ITALY
595 SANTUARIO DELLA VERNA

This thirteenth-century hermitage enjoys a verdant cliffside setting atop Mount Penna, with sweeping views across the Tuscan countryside below. The cluster of medieval stone buildings feels like a place out of time, with silent processions of white-robed monks making their way through the morning mist to mass.

APULIA, ITALY
596 LECCE

Sometimes called "the Florence of the South," Lecce is a baroque masterpiece of a town. Strolling through the lanes of the ancient quarter, you will notice that buildings are decorated ornately. Lecce is the ideal base for visiting the smaller towns of the southern coast. Pause awhile in the pretty courtyard of the Palazzo dei Celestini on your way to the quiet gardens.

SICILY, ITALY
597 WINDMILLS OF MOZIA

The bright orange domes of the white windmill towers stand out in stark contrast with the soaring blue of the Sicilian sky. Their reflection in the shallow lagoon, lined with salt flats, shifts with tints of pink and purple and white. Head to the hilltop town of Erice to see the bewitching sight in one stunning panorama at sunset.

Cagliari, Sardinia;
Windmills of Mozia, Sicily

VERONA, ITALY

598 SANCTUARY OF MADONNA DELLA CORONA

This impressive church sits on a thin rock shelf on Monte Baldo on the site of a remote hermitage. It is still a place of quiet reflection, where pilgrims make the journey to contemplate the nature of their faith, and other visitors come to marvel at how it appears to be suspended in mid-air. It has been reconstructed and strengthened over the years, but still retains many original features. You can take a minibus from Verona up to the church, or choose the pilgrims' staircase and climb the 1,540 steps on foot.

FLORENCE, ITALY

599 CAFFÈ DEL VERONE

A great spot with fifth-floor views of Florence's iconic red rooftops, as well as a breathtaking vista of the Duomo and the surrounding Florentine hills.

FLORENCE, ITALY

600 LAURENTIAN LIBRARY

An uncrowded Michelangelo masterpiece built upon a cloister of the Basilica di San Lorenzo houses the private library of the Medici family, the most important collection of antique books in Italy.

VENICE, ITALY

601 SAN GIORGIO MAGGIORE

A quiet monastery island where a monk will accompany you up the church bell tower for unbeatable views of St. Mark's Basilica.

HIDDEN GEM

VENICE, ITALY

602 LIBRERIA ACQUA ALTA

In a city that regularly floods, this whimsical bookstore solves the problem by keeping its stacks of books in boats and bathtubs.

VENICE, ITALY

603 HILTON MOLINO STUCKY VENICE

The Skyline Terrace at this smart hotel offers incredible panoramas across the whole of Venice and the southern lagoon. Hotel guests can use the swimming pool.

VENICE, ITALY

604 THE VENICE–SIMPLON ORIENT EXPRESS

Ride the world's most famous luxury train. Three new suites on the train's key routes include private living rooms and bathrooms.

Navigli District, Milan

ROME, ITALY
605 IL MUSEO DEL LOUVRE
This is a mix between a bookshop, an art gallery, and a collection of curiosities focusing on photography, art history, and vintage prints.

ROME, ITALY
606 HOTEL INDIGO ROME–ST. GEORGE
This hotel mixes modern Italian furniture with ancient Roman arches. Head upstairs to the peaceful rooftop bar and courtyard.

ROME, ITALY

607 SANTI QUATTRO CORONATI

In the late 1990s, restoration work in the Gothic hall at the fortified abbey of Santi Quattro Coronati (Four Crowned Saints) revealed a superb specimen of thirteenth-century painting featuring depictions of the seasons, zodiacs, and scenes from pagan mythology. Booking requests for rare private tours can be made on the hall's website.

MILAN, ITALY

608 3 ROOMS

A boutique hotel consisting of three residences, each with its own private entrance. Plants spill from the balconies above the interior courtyard and tea garden, while the rooms are large and filled with stylish designer furniture. The hotel is above a popular gallery, boutique, and bar on trendy Corso Como, but feels peaceful and a world away.

MILAN, ITALY

609 VIVAIO RIVA

A family-managed garden of antique greenhouses and quiet corners. Locals come here to purchase roses and azaleas or to simply enjoy the flowers.

MILAN, ITALY

610 NAVIGLI DISTRICT

Navigli is an arty neighborhood of canal-side studios, charming galleries, and boutiques. Make time to stop in the independent cafés alongside the canal, parts of which are 800 years old. Here you will also find the fourth-century Basilica of Sant'Eustorgio—one of the capital's oldest churches—which originally housed the relics of the three kings.

LOMBARDY, ITALY
611 THE VILLAGES OF LAKE COMO

The beauty of Lake Como, in northern Italy's Lombardy region, has attracted wealthy and famous people to build holiday homes along its winding shoreline since the early years of the Roman Empire. However, these palatial villas, half submerged by exquisite greenery with walls of oleander and poplar trees, are only part of the attraction.

Visitors to Lake Como are mesmerized by the magnificent mountain views and the intense color of the lake. You can explore the enchanting medieval centers of quaint lakeside towns and ancient villages nestled into chestnut forests in the shadow of the Alps' snowy slopes. Here, you will discover tiny cafés and traditional trattorias hidden down cobbled alleyways, boats bobbing about in pretty harbors, and markets laden with ripe fruits and vegetables.

Charter a luxury yacht and sail the still waters, or rent a car to explore tiny villages such as Pescallo, southeast of the Bellagio promontory. Like others along the lake, this fishing village boasts a small harbor, historic ivy-covered houses, and narrow cobblestone alleys dripping with fuchsias, opening on to beautiful lake views.

Ten minutes' walk from Pescallo, Bellagio itself is an elegant and long-established tourist resort situated on the promontory between the two southern branches of Lake Como. Out of season, it is relaxing and romantic, with classy boutiques along the Via Garibaldi, picturesque lanes winding to the main squares, and two beautifully manicured Italian gardens to visit. One is in the grounds of Villa Serbelloni, which used to belong to a whisky heiress. She left the property to the Rockefeller Foundation, which now uses it as a venue to host conferences and retreats for artists, who work in little chalets dotted around the grounds. The second is a charming sloping garden on the lakeshore at Villa Melzi, with a pretty blue-roofed pavilion at the water's edge, and a shady water garden.

A stroll through the surrounding olive groves around Bellagio will bring you to other villages that you can explore at a leisurely pace. Those in the know make their way to the hamlet of Careno for lunch at the Trattoria del Porto, where the fish is fresh from the lake, and the food is voted among the best in the region. However you choose to spend your time here, Lake Como is a gloriously tranquil destination for those seeking the aspirational Italian lifestyle.

LJUBLJANA, SLOVENIA

612 **KAVARNA NEBOTIČNIK**

Occupying the top floor of one of Ljubljana's
tallest buildings, Nebotičnik Café and terrace
is the perfect place to unwind after a busy day
sightseeing around this delightful city. Choose
a table on the terrace of this art deco skyscraper
for 360-degree views of the Alps, Ljubljana Castle,
and the sprawling Tivoli Park below.

LJUBLJANA, SLOVENIA

613 **NATIONAL AND UNIVERSITY LIBRARY OF SLOVENIA**

The national library was designed—like many
important buildings in Ljubljana—by prolific
Slovenian architect Jože Plečnik. As you enter, you
climb a monumental staircase, flanked by pillars of
black marble, leading you into the library's grand
reading room with its huge glass walls. Entry is by
tour only.

Kavarna Nebotičnik

Lake Bohinj

UPPER CARNIOLA, SLOVENIA
614 LAKE BOHINJ

Lake Bohinj may not have a church on an island in the middle of it, as tourist favorite Lake Bled does, but it is far quieter and feels more authentic. Explore the picturesque hamlets on the shores of the impossibly still waters, such as peaceful Ribčev Laz with its fifteenth-century church.

UPPER CARNIOLA, SLOVENIA
615 VELIKA PLANINA

Grassy mountaintop plateau with wooden shepherds' dwellings and church. One of the largest herdsmen's settlements in Europe occupy the huts from June to September.

BOVEC VALLEY, SLOVENIA
616 CAMP LIZA

This is a beautiful place to camp amid the peaks and pastures of the Bovec Valley, through which the mesmerizing emerald-green Soča river flows.

TRIGLAV NATIONAL PARK, SLOVENIA
617 VRSIC PASS

Road trip through Slovenia's highest mountain pass, negotiating dramatic switchbacks and pausing at the many clearly marked photo opportunities.

Veli Rat

DUGI OTOK, CROATIA
618 **VELI RAT**
This lighthouse is surrounded by pine trees and pebble beaches and is considered to be one of the most beautiful lighthouses on the Adriatic.

ZADAR, CROATIA
619 **THE SEA ORGAN**
Located at the edge of the sea, this sound installation uses underground pipes to create music from the waves lapping against the shore.

ZAGREB, CROATIA
620 **CAFÉ U DVORISTU**
A tucked-away organic courtyard café and art gallery with a creatively decorated terrace found in a peaceful street surrounded by old buildings.

ZAGREB, CROATIA
621 **DVORIŠTA**
Privately owned courtyards are opened to the public for ten days during July. Join a small group tour to peek inside the city's secret spaces.

LIKA-SENJ COUNTY, CROATIA
622 **PLITVICE LAKES NATIONAL PARK**
You could spend several days exploring the wooden footbridges and dirt pathways that snake around the edges of the crystalline lakes within this national park. The waters of the lakes and waterfalls take on brilliant shades of emerald green and sapphire blue, giving the Plitvice Lakes the nickname "the Jewel of Croatia." Ask a guide at the entrance for directions to the unmarked lookout point Veliki Slap for a picture-postcard view of the lakes drenched in their surrounding greenery. Swimming is prohibited in the lakes, so rent a rowing boat instead.

Maksimir Park

ZADAR, CROATIA

623 KAVANA LOVRE CAFÉ

Visit the secret chapel hidden at the back of this café, constructed in the eleventh century with a mismatch of ancient columns.

ZAGREB, CROATIA

624 MAKSIMIR PARK

The oldest park in Croatia is landscaped like an English country garden, with lawns and artificial lakes, plus two beautifully restored pavilions.

OHRID, MACEDONIA
625 **OHRID**
Visit this sleepy, atmospheric town on the edge of a serene lake. Take a daytrip out to Sveti Naum Monastery, with its own beach and rose gardens.

BUDVA, MONTENEGRO
626 **BUDVA OLD TOWN**
See the sites of the ancient settlement early in the morning, then take a taxi-boat from the seafront to the quiet beaches of Sveti Nikola Island.

BANAT, ROMANIA
627 **DEVIL'S LAKE**
Hike through the Nera Gorges and you'd be forgiven for thinking you could be the first person to travel through this land. It is an area filled with folklore and fairy tale, not least that of the Devil's Lake (Lacul Dracului).The greenish-blue water hiding here in the verdant forest is said to be bottomless and that those who dare swim in it will never return to shore. While superstitious locals may steer clear of swimming in the lake, visitors ignore the tale and return unharmed.

MOSTAR, BOSNIA AND HERZEGOVINA
628 **KONOBA TAURUS**
Set in a beautiful stone building, this tiny restaurant, tucked off the tourist trail in Mostar, benefits from two light-filled outdoor terraces.

RILA MOUNTAIN, BULGARIA
629 **RILA MONASTERY**
Immerse yourself in silence for an overnight monastery stay, high up in the middle of the fragrant conifer forests of the Rila mountains.

VARIOUS LOCATIONS, ALBANIA
630 **ABANDONED BUNKERS**
Ubiquitous concrete bunkers were abandoned following the collapse of communism. Whichever you visit, ask the locals where to find the most interesting ones.

Rila Monastery, Bulgaria

KOTOR, MONTENEGRO

631 BAY OF KOTOR

The jewel in the crown of the tiny country of Montenegro is without doubt the Bay of Kotor. Photogenic medieval towns are scattered along the shores of cobalt coves, sewn together by serpentine roads winding their way along soaring cliffsides. Naturally sheltered and cradled by calm seas, the walled town of Kotor is many explorers' first stop. However, head onward to laid-back Lepetane village, and you'll find yourself immersed even further into solitude. Rent a room at the Apartments Okuka, kick back, and watch the boats sail across the bay from your balcony.

THESSALY, GREECE

632 METEORA

In the foothills of the Pindus Mountains, a spectacle of gigantic wind-carved sandstone pillars stretches into the sky. Perched atop these rocks are ancient monasteries dating from the Ottoman conquest. Six of the original monasteries remain open; the most difficult to access—and therefore the quietest—is Agia Triada, the Monastery of the Holy Trinity.

You can also head away from the main tracks, onto old monk's trails to find cave hermitages cut into the rocks where hermits escaped the material world.

ATHENS, GREECE
633 ALICE INN ATHENS
On a quiet backstreet with only four rooms. The Harry Belafonte suite has a great view of the Acropolis from the roof terrace.

ATHENS, GREECE
634 BIOS
Visit this impressive city center roof terrace bar above a tiny art house cinema. Avoid the popular live performances if you want a quieter view of the Acropolis.

PELOPONNESE, GREECE
636 AMANZOE
Soaring pillars and colonnades surround your own private marble-edged pavilion at this ultra-exclusive hilltop health resort. Soak in the panoramic views of the shimmering Aegean Sea, cypress trees, and olive groves from the seclusion of your private pool, or borrow a classic from the well-stocked library. Privacy is of the utmost importance here.

CRETE, GREECE
635 BALOS
Famed for its vivid turquoise waters, white sand, and devastatingly beautiful setting, Balos possesses an unforgettable sense of remoteness. The sea is shallow and warm, and the crushed shells on the beach lend the sand an iridescent pink shine. Arrive in the morning before the tour boats for a few hours of blissful solitude.

637 SILVER ISLAND YOGA RETREAT

With no Internet service and no phone signal, this sixty-acre island yoga haven is a place where you can completely unwind.

HIDDEN GEM

PATMOS, GREECE

638 SERENDIPITY VILLAS

Barely on the radar of most Grecians, the remote island of Patmos has crystal coves, thyme-scented valleys, and divine isolation: St. John is said to have written the Book of Revelations here. Exquisite sun-drenched mansions—like Serendipity Villas with its traditional wooden ceilings and flagstone floors—have been sympathetically converted into exclusive vacation hideaways.

Serendipity Villas

Hot-air ballooning, Cappadocia

CAPPADOCIA, TURKEY
639 HOT-AIR BALLOONING

Take off for sunrise to experience the changing colors of the landscape below. Two-hour flights will take you over the "fairy chimneys" to see Bronze Age homes and churches carved into the rock faces. The sight of hundreds of other balloons gracefully rising up is also unexpectedly serene.

BODRUM, TURKEY
640 TURKISH GULET

Cruise in relaxed luxury on a traditional gulet. These 80-ft (24-m) polished-wood-and-gleaming-brass boats sail from the city's harbor to drift from cove to cove through blue waters. You can stop and explore ruins, stroll around coastal villages, or jump in to join the fish that dart about the hull.

OCAKLI, TURKEY
641 ANI GHOST CITY
In the remote highlands of northeast Turkey, the magnificent medieval city of Ani was once home to hundreds of thousands of people. Ruled by many different empires, it was repeatedly raided and ransacked until finally being abandoned. It is now a site of impressive ruins, including a 1,000-year-old mosque, perched precariously on the edge of a cliff, and an imposing basalt cathedral.

ISTANBUL, TURKEY
642 BEBEK CAFÉ
Sit outside in the shade by the Bosporus, sipping tea at this atmospheric waterside café dating back to the 1940s. The area used to be a sleepy fishing village before it became an upmarket part of town, but the café retains its charming roots and relaxed atmosphere. Try the classic *kasarlı simit* bread.

HIDDEN GEM
ANTALYA, TURKEY
643 KALE PANSIYON
The Kale Pansiyon's ten airy rooms are only accessible by boat from Ucagiz on the mainland. This is the place to switch off from an always-on world, where the only thing disturbing the silence is the lapping of water against the private jetty. Come off-season to avoid the noise of passing tour boats.

ISTANBUL, TURKEY
644 ÇEMBERLITAŞ HAMAMI
No trip to Istanbul would be complete without an authentic hammam experience. The Çemberlitaş, dating back to 1584, is one of the oldest hammams in the city. Bathe in the waters or lie on the central hot stone, as sunlight streams through the apertures of the Ottoman dome above.

Tbilisi Old Town

TBILISI, GEORGIA
645 SOLOLAKI

From its dramatic setting in a deep valley, the Old Town of Tbilisi hugs the Mtkvari River and climbs the slopes of the surrounding hills. Sololaki neighborhood is a labyrinth of winding roads linking leafy squares lined crumbling brick houses. Explore the fascinating abandoned buildings, such as the stained-glass house on Betlemi Street.

TBILISI, GEORGIA
646 BOOK CORNER CAFÉ

Retro-style art café hidden in an old neighborhood in the heart of the Georgian capital. Low-key music provides the perfect backdrop to sit and read the vintage books on sale here or to browse the artworks on the walls by local artists. Presentations and literary evenings are regularly held in the pretty courtyard outside.

MTSKHETA-MTIANETI, GEORGIA
647 STEPANTSMINDA

The two-hour hike from Stepantsminda brings you
to the fourteenth-century Gergeti Trinity Church,
a small stone building set against the stunning
backdrop of Mount Kazbek. Due to its remote
position, valuables were sent here for safekeeping
in times of danger. Visit during the low season, and
you will be alone, bar a few cows and stray dogs.

YEGHEGNADZOR, ARMENIA
648 NORAVANK

This hauntingly preserved monastery complex
sits in an isolated, picturesque valley and is a
wonderful example of thirteenth-century Armenian
religious architecture. The site consists of three
churches, but the beautiful St. Astvatsatsin is
perhaps the most interesting, with its exterior
steps leading to an upper level. Exploring the cave
complex is a must.

SYUNIK PROVINCE, ARMENIA
649 SHIKAHOGH STATE RESERVE

Mt'nadzor village is set so deep within a canyon
that its days are passed in almost perpetual
twilight. Here, the communities within the remote
reserve still maintain old Armenian traditions and
customs. Trek out from the village to find a steep
terrain of red rock and virgin oak forest hiding
abandoned settlements, medieval churches,
and Iron Age tombs.

BAKU, AZERBAIJAN
650 MINIATURE BOOKS MUSEUM

A museum dedicated to miniature editions of
books. There are several thousand tiny books,
including many important works in numerous
languages. The oldest book is a seventeenth-
century copy of the Quran. The smallest book
in the museum—at .25 x .35 inch—requires
a magnifying glass to be read.

SAKHA REPUBLIC, RUSSIA
651 OYMYAKON

Those seeking extreme isolation as part of a wintry Russian adventure may enjoy the bleakness of the coldest permanently inhabited place on Earth. Deep in Siberia, temperatures in Oymyakon have previously hit a low of -96.2°F (-71.2°C), yet some homes still have outside toilets. The name Oymyakon means "nonfreezing water" and came about due to a nearby hot spring.

SIBERIA, RUSSIA
652 TRANS-SIBERIAN RAILWAY

Book a luxury cabin with Golden Eagle Luxury Trains on the Trans-Siberian Railway. While onboard, you will lose yourself in the endless stream of thoughts that drift through your mind as you speed through the vast panoramas of forests, plains, steppes, lakes, and remote villages. The full route from Moscow to Vladivostok takes seven days.

MOSCOW, RUSSIA
653 GARAGE MUSEUM OF CONTEMPORARY ART

One of the Russian capital's ambitious new modern-art venues, this renovated Soviet-era restaurant in a city park now hosts exhibitions and lectures featuring Russian and international artists. Inside, a conservation project allows you to admire partially ruined Soviet-era wall mosaics. There's also a good café and large bookstore dedicated to art.

LAKE VUOKSA, RUSSIA
654 CHURCH OF ANDREW THE APOSTLE
Visit this tiny island with a church that was once a
Guinness World Record contender. Ask a local to
row you across.

RUSSIAN FAR EAST, RUSSIA
655 KAMCHATKA COAST
Spot Kamchatka brown bears as part of a cruise
along Siberia's eastern coastline, surely one of the
world's least-visited regions.

ST. PETERSBURG, RUSSIA
656 PRIVATE BOX IN MARIINSKY THEATRE
Enjoy a glass of champagne with the ballet. Treat
yourself to the extravagance of a private box for the
most comfortable experience.

Mariinsky Theatre

AFRICA & THE MIDDLE EAST

From the largest sand desert in the world in the north, through the verdant rain forests of the Congo basin and the great plains of Kenya to the cosmopolitan cities of South Africa at the tip, Africa is home to almost every environment on Earth. Trek high into the Atlas Mountains; take a camel into the swirling expanse of the Sahara; or safari across wide-open savannahs. Beyond the plains are white sand beaches, coral reefs, and the private islands of Zanzibar, Pemba and Fanjove. The Middle East, meanwhile, is the birthplace of religion, magic, and storytelling. It is a region that lays claim to towering pyramids in Sudan and otherworldly tombs at Petra; and to spiritual Jerusalem, sacred to Jews, Muslims, and Christians alike.

Pyramids of Meroë, see page 293

Surf Star

TAMRAGHT, MOROCCO
657 SURF STAR MOROCCO

Combine surfing and yoga in the glorious
Moroccan sunshine. You will be inspired by the
backdrop of Tamraght's sandy beach and endless
coastline, with its relaxed beachfront cafés.

CHEFCHAOUEN, MOROCCO
658 CHEFCHAOUEN

Play Ludo with locals in rooftop cafés overlooking
the narrow lanes of blue-washed walls and
red-tiled roofs. This is Morocco's prettiest village,
and it sits secretively in the Rif mountains.

HIDDEN GEM

MERZOUGA, MOROCCO
659 ALI & SARA'S DESERT PALACE

Watch the sun set from the sand dunes before
spending a magical night under the Saharan stars
in a luxury Bedouin tent, in this secluded glamping
site in Merzouga.

FEZ, MOROCCO
660 MERENID TOMBS

On a hill outside the city walls, the remains of
these fourteenth-century tombs lie crumbling and
looted. The view is outstanding. Below you, the
maze of the medina sprawls in a patchwork of
minarets, courtyards, and clothes lines.

OUARZAZATE, MOROCCO
661 AIT-BEN-HADDOU
This UNESCO-protected red mud-brick fortress seems frozen in time, still resembling its days in the eleventh-century as a caravanserai. Its claim to fame is that it was featured in the movie *Lawrence of Arabia*.

ASNI, MOROCCO
662 KASBAH TAMADOT
High in the Atlas Mountains, the peaceful courtyards and landscaped gardens of exclusive Kasbah Tamadot offer breathing space and tranquility in which you can truly unwind from the buzz of busy Marrakech.

HIGH ATLAS, MOROCCO
663 IMLIL
Escape the chaotic souks of Marrakech and head into the mountains where the air is crisp and cool. This small Berber town is nestled in a valley in High Atlas and makes a good starting point for mountain treks.

Ait-Ben-Haddou

El Fenn

MARRAKECH, MOROCCO
664 EL FENN

Head up to the roof of one of Marrakech's most stylish riads, where you will discover a Berber tent filled with colorful cushions waiting for you on the spacious terrace. Borrow a watercolor set from reception to capture the sweeping views across the rooftops to the Atlas Mountains.

MARRAKECH, MOROCCO
665 BELDI COUNTRY CLUB

Ten minutes by taxi from the medina, at the end of a dusty road, is the Beldi Country Club. The buildings are arranged like a traditional village, and are set within gardens of palms and rose bushes. At night, lanterns light the way through a courtyard and lead you back to your room.

MARRAKECH, MOROCCO
666 ES SAADI MARRAKECH RESORT
The Es Saadi offers yoga retreats in partnership
with Le Tigre Yoga Club. The idea is to rest,
restore, and revive over the course of three days, in
a beautiful, tranquil setting that is a world away
from the city's dusty souks. Leave breathing deeper,
with a refreshed spirit and improved mood.

MARRAKECH, MOROCCO
667 RIAD JARDIN SECRET
The traditional Islamic gardens of this elegant
nineteenth-century palace follow the geometric
orderliness of the Koranic description of paradise.
Leave the intensity of the city behind and walk
around the exotic garden to the sound of running
water that flows through here from the mountains.

HIDDEN GEM
ESSAOUIRA, MOROCCO
668 AUBERGE TANGARO
Dine by candlelight in the restaurant and bathe
in sunshine on the terrace by day. The Tangaro
is a whitewashed oasis in this laid-back Atlantic
seaside town. Practice yoga in the driftwood
spa, or watch the blue-tailed fishing boats
bobbing in the harbor from the terrace.

TAN TAN, MOROCCO
669 WESTERN SAHARA COAST ROAD
The road from Morocco to Mauritania passes
through a sparsely populated, desert-dominated
landscape. On the way, you can spot shipwrecks on
the beaches where the Sahara meets the sea.

670 **LEPTIS MAGNA**

This was once one of the most beautiful cities in the Roman Empire; now weeds grow among the cracks in the cobblestones. Leptis Magna lay forgotten but well preserved for 900 years beneath sand dunes until it was recently excavated. With Libya currently avoided by tourists, Leptis lies abandoned once again.

TRIPOLITANIA, LIBYA
671 GHADAMÈS
Covered alleyways allow travel around this Roman oasis town, known as "the pearl of the desert," protected from the blistering desert heat. The narrow lanes weave around the buildings that are entirely made of mud in the Old Town. Keep walking and you will be led to a refreshing spring-water pool.

CARTHAGE, TUNISIA
672 BATHS OF ANTONINUS
Tucked among pink oleander in the ruins of the capital city of the ancient Carthaginian civilization, are the crumbling remains of the largest Roman baths built on the African continent. Here, you will find Roman relics without the crowds of their Italian counterparts.

TOZEUR GOVERNORATE, TUNISIA
673 CHEBIKA
The green palms of the oasis are visible for many miles across the desert. From the Old Town, walk through a narrow cleft in the mountains and into the small canyon filled with huge palm trees. You will arrive at an amazing oasis pond of azure water with an attractive waterfall.

DAQAS, TUNISIA
674 SIDI BOUHLEL
More commonly known as "the *Star Wars* canyon," since many of the scenes from the famous films were shot here. The location has also starred in *The English Patient* and *Indiana Jones and the Raiders of the Lost Ark*. The canyon—which is located close to the town of Tozeur—is named after a nearby shrine to a holy man.

SOUSSE, TUNISIA
675 MEDINA OF TUNIS
The main souks in the Old Town are far from peaceful, but slip out to the smaller alleys and cobblestone streets around the edges, and you'll find quieter courtyards lined with palm trees. Climb up the stone steps of the fortified monastery to the circular watchtower for far-reaching views across the medina.

LUXOR, EGYPT

676 THE NILE

Navigate the Nile on a traditional Egyptian felucca, the ubiquitous wooden sailing boats that have sailed along this mighty river since ancient times. Let the wind carry you and your crew past the colorful sights of the river and its lively bank, stopping to swim or explore remote villages. Lounge on the deck while listening to the soft sound of the magical river and the creatures that make it their home. You will drop anchor as the sun sets and bathes the world in its golden glow, then settle down to sleep on deck under a canopy of stars.

Felucca on the Nile

CAIRO, EGYPT

677 SUFI

This Arabic and English bookshop is set within a palatial old apartment in downtown Cairo. Arabic music, plush red velvet cushions, and intricate Moroccan lamps create a comfortable ambience in which to peruse the shelves and lose yourself in a book.

MINYA, EGYPT

678 BENI HASAN TOMBS

Rock-cut tombs carved into the high limestone cliffs on the east bank of the Nile with beautifully painted scenes of daily life and ancient deities.

SOMA BAY, EGYPT

679 YOGA ESCAPES

Practice yoga steps from the Red Sea. Stay in a five-star hotel on Soma Bay on a peninsula surrounded by blue water—the perfect location to find peace.

HIDDEN GEM
CAIRO, EGYPT
680 ZEINAB KHATOUN TEAHOUSE
Add herbs and spices to your teapot at this teahouse on the rooftop of a
recently restored Ottoman-era manor house. Your morning brew
will be accompanied by superb views of Cairo's minaret-studded skyline.

ASWAN, EGYPT
681 OLD CATARACT HOTEL
Take in the iconic view of the Nile from the
terrace. Agatha Christie is believed to have written
Death on the Nile while staying here, so you might
unlock your inner writer during your stay.

WADI EL-NATRUN, EGYPT
682 COPTIC MONASTERIES
Journey one hour north of Cairo to the ancient
fortified churches dating back to fourth-century AD.
The short journey will be rewarded by beautiful
frescoes in the monastery of the Syrians.

Coptic Monasteries

NIANI, GAMBIA

683 WASSU STONE CIRCLES

In the Central River Region of Gambia, eleven
stones in a circle mark a 1,200-year-old royal burial
site. Little is known about the origins of this, or
indeed the hundreds of others found across the
region. Join the custom of visitors who have
passed through here before by leaving a small
rock on top of the stones as a sign of respect.

BIJILO, GAMBIA

684 COCO OCEAN RESORT & SPA

Monkeys jump through the canopies, and hornbills
call from the branches of the coconut trees at this
luxurious beach and spa resort. Its traditional
whitewashed Moorish architecture is framed by
pink bougainvillea and tropical flower beds. The
interior is ornate and strikingly elegant.

MAKASUTU FOREST, GAMBIA

685 BIRD-WATCHING

Top birding destination packed with more than
540 species of bird in relatively close proximity.
Many will even visit your hotel garden so there's no
need to wander too far on lazy days. The Gambia
Experience run bird-watching vacations with
world-renowned ornithologist Chris Packham.
Choose from tranquil lodges and visit different
habitats, such as rice fields and fishing villages.

BANDIAGARA CIRCLE, MALI

686 DOGON VILLAGES

The spiritual Dogon people have inhabited the
area for more than 1,000 years, living in secluded
villages that are carved into the spectacular
cliffside. Start your exploration in Bandiagara and
then trek to smaller villages that are perched on
the plateau or down in the sandy lowland. Local
homestays are often available, should you wish
to experience an authentic slice of Malian life.

Île de Gorée

SENEGAL

687 THE LITTLE BAOBAB

Experience *taranga*—the Wolof word for "hospitality"—at this thatched guesthouse in a small Senegalese village. You will enjoy homemade meals made using ingredients from the organic garden. Borrow a book from the eclectic library and hang out in a hammock with the chickens.

SENEGAL

688 ÎLE DE GORÉE

The island of Gorée was the largest slave-trading center on the African coast between the fifteenth and nineteenth centuries. On its now-quiet colonial streets, draped in trailing bougainvillea, you can see the contrast between the grim slave quarters and the elegant pastel-painted houses of the traders.

AHANTA WEST DISTRICT, GHANA

689 **BUSUA**

Popular with laid-back budget travelers since the 1960s, Busua has retained the relaxed vibe that they brought with them in their backpacks. While upscale resorts have recently been setting their sights on this pristine patch of sandy real estate, it still remains distinctly chilled out, due to its distance from Accra.

While the sandy beach and safe swimming waters are the main draw, you can also rent a bike and ride out to Butre and Fort Batenstein.

Ben Abeba

LALIBELA, ETHIOPIA
690 **BEN ABEBA**

On a hilltop overlooking a holy city known for its ancient rock-carved churches, this unusual restaurant looks like a surreal snail's shell. Its outdoor dining spaces jut out from the central spiral staircase, linked by walkways and lined with plants. The highest platform offers views of the river valley below, while a fire pit keeps you warm and offers a companionable glow as the sun goes down in the evening.

ADDIS ABABA, ETHIOPIA
691 **HILTON ADDIS ABABA**

Visitors are welcomed to the grand hotel with a traditional coffee ceremony—an integral part of Ethiopian social life—in the lobby.

AMHARA, ETHIOPIA
692 **SIMIEN MOUNTAINS**

Visit this dramatic landscape of misty peaks, ancient forests, exquisite flora, and exotic fauna. A ten-day trek takes in jagged pinnacles, deep ravines, alpine meadows, and lush plateaus—and the chance to discover a lesser-known landscape of the African continent.

Pyramids of Meroë

BAHIR DAR, ETHIOPIA

693 BLUE NILE FALLS

As the Blue Nile flows to Khartoum to form the Great Nile, it thunders over the cliff face south of Bahir Dar. Here, it drops into a chasm more than 148 ft (45 m) deep and creates the dramatic spectacle of Blue Nile Falls waterfall. The name means "great smoke" in Amharic. The trek to the east bank behind the falls is rewarding.

GONDAR, ETHIOPIA

694 FASILIDES BATH

Walk around the rock wall surrounding the seventeenth-century three-storied bathing palace in the center of a pool. It is only filled with water for the Orthodox Christian celebration of Epiphany.

NILE, SUDAN

695 PYRAMIDS OF MEROË

Egypt's pyramids may be the most famous in the world but they are not the only ones in North Africa. Meroë boasts nearly 200 of the ancient royal tombs. Smaller than their counterparts in Giza, some are nearly 4,000 years old. Sanctions mean the area receives fewer than 15,000 tourists annually, so you can explore without the crowds.

KAMPALA, UGANDA
696 EMIN PASHA HOTEL

Evoking a bygone era, this boutique hotel exudes elegance and comfort. Set in two acres of tropical gardens, the Emin Pasha is an oasis offering privacy and calm in a busy, dusty city. The restaurant terrace is one of the best places to eat in Kampala.

KAMPALA, UGANDA
697 PRUNES

If you are big on brunch, head to this converted bungalow in Kololo suburb. Light and airy, with a refreshing garden, Prunes serves healthy fresh food that is sourced from the nearby farmers' market. The indoor reading room is a quiet space to take your coffee made from local Ugandan beans.

SOUTHWESTERN UGANDA, UGANDA
698 LAKE BUNYONYI

Bunyonyi translates to "place of many little birds"—aptly more than 200 species live on the lake and the green-terraced hillsides that slope down to its shore. In the morning mist, the many islands across the lake look magical. Rent a dugout canoe to explore its otherworldly beauty close up.

RUWENZORI RANGE, UGANDA

699 **MOUNT STANLEY**

Africa's third-highest mountain is in one of the
most beautiful and dramatic environments the
country has to offer. The area is wild and
untouched by human habitation. In a bid to
attract more visitors to the mountain, the trails
have been restored, and the refuge huts have
been renovated. But you will still be
unbothered by crowds as you ascend.

QUEEN ELIZABETH NATIONAL PARK, UGANDA

700 **ISHASHA PLAINS**

There are plenty of hippos and not many tourists
in the Ishasha sector of Uganda's most popular
savannah reserve. This is one of only two places
you can find the tree-climbing lions that hang out
on the branches of huge fig trees.

HIDDEN GEM
GABON

701 **LOPÉ NATIONAL PARK**

Stay at the park's research center and assist in the
day-to-day research program, which is studying the
behavior of the animals in the park. You can spend
the day tracking mandrills through the rain forest,
or observing the animals that are drawn to the
banks of the Ogooué river.

Samburu National Reserve

RIFT VALLEY PROVINCE, KENYA

702 SAMBURU NATIONAL RESERVE

Explore the rugged, semidesert reserve inhabited by the remote nomadic Samburu tribe. Predominantly unfenced savannah grassland with clusters of acacia and dramatic forests, the reserve is cut through by the Ewaso Ng'iro river, which draws a rich diversity of wildlife. Elephants are the dominant mammal in the park, with up to 900 individuals hanging out here.

SERA CONSERVANCY, KENYA

703 RHINO TRACKING

In the vast untouched wilderness of Kenya, luxury safari camp Saruni Rhino offers a rare black rhino tracking experience, which funds its conservation projects in the region.

LAIKIPIA COUNTY, KENYA

704 ARIJIJU

Arijiju is a beautiful private home on a hillside. From the fragrant green spaces to the cool shade of the vaulted walkways and the closed courtyards, the retreat has an air of monastic calm. Profits are fed back into Rhino conservation projects.

MAASAI MARA, KENYA

705 MAASAI MARA HOT-AIR BALLOON

For a unique and exclusive Tour of Maasai Mara National Reserve, ride a hot air balloon over areas of the reserve that are off-limits to safari vehicles.

HIDDEN GEM

KIAMBU, KENYA

706 PARADISE LOST

Paradise Lost is a little oasis in the middle of a coffee farm. The main attraction is a maze of caves eroded by the river, the entrance hidden behind a cascading waterfall.

MAASAI MARA, KENYA

707 MAASAI MARA VILLAGE STAY

Stay in a traditional Maasai hut hosted by a Maasai family, where you can experience the pace of a culture that has remained unchanged for hundreds of years. After helping with the daily activities, you will share a cup of smoky chai before letting the cattle low you to sleep. Groups are kept small in order to minimize impact on traditional village life.

LAMU ISLAND, KENYA
708 LAMU

The oldest and best-preserved Swahili settlement in East Africa retains its traditional way of life on a peaceful tropical island of endless beaches and tiny villages amid mango plantations. Donkey carts replace motor vehicles on the narrow streets, so life is taken at a more sedate pace. Beautiful Shela Beach is 7 mi (12 km) of pristine sand that has been practically left to nature.

GREAT RIFT VALLEY, KENYA
709 CHALBI DESERT

The great shimmering whiteness of this huge salt pan is home to oryx, ostrich, and zebra that have adapted to the hostile environment. It is an eerie landscape of cracked earth and bare skies that shouldn't be entered without an experienced guide. The desert's secret is the northern fringe of palm-shaded oases used by the Gabra people to water their camels.

WATAMU, KENYA
710 GEDI

With no written account of it in any historical records, this abandoned thirteenth-century city is shrouded in mystery. Buried deep in a tropical forest on the edge of the Indian Ocean, the site contains a palace. This comes complete with tunnels and secret rooms, coral brick houses, and a temple. Local people say that it is haunted by the "Old Ones."

HIDDEN GEM

NAIROBI, KENYA
711 TIN ROOF CAFÉ

Visit this intimate garden café in a converted home, with a commitment to healthy eating. Play board games on the bright and airy African veranda while you enjoy freshly prepared food that will nourish both your body and soul.

NAIROBI, KENYA
712 GIRAFFE MANOR

A lanky-necked companion might join you for breakfast through the window at this beautiful 1930s manor house next to the city's giraffe center.

Entamanu Ngorongoro

NGORONGORO CRATER, TANZANIA
713 ENTAMANU NGORONGORO

Watch the sun rise over the Ngorongoro Crater and set over the Serengeti from the stylish tented camp on the crater's rim. During the day, you can descend into the crater itself for guided game drives. Almost 30,000 animals inhabit a mere 100 sq mi (259 sq km) in the perfectly formed caldera, including many of the big cats and the rare black rhino.

HIDDEN GEM

SAADANI NATIONAL PARK, TANZANIA
715 BABS' CAMP

The talking point at Babs' Camp is a 66-ft (20-m) viewing tower with a crow's nest. Head to the top, and you can enjoy stunning views of the Indian Ocean and the surrounding forest.

IRINGA, TANZANIA
714 RUAHA NATIONAL PARK

Hot, dry, and dramatic, Ruaha's relative difficulty to access leaves it with lower visitor numbers than Tanzania's better-known parks. You can catch the same wildlife congregating on the banks of the Great Ruaha river, as it rushes through woodland.

Lake Tanganyika

LAKE TANGANYIKA, TANZANIA

716 LAKE TANGANYIKA

The turquoise water of Lake Tanganyika shimmers at the foot of the forested slopes of the giant Mahale mountains. Misty, dark green hills loom above its remote white shores. One of the world's largest populations of wild chimpanzees live in the surrounding forest. A guide from Greystoke Mahale can take you out to track them.

SERENGETI, TANZANIA

717 FOUR SEASONS SAFARI LODGE SERENGETI

Cool down in your own private infinity pool after an exhilarating day tracking game in Tanzania's most famous safari area. As you swim, you may spot zebra and elephants at the waterhole. Sitting on a hillside, the camp is in prime position for watching the annual migration of wildebeest.

SONGO SONGO ARCHIPELAGO, TANZANIA

718 FANJOVE PRIVATE ISLAND LODGE

Fling back the folding doors of your traditional thatch-roofed banda for uninterrupted views of the ocean from the comfort of your four-poster bed. During your stay, you can wander along the beach to explore the crumbling lighthouse, or simply snooze the day away.

HIDDEN GEM

DAR ES SALAAM, TANZANIA
719 UPEPO GARDEN

Stay at this relaxing and peaceful guesthouse with just five rooms on the beachfront in Mbezi. Sip a refreshing juice at the private beach bar overlooking the Indian Ocean or catch a nap in the shaded garden before heading to bed to sleep until the sun rises through your window.

DAR ES SALAAM, TANZANIA
720 MASJID AL-QIBLATAYN

Located in the Kariakoo area of Dar es Salaam, this mosque is one of the most important in the city. Visitors can look around the impressive interior, but it is best to avoid Friday prayers if you're looking for a sanctuary of cool and calm. Check and respect the dress code before entering.

ZANZIBAR, TANZANIA
721 ANNA OF ZANZIBAR

Stay at this boutique lodge on its own private stretch of beach, offering barefoot luxury and five-star services. Named after the traditional trading currency in the days of the spice trade, Anna of Zanzibar is a gem. The five villas are dotted around a garden and swimming pool.

PEMBA ISLAND, TANZANIA
722 MANTA RESORT

Descend below the surface of the sea to a cozy room with just one bed, encapsulated within a glass bubble that looks straight out to the Indian Ocean. This is the Underwater Room at the Manta Resort. The daybeds on the top deck make the perfect place for stargazing.

ZANZIBAR, TANZANIA
723 BWEJUU BEACH

Possibly the best beach on Zanzibar if you want to find a much sought after and hard to come by spot of sand to yourself. The 12-mile long sandbank is home to a small fishing community who you'll see returning to the shore, where the women gather seaweed as children play.

LIVINGSTONE, ZAMBIA
724 TONGABEZI LODGE

This stunning, luxury lodge on the banks of the mighty Zambezi
river is the ideal place to unwind at the end of your day on safari.
Tongabezi is only eleven miles upstream of the majestic Victoria Falls,
where you might be lucky enough to witness the lunar rainbow over
the water when the moon is full. Choose the Honeymoon House for
romantic luxury. This particular suite has a private pool overlooking
the river, and you can enjoy a secluded candlelit dinner on your deck
under the stars. Afterward, sink into the open-air bath and be
serenaded by the sounds of the African evening.

EASTERN PROVINCE, ZAMBIA
725 LUANGWA VALLEY

The concentration and diversity
of animals around the Luangwa
river and its oxbow lagoons is
one of the most intense in
Africa, so this is a must-do for
big-game enthusiasts.

Tongabezi Lodge

LAKE MALAWI, MALAWI
726 MUMBO ISLAND CAMP
There is little to do in this tiny jungle-clad
hideaway in the middle of the lake except
test out the hammocks and gaze into the
clear, fish-filled waters.

LIVINGSTONE, ZAMBIA
727 VICTORIA FALLS
Witness the thundering Zambezi and the power of
the Victoria Falls from above on an exhilarating
microlight flight. You will feel the freedom of birds
as you soar through the mist and swoop low over
the rain forest.

MUA, MALAWI
728 CHAMARE MUSEUM
Beautiful museum dedicated to Malawian
history. See the "tree of spirits," hung with almost
300 traditional Gule Wamkulu masks, alongside
panels that explain their meanings.

BLANTYRE, MALAWI
729 MANDALA HOUSE
Tour this colonial-style house and gardens from the
late nineteenth century. It houses the artwork-
adorned Mandala Café and La Caverna art gallery,
which showcases local artists.

THYOLO, MALAWI
730 HUNTINGDON HOUSE
This grand old colonial-style 1920s guesthouse
is nestled on the rolling hills and emerald green
plantations of the Satemwa Tea & Coffee Estate.
Enjoy the relaxed ambience of a bygone era.

WALVIS BAY, NAMIBIA

731 LIGHTHOUSE AT PELICAN POINT

Bask in the sun with the seals on a remote peninsula—the untouched beauty of the Atlantic Ocean on one side and Walvis Bay lagoon on the other. The Captain's Cove Suite at the top of the former harbor control tower has absolute privacy and 360-degree views across the Namibian skyline.

KAVANGO REGION, NAMIBIA

732 CAPRIVI STRIP

The Caprivi Strip is on the elephant migration route, making it the ideal destination to see the herds up close and personal. The waterways and wildlife are copious, while human inhabitants are few and far between—though more lodges are being built. Visit now while it's still unknown.

HIDDEN GEM

KARAS REGION, NAMIBIA

733 KOLMANSKOP

A diamond-rush town abandoned more than fifty years ago is being slowly swallowed by the desert. The ghost town is now an open-air museum. It is an incredible place to wonder and wander around the once-grand houses half submerged beneath the dunes. Their former glory has been ravaged by years of strong winds and desert sand, but they retain an eerie beauty.

OKAVANGO DELTA, BOTSWANA

734 SANDIBE ECOLODGE

Set against the shimmering water of the magnificent Okavango Delta, Sandibe flourishes in a stunning setting of wild palms and gnarled fig trees as the golden-grassed floodplains stretch into the distance all around. The design is inspired by the curved shape of the delta's elusive pangolin, while the suites mimic the nests of the golden weaver bird.

OKAVANGO DELTA, BOTSWANA

735 SANCTUARY BAINES' CAMP

Request that your bed be wheeled out onto your private deck at night to curl up beneath the cosmos with the shimmering waters of the Boro river below you. The backbone of this ecofriendly camp is built from recycled aluminum cans that were collected by the local community in Maun.

NXAI PAN, BOTSWANA

736 NXAI PAN NATIONAL PARK

When the flamingos flock to the Nxai Pan inland lake, the horizon is pink to its edges with the magical sight. Game spotting in African parks is often better in the dry season, but Nxai Pan comes into its own in the rainy season when the whole flat pan is teeming with life.

Sandibe Ecolodge

Time + Tide Miavana

NOSY ANKAO, MADAGASCAR
737 TIME + TIDE MIAVANA

Even before the helicopter touches down at this
enchanted beachside bolt-hole, you feel like you
have escaped daily life. A cluster of stone fortress
villas straight out of a fairy tale open out to an
infinity pool overlooking the Indian Ocean. Your
helicopter is on hand to take you to nearby islands
where you can trek to find lemurs in the rain forest.

HARARE, ZIMBABWE
738 THE SHONA SCULPTURE GALLERY

Visit this beautiful green garden showcasing stone
sculptures that portray the values of family, love,
life, and nature. The sculptures have been
hand-carved by the Shona people using traditional
methods that are thousands of years old.

SAVA, MADAGASCAR
739 MASOALA NATIONAL PARK

The rain forest meets the sea in this incredibly
diverse reserve that represents the largest of
Madagascar's protected land areas and also
some of its least visited.

HARARE, ZIMBABWE
740 NATIONAL HERBARIUM
& BOTANIC GARDENS OF ZIMBABWE

Visit a center for research and information on the
indigenous plants of Zimbabwe, where you can
spend the day discovering tranquil gardens.

VILANKULO, MOZAMBIQUE
741 BAZARUTO ARCHIPELAGO
Once the realm of spice traders and buccaneers, the islands of the
Bazaruto Archipelago are beginning to attract a new wave of
explorers to the wild, dune-backed shoreline of Mozambique. Lodges
on Bazaruto and Benguerra Islands have grown organically out of
small fishing camps set beside white sand and blue waters.

MENABE, MADAGASCAR
742 AVENUE OF THE BAOBABS
Centuries-old giant baobab trees
line the dirt road linking
Morondava and Belo Tsiribihina,
creating a unique, otherworldly
scene. Photographers will
particularly appreciate the site
at sunrise and sunset, when the
colors of the tree trunks change
and their long shadows become
dramatic. The baobabs are
considered sacred by locals,
who say that the spirits of the
deceased live within them.

Avenue of the Baobabs

"Underwater waterfall" in south Mauritius

BELLE MARE, MAURITIUS
7+3 LUX* BELLE MARE

On a glorious stretch of coastline, tucked away in tropical gardens near a sleepy Mauritian village, the LUX* terrace is a blissful spot from which to gaze at azure waters. Book a helicopter tour to view incredible sights around the island, such as the "underwater waterfall" at La Morne.

PORT LOUIS, MAURITIUS
7++ INSTITUTE OF CONTEMPORARY ART INDIAN OCEAN (ICAIO)

A cultural space featuring exhibitions and workshops, with an emphasis on the artistic development of Mauritius. The institute hosts visiting international artists, so the exhibitions are constantly rotating.

BELLE MARE, MAURITIUS
745 LA MAISON D'ÉTÉ

Stay at this intimate boutique hotel with a family home vibe, nestled between volcanic rocks and coves. The cocoon-like rooms are the perfect place to retreat and relax.

TROU D'EAU DOUCE, MAURITIUS
746 LE CAFÉ DES ARTS

Fine dining in an old sugar mill showcasing landscapes and sculptures by the owner's mother. This lady happens to be the last private pupil of French artist Henri Matisse.

LA POSSESSION, RÉUNION
747 LODGE ROCHE TAMARIN & SPA

Built upon a mountainside with spectacular sea views, the lodge is constructed entirely of wood and is an invitation to rest the body and soul in utter seclusion.

HIDDEN GEM

SALAZIE, RÉUNION
748 HELL-BOURG

Despite its rather sinister-sounding name, the village of Hell-Bourg is possibly the most beautiful on Réunion Island. In the lush, green, mountainous interior of the island, the high-altitude village enjoys a pleasant climate and is a hiking heaven. Once a popular spa town, Hell-Bourg's quaint streets are lined with the picturesque and colorful facades of Creole homes. A day can be spent exploring the relics of the old thermal baths by the river nearby and at colonial-style Maison Folio. Its tangled tropical gardens are exotically fragrant, while the charming fountain and traditional *guétali* kiosk evoke a romantic nostalgia for days gone by.

SAINT PIERRE, RÉUNION
749 LA DIAGONALE DES FOUS

If running in the mountains lets off steam for you, the Madman's Diagonal is a 103-mi (165-km) ultramarathon through Réunion Island's thrusting wilderness of mountain peaks and canyons.

750 LION'S HEAD MOUNTAIN

Lion's Head Mountain is one of Cape Town's most iconic sights. Considered to resemble the shape of a crouching lion, the distinctive pointy slope overlooks the Table Bay on one side and the Atlantic coastline on the other. Hiking up Lion's Head is a treat at any time of the day, but there is something special about undertaking the climb on a sunny South African evening.

While most hikers head straight to the peak to catch the sunset from the summit, Lion's Head hides many spectacular secrets that most will miss. Hidden caves along the route harbor peaceful places to admire the awe-inspiring views. When you are ready, head back to the main trail before it gets dark, unless you have a good flashlight with you. You can also continue up to the top of the mountain following the old trail. At 2,195 ft (669 m) above sea level, the views from the peak are spectacular. On a clear day, you can see across to Robben Island, where Nelson Mandela was imprisoned for twenty-seven years. It is a fairly strenuous climb, but anyone who is fit and healthy should be able to do it.

Londolozi Game Reserve

OVERBERG, SOUTH AFRICA
751 HEARTH & SOUL

This ecofarm and spiritual
retreat is so remote that it
doesn't have a postal address.
It's surrounded by trees and
mountains, and seclusion is part
of the spiritual prescription here,
alongside yoga and meditation.

WESTERN CAPE, SOUTH AFRICA
752 KNYSNA

This heavenly town is in the
heart of the Garden Route.
Long, white sand beaches line
crystalline waters of the clear
blue lagoon, and you are
surrounded by the stunning
Outeniqua mountains.

WESTERN CAPE, SOUTH AFRICA
753 LANGEBAAN LAGOON

Rent a luxury houseboat on the
azure waters of the Langebaan
Lagoon. Take life at a slower
pace and enjoy all the natural
wonders of the local area
literally on your doorstep.

ELEPHANT COAST,
SOUTH AFRICA
754 KOSI BAY

Spot hippos wallowing at
secluded Kosi Bay, a pristine
network of lakes on the Indian
Ocean coastline that is still
unexplored and unexploited.

PRETORIA, SOUTH AFRICA
755 TSWAING METEORITE CRATER

An impact crater filled with a
salt lagoon that was created by
an asteroid 200,000 years ago.
With a small on-site museum.

NAMAQUA NATIONAL PARK,
SOUTH AFRICA
756 NAMAQUA FLOWER BEACH CAMP

See this mobile tented camp that
sets up temporarily on the
Northern Cape beach each year
for an amazing wildflower show.

PRETORIA, SOUTH AFRICA
757 ROVOS RAIL PRIDE OF AFRICA

Take an escorted rail tour from
Pretoria to Cape Town on the
elegant Rovos Rail Pride of
Africa route.

SABI SAND, SOUTH AFRICA
758 LONDOLOZI GAME RESERVE

The name of this private family-run game reserve comes from
the Zulu word meaning "protector of all living things." This gives
you an idea of the importance of conservation at Londolozi. The
reserve offers a photography safari in a location that is unparalleled
for wildlife, with great light, an incredible set, and magnificent
subjects. The lodge rents equipment, so you could catch a fish eagle
in flight or leopards in trees—without getting too close for comfort.

PRETORIA, SOUTH AFRICA
759 THE BLUE TRAIN

If you are traveling from Pretoria
to Cape Town, do it in luxury on
the modern The Blue Train.
Enjoy the journey through some
of the most spectacular scenery
on the continent from the
comfort of your five-star cabin.

KRUGER NATIONAL PARK,
SOUTH AFRICA
760 SINGITA
BOULDERS LODGE

A refined lodge set along the
banks of the Sand River, inspired
by the geometry of the boulders
on which it rests.

MOOINOOI, SOUTH AFRICA
761 EMOYENI
RETREAT CENTER

Run on Buddhist principles and
meditation techniques, Emoyeni
seeks to foster mindfulness and
compassion among its guests.
The facilities are functional
rather than luxurious and, as
introspection and inquiry are
encouraged, there are no
distractions in the form of
televisions or a swimming pool.

EASTERN CAPE PROVINCE, SOUTH AFRICA
762 COFFEE BAY

A popular backpackers' bolt-hole with a laid-back barefoot vibe on the Wild Coast of the
Eastern Cape Province. The stunning beach is set against the backdrop of black-faced
cliffs, powder-white sands, and emerald hills. The five-day hike from Port St. Johns to
Coffee Bay is unimaginably beautiful.

THE KALAHARI, SOUTH AFRICA
763 TSWALU KALAHARI RESERVE
The two elusive luxuries of silence and space can be found in abundance at Tswalu Kalahari Reserve in South Africa's Kalahari savannah. The lodge has a stunning sleep-out deck named Malori, meaning "dreamer in Tswana." You can sleep safely in the wilderness under the diamond skies.

KWAZULU-NATAL PROVINCE, SOUTH AFRICA
764 iSIMANGALISO WETLAND PARK
iSimangaliso means "miracle and wonder," an apt description for this park on the Zululand coast. The centerpiece of iSimangaliso is the vast Lake St. Lucia, home to large numbers of hippos, crocodiles, pelicans, and flamingos. Beyond the lake is an incredibly beautiful series of beaches, coral reefs, swamps, and coastal forests.

JOHANNESBURG, SOUTH AFRICA
765 SATYAGRAHA HOUSE
This former home of Mahatma Gandhi, where he developed his philosophy of passive resistance, is now a museum and guesthouse in a garden setting.

Above: Saxon Hotel Villas & Spa

Top: Nirox Foundation Sculpture Park
Above: Living Room's rooftop café

JOHANNESBURG, SOUTH AFRICA
766 SAXON HOTEL VILLAS & SPA

Nelson Mandela wrote his biography *Long Walk to Freedom* here, amid the beautifully landscaped gardens in the middle of a tranquil ambassadorial district in Johannesburg. It is easy to imagine how the peace encouraged his creative flow. Contemporary African design blends with traditional influences to create an elegant sanctuary.

JOHANNESBURG, SOUTH AFRICA
767 NIROX FOUNDATION SCULPTURE PARK

A former fishing farm has been repurposed into a serene sculpture park. The landscaped gardens and waterways are scattered with impressive artworks created by the artists in residence and temporary exhibiting artists. Jeremy Rose's *The Cell* is a thought-provoking replica of Nelson Mandela's prison cell, juxtaposed with the freedom of the reserve.

HIDDEN GEM

JOHANNESBURG, SOUTH AFRICA
768 LIVING ROOM'S ROOFTOP CAFÉ

The owner's ethos that plants make people happy is put into play at this laid-back garden in the sky, with a fantastic city view. The organic café sits in a leafy slice of paradise that blends natural and urban to create a thriving rooftop jungle that epitomizes relaxation in the city.

CAPE TOWN, SOUTH AFRICA
769 TABLE MOUNTAIN
A cable car carries passengers to the top of the iconic Table Mountain. Instead, put on your walking boots and trek through the lush Kirstenbosch National Botanical Garden.

CAPE TOWN, SOUTH AFRICA
770 THE OM REVOLUTION
Mobile yoga studio that takes classes to calm and beautiful outdoor locations around the city. Private classes at your accommodation are available at a time of your choosing.

DURBAN, SOUTH AFRICA
771 DURBAN BOTANIC GARDENS
Africa's oldest-surviving botanical gardens are famous for the original specimen of a cycad that is still recognized as being the rarest plant in the world.

Table Mountain

North Island   *Aldabra Atoll*

NORTH ISLAND, SEYCHELLES
772 **NORTH ISLAND**

Arrive by helicopter to this ecofriendly private
island with plans to reintroduce many of the
critically endangered Seychelles species. Guests
receive a free massage upon arrival.

ALDABRA ATOLL, SEYCHELLES
773 **ALDABRA GIANT TORTOISES**

Visits to the Aldabra Atoll to see the world's largest
tortoises must be approved by the Seychelles
Islands Foundation. The gentle giants can also
be found on Curieuse.

PRASLIN, SEYCHELLES
774 **VALLÉE DE MAI NATURAL RESERVE**

This is a nature reserve and UNESCO World
Heritage Site; one of only two places in the world
where the rare coco de mer grows in its original
palm jungle.

HIDDEN GEM
MAHÉ ISLAND, SEYCHELLES
775 **VICTORIA**

One of the world's smallest capitals is little more
than a cluster of roads around Creole-style houses.
The tiny Hindu temple is particularly peaceful.

LA DIGUE, SEYCHELLES
776 **ANSE SOURCE D'ARGENT**

Take an oxcart from the ferry to Anse Source
d'Argent; the granite rock formations make it one
of the most picturesque beaches in the Seychelles.

FREGATE ISLAND PRIVATE, SEYCHELLES
777 FREGATE ISLAND PRIVATE

Fregate Island Private is the place to come for sublime seclusion. You are unlikely to meet any of the other guests during your stay, though don't be surprised to bump into one of the 2,000 giant Aldabra tortoises that call the tiny granite private island their home. The Rock Spa presides over its slice of cliffside with tumbling views over the sapphire seas of the Indian Ocean. The spa uses products made from the island's native plants. Away from the resort, the rest of the island is a wild and untamed tangle of forest waiting for you to explore.

FÉLICITÉ ISLAND, SEYCHELLES
778 SIX SENSES ZIL PASYON SPA

An African-inspired spa treatment here includes a two-hour Floating Journey with an African foot ritual, and sound therapy with traditional African instruments.

Six Senses Zil Pasyon Spa

Temple Mount, Jerusalem

779 ETZ CAFÉ

All profits from Etz Café in downtown Jerusalem go to helping the homeless and those in need, providing them with free meals and counseling. Mark your home on the map, then order a *limonana*—lemonade and fresh mint with crushed ice—and sit on pavement seats to people watch.

780 DEIR ES-SULTAN

A short walk from Temple Mount lies this incense-filled Ethiopian Coptic monastery. Enter through a low stone doorway off the rooftop courtyard of a medieval annex of the Church of the Holy Sepulchre—the place where Jesus is believed to have been crucified and buried.

JERUSALEM, ISRAEL
781 TMOL SHILSHOM
Hidden on a winding alley is a cozy bookstore-café
whose name means "Those were the days" in
Hebrew. This suits the café's nostalgic ambience;
its eclectic mix of furnishings amid piles of dusty
books written in Hebrew. The café is popular for
the traditional Israeli breakfast, *shakshuka*.

JERUSALEM, ISRAEL
782 SHRINE OF THE BOOK
The first copy discovered of the 2,000-year-old
Dead Sea Scrolls is housed in a contemporary
building shaped like the lid of the jar it was found
in. The white tiles contrast with the black basalt
wall as a metaphor for the battle between good
and evil.

NAHARIYA, ISRAEL
783 AKHZIVLAND
With a mermaid on its flag and the sound of
the sea as the national anthem, the micronation
Akhzivland fully lives its ideals of pacifism and
freedom. Visitors can camp at the independent
state that has a population of just two, self-
proclaimed President Eli Avivi and his wife.

UPPER GALILEE, ISRAEL
784 ROSH PINA
One of modern Israel's first towns is now home
to a thriving artists' colony. Pass a day in the
HaBaron Garden's olive and almond trees, the
scent of the fragrant herbs planted on the hillside
ever present. The local *zimmers* offer peaceful bed
and breakfasts.

785 BEIT EL NESSIM

Hidden among the walled gardens of El Mina's Old Town, this ancient mansion has been lovingly restored by its yogi owners into a jasmine-scented guesthouse with rambling grapevines and knockout views over the bell towers and fruit trees. Beit El Nessim also doubles as Tripoli's first yoga retreat.

786 MAYOULI

Hang out in the hammocks in the serene gardens while cats and chickens roam freely through the peaceful orchard. Mayouli is the perfect place to forget about the city you left at the door. The white sands of Batroun beach are within walking distance, as is the abandoned Mseilha Fort.

787 RUINS OF SEBASTIA

These remains of an important settlement are on a hillside above a village believed to be one of the oldest continually inhabited places in the West Bank.

788 AL-KAYED PALACE GUESTHOUSE

Tourists flock to the ancient ruins on a hilltop above Sebastia, but few visit the village below with its picturesque houses, stunning views, and thousands of years of history. In the center, a nineteenth-century Ottoman palace has been converted into a gorgeous guesthouse.

MAR SABA, PALESTINIAN TERRITORIES
789 MAR SABA MONASTERY
One of the oldest inhabited monasteries in the world climbs dramatically up a cliff edge in the wilderness of the Judean Desert. Explore the quiet inner maze of Mar Saba's Greek Orthodox halls, its small chapels, caves, and endless stairs and gates. Women are only allowed in the Women's Tower.

RAMALLAH, PALESTINIAN TERRITORIES
790 AL-SNOBAR
At the top of a long staircase in the heart of Ramallah, you will discover a secluded swimming spot surrounded by the pine trees that give this place its name. Cushion-covered couches draped in woven red blankets adorn the terraces, enticing you to stay awhile and unwind.

NABLUS, PALESTINIAN TERRITORIES
791 HAMMAM ESH-SHIFA
This well-preserved bathhouse was founded in the thirteenth century and is one of the oldest in the old city of Nablus. Hammam esh-Shifa retains most of its original features, including the dome that filters sunlight through small, stained-glass openings. Women are permitted twice a week.

Wadi Ghwayr, near Feynan Ecolodge, Jordan

Nasir al-Mulk

ISFAHAN, IRAN

792 ROYAL MOSQUE

Admire the stunning architecture and decoration of this elegant mosque at the head of Isfahan's main square. The sheer size of the entrance portal will take your breath away.

SHIRAZ, IRAN

793 NASIR AL-MULK

From the outside, this mosaic-clad mosque looks like many of the other beautiful Islamic temples found throughout the Middle East. Step inside in the early hours after sunrise, however, and you'll soon see why the Nasir al-Mulk is also known as the "Mosque of Many Colors." As the morning sun hits the building, the light streams through the magnificent stained-glass windows, drenching the carved pillars and spilling across the tightly woven Persian carpets of the winter prayer hall in glorious Technicolor, picking out the pink of the ceramic tiles and bathing the interior in a rose-tinted glow.

HIDDEN GEM

OROST, IRAN

794 BADAB-E SURT

The sky-reflecting pools of hot spring water that run down the rusty-orange limestone terraces shift in hue as the sun travels across the sky.

WADI RUM VILLAGE, JORDAN

795 WADI RUM

Sleep at a traditional Bedouin camp in the moody desert wilderness. Sip cardamom coffee boiled over an open fire and eat chicken cooked in an under-the-sand barbecue.

DANA BIOSPHERE RESERVE, JORDAN

796 FEYNAN ECOLODGE

At night, hundreds of candles light the way through the courtyards and corridors of this unforgettable ecolodge in the heart of the magnificent Wadi Feynan.

PETRA, JORDAN

797 HIGH PLACE OF SACRIFICE

Few people climb the 800 steps up the ancient ceremonial procession route to the sacrificial altars high above the Royal Tombs.

Museum of Islamic Art

RIYADH, SAUDI ARABIA
798 THE SKY BRIDGE

This walkway is on the
ninety-ninth floor, where you
can see the whole city laid out
below you. Magical at night if
you don't mind sharing with
a crowd.

HIDDEN GEM
AL-'ULA, SAUDI ARABIA
799 AL-'ULA

This 2,000-year-old ghost town
is a maze of mud-brick and
stone houses that have been
abandoned in the hot sun for
more than thirty years. The
walled city was once a thriving
oasis town on the "incense
road"; now you can find yourself
utterly alone in the silent streets.

DOHA, QATAR
800 MUSEUM OF ISLAMIC ART

Built on its own man-made
island in the sea off Doha's
waterfront, the Museum of
Islamic Art looks like a Cubist
fortress rising from a moat.
Beyond the palm-lined entrance,
a five-story-high domed atrium
creates a spectacle of light and
space and is the perfect place to
contemplate the craftmanship of
the ancient Islamic artists.

AL ZUBARAH, QATAR
801 AL ZUBARAH FORT

All that remains of the once thriving port that bustled with fishermen and merchants are the archaeological skeletons of the city. While Al Zubarah itself is off-limits, its fortress is open and offers bleak views from its battlement of the abandoned pearling town being slowly consumed by the sands of the desolate desert.

DOHA, QATAR
802 KHAWR AL 'UDAYD

Tranquil beach surrounding a vast inland lake in the middle of the desert, which arrives with the morning sun and slinks back to the sea once more as night falls.

Al Zubarah Fort

ABU DHABI,
UNITED ARAB EMIRATES
803 MASDAR CITY

Wander the silent streets of a modern-day ghost town. Work began in 2006 on Masdar City, next to Abu Dhabi International Airport. The aim was to build a carbon-neutral city from scratch, powered entirely by the sun and wind, with no cars and zero waste. It was to be the world's most sustainable city. Ten years after work started, recession hit, and the project was all but abandoned with only 5 percent of the buildings complete. Now less than 2 percent of the intended 40,000 people inhabit the city's space. Take a lonely walk to find the organic café.

Masdar City

DUBAI, UNITED ARAB EMIRATES
804 MAJLIS CAFÉ

Hidden inside the grand Jumeirah Mosque, shaded by old ghaf trees, Majlis is, by its own admission, the "first and finest camel milk café in Dubai."

DUBAI, UNITED ARAB EMIRATES
805 LIFE'N ONE

This vegan café and wellness center is near the coast, offering meditation and yoga in a villa-style venue with a large garden and swinging sun seats.

Sheikh Zayed Grand Mosque in Abu Dhabi

ABU DHABI,
UNITED ARAB EMIRATES
806 SHEIKH ZAYED GRAND MOSQUE

Although it is one of the largest mosques in the world with a capacity for many thousands of worshippers, there are plenty of peaceful spaces in which to reflect. Avoid the heat of the day and take the 5 p.m. sunset tour.

DUBAI, UNITED ARAB EMIRATES
807 XVA ART HOTEL

This boutique hotel is also one of Dubai's best art galleries. Pop in for an exhibition, stay for a coffee in the courtyard café.

DUBAI, UNITED ARAB EMIRATES
808 AL BARARI

Environmentally conscious community with a focus on sustainability and living in harmony with nature. Take a book and hang out by the lake in the gorgeous gardens.

HIDDEN GEM
DUBAI, UNITED ARAB EMIRATES
809 COFFEE MUSEUM

This shrine to caffeine consumption explores coffee's Middle Eastern heritage. Wander a maze of exhibits before having a cup of the black stuff in the café.

Al Baleed Resort Salalah

SANA'A, YEMEN
810 MOCHA COFFEE SHOP

A café on the sixth floor of the Taj Talha Hotel, a former eighteenth-century palace with an open view over the Sana'a Old City. It is particularly magical to visit at night when the sun drops below the horizon and the lights of the city switch on. Guests at the hotel can have breakfast on the roof as the Old City awakes.

MUSCAT, OMAN
811 SULTAN QABOOS GRAND MOSQUE

The Grand Mosque of Muscat dominates the city skyline, embellished in beautiful mosaics and handcrafted architectural details, including a 46-ft (14-m) wide chandelier with 600,000 Swarovski crystals and a 230-ft (70-m) handloomed carpet that took 600 women more than two years to make. Inside is peaceful, quiet, and cool.

SALALAH, OMAN
812 AL BALEED RESORT SALALAH

Salalah is known as the "Perfume Capital of the World," partly in thanks to the important role it played in the early trade of frankincense. This has inspired the Al Baleed Resort's signature spa treatment, the Frankincense Ritual, a four-handed massage technique enhanced with frankincense oil.

MUSANDAM PENINSULA, OMAN
814 MUSANDAM

Dramatic scenery of stunning fjords, winding mountain roads, and small fishing villages has earned the Musandam Peninsula the nickname "the Norway of the Middle East." A trip to the peninsula is an isolated but accessible escape into the wilderness, away from the glitz of the modern Gulf cities.

HIDDEN GEM
SUR, OMAN
813 WADI SHAB

Follow the gorge cut into the rock face by a freshwater stream to find a half-submerged cave filled with a turquoise pool and raging waterfall. The hike is an unsignposted adventure and you'll be leaping across rocks and paddling through streams. Jump into the clear blue natural swimming pools along the way to keep cool.

SALALAH, OMAN
815 EMPTY QUARTER

Could anything sound better to the serious solitude seeker than a place enigmatically named "the Empty Quarter?" This fabled sea of sand – 250,000 square miles of nothing but dunes – fascinated Lawrence of Arabia. Mobile camps allow explorers to sleep under canvas surrounded by the silence of the great forbidding desert.

ASIA PACIFIC

A continent of intrigue, solace, and spirituality, Asia blends modern with ancient, turns rain forest to desert, and transforms jungle into powder-white sand. Head high into the Himalayas to myriad temples, or travel south, following spice routes to the heavenly beaches of Goa.

Venture to the islands of the Pacific for the kaleidoscopic colors of the coral reefs, dramatic volcano peaks, and a laid-back barefoot vibe. Here you can explore the underwater caves of Samoa's To Sua Ocean Trench or be one of the few people to hike to the sacred mysterious ruins of Nan Madol deep in the jungle on Pohn Pei. Beyond the islands, the Pacific Ocean laps the shores of breathtaking New Zealand and Australia, with their medley of dramatic landscapes and multicultural cities.

Keemala, see page 370

PELLING, INDIA
816 THE ELGIN MOUNT PANDIM

Cocooned within eight acres of virgin forest and landscaped gardens, the Elgin Mount Pandim oozes old-world charm. This is not really surprising, since it was first owned by the royal family of Sikkim (formerly a kingdom; now an Indian state). The 300-year-old Pemayangtse Monastery is nearby, or you can explore the Rabdentse ruins that are hidden in an orchid-filled forest grove.

The Elgin Mount Pandim

UTTARAKHAND, INDIA

817 THE GAUMUKH GLACIER

The source of the Ganges is so deep in the Himalayas that few people tread the trail there. The 12-mi (20-km) pilgrimage begins at Gangotri village, climbs through spectacular mountains to the Gaumukh Glacier, and then on to the icy source of the holiest river in Hindu mythology. It is a challenging route, but the rewards are worth it.

UTTARAKHAND, INDIA

818 RAMGANGA RIVER

Sit back with a book and wait for the fish to bite with the sounds of the forest all around you. The Ramganga winding through the verdant forest of the Corbett National Park on the gentle slope of the Himalayan foothills is an angler's paradise. However, you don't need to arrive with rod and bait to appreciate its beauty.

NARENDRANAGAR, INDIA

819 ANDANA SPA

In the foothills of the Himalayas, the Andana's Dhyana Seven-night Self-realization Program aids emotional and spiritual balance and reconnects participants more deeply with their physical and mental faculties. Daily meditations, yoga nidra, mantra chanting, and silent flame-gazing is followed by self-study, in which visitors are encouraged to reflect on the day's experiences.

NEW DELHI, INDIA

820 LODHI GARDENS

This 90-acre park is an oasis in the heart of the city. The resting place of Mohammed Shah and full of architectural gems and shaded pathways, the gardens offer a tranquil respite from the heat and dust. Arrive early in the morning and the gardens will be quiet and cool.

NEW DELHI, INDIA

821 PALACE ON WHEELS

India's first luxury train evokes a bygone era of indulgence, elegance, and jewel-studded maharajas, seamlessly blended with contemporary style. Enjoy the passing scenery from the Ayurvedic Spa car, which offers massages.

NEW DELHI, INDIA

822 HAUZ KHAS VILLAGE

Walk through the pedestrianized area with its array of bars and restaurants, and you reach a tranquil, eerily quiet complex containing a fort, tomb, and other buildings with a history that dates back to the thirteenth century.

NEW DELHI, INDIA

823 LOTUS TEMPLE

This temple of the Baha'i faith is
in the shape of a lotus flower
and made from marble. The
inner sanctum is open for silent
prayer and meditation.

MAHARASHTRA, INDIA

824 CARPENTER'S CAVE

Cave 10 is the most famous of
the Buddhist caves at the Ellora
Caves complex of Buddhist,
Hindu, and Jain cave temples.
The cathedral-like stupa hall
known as Carpenter's Cave
features a ceiling carved to look
like wooden beams.

MADHYA PRADESH, INDIA

825 MANDU

Surrounded by baobab trees,
the city of Mandu is full of
spellbinding Afghan architecture
and grand romantic palaces
awash with lakes and gardens.

Lotus Temple, New Delhi

Marine Drive, Mumbai

MUMBAI, INDIA

826 **KALA GHODA CAFÉ**

Bag yourself the leather sofa upstairs in this former barn in the heart of Mumbai's art district for a bird's-eye view of the street below.

MUMBAI, INDIA

827 **MARINE DRIVE**

Walk along the 2-mi (3-km) coastal walkway as the sun sets and enjoy the sparkling waters of the Arabian Sea, nicknamed "the Queen's Necklace" for its twinkling night lights.

HIDDEN GEM

MUMBAI, INDIA

828 **FLYOVER FARM**

Mumbai's first urban farm on a rooftop is run by Fresh & Local, an organization that specializes in urban farming, where residents produce and consume organic food on top of their own buildings. Seasonal fruits, vegetables, and herbs are grown by the families, then distributed through a rooftop grocery. The project takes on volunteer workers on Wednesdays and Sundays. This is an ideal way to get up above the swirling mess of traffic, enjoy health-boosting outdoor work, and provide a service to the community. The project started because residents had no organic produce within walking distance of their homes and were keen to cook with chemical-free ingredients.

829 **AGONDA BEACH**

Wide, quiet, and picturesque Agonda Beach has endless miles of pristine palm-lined sands, where the scent of spices waft from the simple ocean-side shacks. Try a sunset yoga session then camp out under the starry skies; or, choose a temporary home among several clusters of simple wooden beach huts with sea-facing verandas.

KERALA, INDIA

830 **ALAPPUZHA (ALLEPPEY)**

Experience life on the laid-back backwaters of Kerala, a watery world of sleepy hamlets and paddy fields. Explore the canals of Alappuzha, a city that is the hub for thousands of thatched-roof houseboats that used to house the area's rice and spice traders. Some of these boats are now available to rent and have been renovated to include modern comforts. From your waterborne base, you can visit the red-and-white lighthouse at Alappuzha beach. Built in 1862, the lighthouse is now open on weekdays to visitors and is a local landmark.

CHETTINAD, INDIA

831 **CHETTINAD**

The starry nights above the abandoned mansions and ghost villages of Chettinad are as peaceful as any in India. When the community migrated away from the area in the nineteenth century, they left behind their grand ancestral homes. Some of these have been left to ruin, while others have been renovated and opened as guesthouses.

HIDDEN GEM

ABHANERI STEPWELL, INDIA

832 **ABHANERI**

This is an impressive and ornate 1,200-year-old well in a dusty village. It is deep, with a maze of more than 3,500 steps descending to the base, and dozens of statues of Hindu gods.

KARNATAKA, INDIA
833 GOKARNA
Visit this small and remote holy town with some of India's most secluded and pristine beaches nearby. Thatched bamboo huts are dotted along its stretches of blissful coastline.

GOA, INDIA
834 DUDHSAGAR FALLS
Legend has it that a modest princess bathed in the lake here every day before drinking a jug of milk. A wandering prince heard her laughing with her handmaidens, and when she saw him looking at her in her bathing clothes, her handmaidens poured the milk in a cascade to create a curtain for her to hide her modesty behind.

Velassaru

MALÉ, MALDIVES

835 VELASSARU

Enjoy endless turquoise-tinged ocean views from the shaded patio of the Deluxe Pool Villa, or dive straight into the crystalline sea from one of the stilted Water Villas. In the evening, dine at a candlelit table on a glistening pearlescent beach, before sinking your toes into the sand and your body into a beanbag. Then, you can watch a film under the stars with lapping waves forming part of the soundtrack.

MALÉ, MALDIVES

836 MALÉ FRIDAY MOSQUE

This ancient mosque is the oldest in the Maldives. It was initially built in 1658 over the foundations of an earlier temple. Constructed mostly out of coral stone, intricate carved patterns can be seen etched into the walls and the coral headstones in the cemetery beside it. The interior is beautifully bedecked in traditional Maldivian woodcarvings and lacquerwork.

RANGALI ISLAND, MALDIVES

837 CONRAD MALDIVES RANGALI ISLAND

Unwind completely with a chakra-balancing massage in the glass-bottomed spa house as you watch life unfolding on the ocean floor beneath you. When you have finished, you can dine beneath the waves at the all-glass underwater restaurant that is surrounded by colorful coral gardens. The restaurant can be transformed into a submarine suite for two, for a more intimate experience.

Yala National Park

TISSAMAHARAMA, SRI LANKA
840 YALA NATIONAL PARK

The second-largest national park in Sri Lanka is one of the best places on Earth to see leopards in their natural habitat. With only thirty-five in the entire park, sightings cannot be guaranteed, but there are plenty of other animals to see. Tented safaris will take you out at dusk and dawn when the chances of spotting a leopard are highest.

GAN, MALDIVES
838 YOGASPHERE

The Five Elements Yoga & Adventure Retreat explores the concepts of earth, fire, water, and spirit in the body. Start the morning with yogic breathing and mindfulness before your first class. Every day there is a life-affirming talk and the evenings end with yoga.

BERUWALA, SRI LANKA
841 BRIEF GARDEN

The inside and outside blur at the former home of landscape architect Bevis Bawa's sylvan refuge. Enjoy the green rooms that are delicately perfumed with frangipani and decorated by local artists.

IHURU, MALDIVES
839 ANGSANA IHURU

This intimate getaway is located on a beautiful palm-dotted island encircled by white-sand shores and crystal clear lagoons. The thatched-roof villas are vibrantly decorated, reflecting the island's verdant greenery and turquoise water. Guests can get involved with the resort's marine conservation projects, which are focused on one of the best-preserved coral reefs in the Maldives.

ELLA, SRI LANKA
842 98 ACRES RESORT & SPA

Stay on a scenic tea plantation to enjoy the beauty and serenity of Sri Lanka's epic hill country. Take time out to stroll across the engineering feat that is Nine Arches Bridge.

VARIOUS LOCATIONS, NEPAL
843 TEMPLE TOURING

Nepal's many temples and monasteries feature high on the list of must-sees. You will find them everywhere you go in tiny town squares, high up on jungle-clad hillsides, or hidden down the back streets of the capital city. Many contain beautiful examples of Himalayan art.

KHUMJUNG, NEPAL
844 EVEREST BASE CAMP

The prize destination for many visitors to Nepal, Everest Base Camp can get crowded, so choose one of the less popular treks to the camp, such as the old access route from Jiri, which is mostly only used by porters and pack animals.

KATHMANDU, NEPAL
845 SOUND PLANETARIUM

Let go of all stress and rejuvenate with a vibrational sound therapy session. Singing bowl treatments are offered for relaxation, vitality, and aura harmonization, and most last for over an hour, giving you plenty of time to relax into the session. If it hits the spot, you can take a training course so you can perform your own therapies, or buy your own singing bowl from the shop. Choose from a selection of off-the-shelf bowls or order a bespoke design to be made for you.

Singing bowls, Nepal

HIMALAYAS, NEPAL

846 ANNAPURNA SANCTUARY TREK

Embark on this classic ten-day trek through the breathtaking Himalayan landscape of the Annapurna massif, part of which forms a natural amphitheater known as the Annapurna Sanctuary. Trek through magnificent forests and past awe-inspiring glaciers. Rest, revive, and refuel in cozy mountain teahouses along the way.

KATHMANDU, NEPAL

847 GARDEN OF DREAMS

Also known as the Garden of Six Seasons, the beautifully restored neoclassical historical garden is an exquisite ensemble of pavilions, pergolas, fountains, and flower beds.

POKHARA, NEPAL

848 THE FULBARI RESORT & SPA

If you've been exploring the Himalayas, treat yourself to a post-trek splurge at this resort. The Fulbari is one of Nepal's most luxurious and exclusive spa resorts, benefiting from the Himalayan mountain range as a backdrop. Although this is a large hotel, a sense of peace and relaxation pervades throughout.

PUNAKHA, BHUTAN
849 PUNAKHA DZONG

Punakha Dzong is arguably Bhutan's most beautiful *dzong*, a fortress that serves as a monastic and administrative center. Also known as the Palace of Great Bliss, the dzong sits at the confluence of two clean, clear turquoise-blue rivers—Pho Chhu and Mo Chhu. Entering the Punakha Dzong is like entering another world. The complex of courtyards, temples, and shrines is overwhelmingly serene, with lilac-colored jacaranda trees softening the towering whitewashed walls, and exquisite murals depicting the life of Shakyamuni Buddha. If you are lucky, you may catch a ceremony taking place during your visit and enjoy the chanting and drumming of the monks.

Punakha Dzong

Phobjikha Valley

PHOBJIKHA VALLEY, BHUTAN
850 PHOBJIKHA VALLEY

Wake at dawn to watch the sunrise break over the mountains and turn the mist in this glacial valley into a warm yellow hue.

PARO, BHUTAN
851 PARO TAKTSANG

Paro Taktsang (the Tiger's Nest Monastery) is one of Bhutan's most photographed sites. It consists of a collection of temples that are perched a precarious 2,953 ft (900 m) above ground on a cliff ledge.

HIDDEN GEM
DAMXUNG COUNTY, TIBET
852 NAMTSO

Tibetan for "Heavenly Lake," the pure blue waters of the highest saltwater lake in the world hold a spiritual significance for the tribes that pitch their tents on its shores.

NAMCHA BARWA, TIBET
853 TSANGPO CANYON

Stretching from deep within the Himalayas out to sea, the Tsangpo Canyon is the deepest canyon in the world. Its exotic flowers and rare wildlife are seldom seen by tourists.

YARLUNG VALLEY, TIBET
854 TRANDRUK MONASTERY

The cloistered courtyard of one of the earliest Buddhist temples in Tibet is shrouded in a sense of contemplative calm. Take your time to explore all the hidden treasures it has to offer.

855 **HANGING TEMPLE**

The fifth-century Hanging Temple clings to a crag more than 164 ft (50 m) above the ground. Built by a monk named Liao Ran with the help of Tao Buddhists, its position protects it from the flooding river below, and from the rain and snow of the mountain peak above. Unusually, the monastery is dedicated not to just one, but to three religious systems: Confucianism, Taoism, and Buddhism. Statues and carvings from each can be found throughout the site. Visit in winter to experience its peace in full solitude.

JIANGSU PROVINCE, CHINA
856 SUZHOU

Explore the waterside gardens, enchanting canals, and sacred landmarks of the ancient city of Suzhou—known as the Venice of the East—located in the Yangtze River Delta.

HUAYIN, CHINA
857 HUASHAN TEAHOUSE

On a remote peak of Mount Hua, a sacred mountaintop teahouse offers refreshment to those daring enough to make the perilous journey along one of the most dangerous hiking paths in the world. The temple teahouse is reached by a series of steep stone steps carved straight into the mountain. From there, you cross a deep valley on a rickety gondola, before shuffling along a thin ledge of scrappy wooden planks lashed to the sheer rock face hundreds of feet above the ground. Make it to the temple in one piece, and you will have truly earned your cup of tea and the sense of total serenity.

MIYUN COUNTY, CHINA
858 THE GREAT WALL AT GUBEIKOU

Wild and unreconstructed, so that it retains its original beauty, this semi-ruined section of the Great Wall of China is rarely visited by tourists. This section of wall was the scene of many battles.

TANGSHAN, CHINA
859 TANGSHAN BUDDHIST SHRINE

Outside Tangshan, a serene Buddhist shrine blends contemporary design with the existing landscape. The building lies beneath a mound of earth covered with grass, blending in to the surrounding fields, trees, and water.

HANGZHOU, CHINA
860 XIHU STATE GUESTHOUSE

Enjoy spectacular sunsets at this state-run guesthouse situated within an impeccably landscaped garden on the edge of a lake. The peach blossom in the spring is poetic in its beauty.

GUIZHOU, CHINA
861 XIJIANG

The green hills and valleys of this remote province are largely unknown to travelers outside China. Opt for a local homestay in Quianhu Miao Village below Leigong Mountain.

BEIDAIHE, CHINA
862 SEASHORE LIBRARY

Sitting on the seashore, the library at Beidaihe looks like a weathered rock. Inside, the contemporary design lets in the light, sound, and breeze of the ocean, reflecting the connection between people and the sea.

798 Art Zone

BEIJING, CHINA
863 **798 ART ZONE**

A complex of Mao-era decommissioned military factories that is now home to a thriving artistic community. Discover contemporary art galleries, art bookshops, and cafés. Of particular note is the Xin Dong Cheng Space for Contemporary Art: a lovely space that showcases up-and-coming Chinese modern artists.

BEIJING, CHINA
864 **YONGHE LAMA TEMPLE**

Also known as the Harmony and Peace Palace, Yonghe Lama Temple is the largest and most perfectly preserved lamasery in China. Set aside ample time to enjoy the frescoes and thousands of Buddha statues, or head up to explore the rooftops.

BEIJING, CHINA

865 LIYUAN LIBRARY

Clad in the small sticks that are used by local villagers for lighting fires, the natural facade of Liyuan Library creates a beautiful reading ambience as the light filters through.

BEIJING, CHINA

866 CAFÉ ZARAH

Sit in the sun overlooking the *hutong* (narrow alley) rooftops while listening to life's gentle banter on the street below. Set in an ancient Chinese courtyard, this calming enclave has been renovated with contemporary steel-and-concrete elements. There is a serene, second-story roof terrace and pretty garden below.

SHANGHAI, CHINA

867 GUYI GARDEN

One of Shanghai's best preserved classical gardens in the Ming style provides a pleasant place for a stroll after tucking into some *xiaolongbao*, the district's famous soup-filled dumplings.

SHANGHAI, CHINA

868 SUBCONSCIOUS DAY SPA

Balance your body, mind, and soul at this high-end organic and ecofriendly day spa located in a shopping mall. When your retail therapy is over, treat your feet to their Blissful Four Foot Massage.

869 HORSE TREKKING

Ride out on an eight-day horseback trek through the mountain passes, taiga forests, and idyllic meadows of the country's northernmost province, traveling through the beautiful Khoridol Saridag mountains to Lake Khövsgöl, the alpine lake known as Mongolia's "dark blue pearl." You will stop along the way to visit Tsaatan families who herd domesticated reindeer.

GOBI DESERT, MONGOLIA
870 THREE CAMEL LODGE

A scattering of felt-covered traditional Mongolian tents makes up the heart of this remarkable ecolodge. Known as *gers*, the spherical structures are made by local nomadic herders and fitted with hand-carved furniture and warm camel-hair blankets. The herders are welcome to use the central well, so expect to see their cast of cattle, sheep, and goats quenching their thirst on occasion. The surrounding landscape is of epic proportions and you can explore local sites, including the Flaming Cliffs, and the town of Bulgan, on excursions from the lodge.

ÖVÖRKHANGAI, MONGOLIA
871 KARAKORUM

Genghis Khan built Karakorum as a base for invading China. You can still see remnants of the old capital in the plain Soviet-built town that stands on its site today. The main attraction is Erdene Zuu Monastery, Mongolia's oldest-surviving monastery. Catch a morning prayer for a divine experience.

ALTAI MOUNTAINS, MONGOLIA
872 MOUNTAIN TREKKING

Nomadic Expeditions lead treks through the magnificent Altai mountains, one of the last untouched wilderness areas of Asia and located at the border of Russia, China, and Mongolia, in relatively unexplored Western Mongolia. Camp beside pristine rivers, explore forests, and meet local Kazakh families in this isolated part of the world that is far from the tourist trail.

BAYAN-ÖLGII, MONGOLIA
873 EAGLE HUNTING

Magnificent golden eagles have been used for hunting in the epic and forbidding landscape of the Altai mountains by nomadic Kazakhs for thousands of years. Steppes Travel can arrange expeditions from ölgii on sturdy Mongolian horses. You will have the opportunity to accompany the eagle hunters in these remote lands, staying with local tribespeople in simple houses as you travel.

HAPCHEON COUNTY, SOUTH KOREA

874 TRIPITAKA KOREANA LIBRARY

Hike up the stunning slopes of Gaya mountain to Haeinsa Temple, home to the Tripitaka Koreana library. The library contains approximately 80,000 original engraved woodblocks, constituting the most complete collection of Buddhist texts in existence today.

The original Tripitaka was completed in 1087, but was destroyed in 1232 during a Mongol invasion. Its remake was ordered in 1237 to please Buddha and to ask for his help against the Mongolian invaders. It took a further eleven years to complete, using wood from the silver magnolias, white birches, and cherry trees of the southern coast of the peninsula.

The library is not generally open to tourists, but access may be granted by request. Otherwise, you can enjoy the temple and catch sight of the woodblocks through a dedicated viewing area, as well as appreciating the exterior of the incredible fifteenth-century building that was created specifically to house them.

The temple itself is named after a passage in the Buddhist Flower Garland Sutra, pertaining to the state of deep concentration that Buddha achieved, in which his mind was like a perfectly placid sea, reflecting things as they really are.

Those interested in gaining a fascinating glimpse inside Korean Buddhist culture can opt for an overnight temple-stay in same-sex dormitories, allowing you to rise with the monks at 3 a.m. and witness the beating of the giant temple drum before participating in the daily chanting and meditation. Haeinsa Temple is located on the fringe of Gayasan National Park.

Amakusa

875 AMAKUSA

The Amakusa area is remote and rural, qualities that enticed sixteenth-century missionaries to convert many of its indigenous people to Christianity before the religion was forbidden. A Romanesque-style church on top of a small hill overlooks a museum that is dedicated to the hidden Christians during this period.

KYOTO, JAPAN

877 TORAYA KARYO KYOTO ICHIJO

One of the longest-standing Japanese sweetshops has a tearoom and terrace overlooking the beautiful gardens and the Inari Shrine. Try their famous red bean *yokan* or *namagashi*; the sweets used in the traditional Japanese tea ceremony. The establishment has been providing sweets for the imperial palace since the sixteenth century. Many of the creations look almost too beautiful to eat.

KYUSHU, JAPAN

876 SEVEN STARS OF KYUSHU

The eight suites of this luxury sleeper train are so sought-after that you must enter a lottery to have a chance of buying a ticket. If you're lucky enough to secure one, over two or four days, you can discover the enigmatic island of Kyushu and its volcanoes and hot springs as it flows past your window.

KYOTO, JAPAN
878 GIO-JI TEMPLE

This magical space houses a tiny thatched-roof hall set within a luxuriant moss-covered grotto so soft-looking that you might be tempted to lie down. Unfortunately, that's not permitted, so you will have to make do with daydreaming. The site is often completely passed by tourists, so you will likely enjoy the quaint spot to yourself.

KYOTO, JAPAN
879 HANAMI

Avoid the overcrowded Maruyama Park when the cherry trees release their pink blossoms into the spring air. The grounds of the Hoshinoya Kyoto hotel host a grove of the trees along the banks of the Hozugawa River, to which it clings. The hotel boat provides the perfect crowd-free viewing spot.

KYOTO, JAPAN
880 TAWARAYA INN

Visit this three-hundred-year-old traditional, family-run Japanese inn in the heart of Kyoto, with a well-stocked multilingual library specializing in Japanese art and design. The eighteen traditional tatami mat rooms overlook exquisite gardens, so even in the city you experience a tranquil idyll in which to enjoy true Japanese hospitality.

Tawaraya Inn   *Hozugawa River*

KYOTO, JAPAN

881 SAGANO BAMBOO FOREST

In the far west of Kyoto, a forest of soaring bamboo stalks sway in the wind, creaking, twisting, rustling—a sound so captivating that it has been added to the Ministry of Environment's list of the 100 Soundscapes of Japan. This project aims to encourage enjoyment of nature's music and introduce people to the diversity of natural sounds.

Hiroshima Peace Memorial Museum

HIROSHIMA, JAPAN
882 HIROSHIMA PEACE MEMORIAL MUSEUM

In a place of such international tragedy, the Hiroshima Peace Memorial Museum is a zone of tranquility, set within a beautiful park with trees, lawns, and contemplative paths in stark contrast with the devastated city around. The museum campaigns for the elimination of nuclear armaments and the realization of world peace.

OKUTAMA, JAPAN
883 FOREST BATHING

Shinrin-yoku is the Japanese practice of metaphorically bathing in the presence of trees. This form of ecotherapy has scientific evidence to support that it lowers heart rate, blood pressure, and stress hormone production, while improving overall feelings of well-being. Okutama has five "Forest Therapy Routes" to explore and engage with.

MIE, JAPAN
884 AMANEMU

Based around the centuries-old Japanese bathing tradition of *onsen*, stone baths are fed by salt-infused mineral water from nearby thermal hot springs set within Zen-like gardens. For more radiance-boosting bliss, plunge in the heated outdoor watsu pool overlooking the smooth waters of Ago Bay.

HIDDEN GEM
FUKUOKA, JAPAN
885 THE ACROS FUKUOKA BUILDING

A series of terraced gardens climb the full height of this giant building in the middle of Fukuoka. Each floor contains beautifully landscaped spaces for meditation, relaxation, and escape from the congestion of the city. Reflecting pools and waterfalls mask the ambient noise of the urban world below.

VARIOUS LOCATIONS, JAPAN
886 PRACTICE ZAZEN

Zazen is the Japanese art of seated meditation, practiced to cultivate stillness and create space in your life. In zazen, you seek a state of letting go while still awake; of experiencing the present moment without attachment to your thoughts or personal story.

Nezu Museum

TOKYO, JAPAN

887 NEZU MUSEUM

Private collection of Japanese and Asian art set within a splendid garden of winding paths, small streams, and beautiful sculptures. Enjoy it all from the wide-windowed café or explore on foot.

TOKYO, JAPAN

888 AMAN TOKYO

This spot is laid out like a traditional Japanese home, complete with meditation garden. However, tradition mixes with contemporary, with floor-to-ceiling windows giving a view of the metropolis.

TOKYO, JAPAN

889 HENN-NA HOTEL

Do you fancy eschewing all form of human contact on your holiday? If so, check in to the Henn-Na Hotel, which is staffed almost entirely by robots.

CHICHIBU, JAPAN

890 CHICHIBU DISTILLERY

Japan is one of the world's biggest whisky markets. Visit the young distillery of Chichibu whisky to learn how one man plies his craft and is dedicated to producing an excellent product.

Chichibu Distillery

Underground Temple

TOKYO, JAPAN

891 UNDERGROUND TEMPLE

The Underground Temple is a nickname given to this colossal, cathedral-like underground surge tank that you can explore. Its size is quite overwhelming.

TOKYO, JAPAN

893 EDO-TOKYO MUSEUM

The reading room on the seventh floor of the cavernous Edo-Tokyo Museum in the Ryogoku district offers an incredible panorama of the cityscape beyond—and naturally, an abundance of reading material, as well as video booths.

YAMANOUCHI, JAPAN

892 JIGOKUDANI MONKEY PARK

A trek through the Nagano woods to this unique park offers visitors the opportunity to see snow monkeys keeping warm in winter in the park's natural hot springs. The Japanese macaques live in large social groups, gathering around and bathing in a large rocky hot tub as they almost completely ignore their human guests. This means that visitors can get unusually close to the monkeys, although obviously, feeding them isn't allowed.

Inle Lake

NYAUNGSHWE, MYANMAR
894 **INLE LAKE**

Life on vast and serene Inle lake is utterly laid-back. Cruise along channels hemmed in by floating gardens, past stilt-house villages that straddle the waterways, and Buddhist temples rising above the misty marsh fringes. Inle Heritage Stilt Houses in Inn Paw Khon Village has six quirky bungalows sitting on stilts, and it doubles as a Burmese cat sanctuary.

SHAN STATE, MYANMAR
895 **INLE PRINCESS RESORT**

Boutique refuge on the serene Inle Lake with a commitment to local cultures and luxury. The secluded lake houses are built from reclaimed teak and bamboo thatch, using traditional Inthar practices. Each residence has a private deck sitting above a lotus flower-filled inlet, and outdoor showers beneath the blue peaks of the Shan Hills.

HIDDEN GEM
MINGUN, MYANMAR
896 **THE GARDEN CAFÉ**

Tables and chairs are scattered across a large shady garden spectacularly set on the banks of the Irrawaddy River. It's tucked down a small lane opposite the Mingun Bell.

RAKHINE STATE, MYANMAR
897 **MRAUK U**

The ancient temples and pagodas of a once-powerful empire form the backdrop of everyday life for the farmers and goat herders working the fields in the beautiful hilly landscape around Mrauk U. Fewer than 5,000 foreigners make the trip through the backwaters to the site each year, compared to Bagan's 300,000 visitors.

BAGAN, MYANMAR
898 HOT-AIR BALLOONING

The balloon rises against a backdrop of ancient temples shrouded in mist, where the only sound is that of your camera's shutter clicking.

KACHIN STATE, MYANMAR
899 KHAKABORAZI NATIONAL PARK

The Ice Mountains of Myanmar's far north is one of the world's last frontiers. You will need to secure a permit in advance, to travel past Putao.

Hot-air ballooning, Myanmar

900 LUANG PRABANG

Landlocked on all sides, Laos remains an authentic corner of Asia untainted by mass tourism. Magical Luang Prabang province is a landscape of green, from the lush tea plantations to the brooding jungle; from rice fields to the grassy wetlands. It is a province of scaling peaks and cascading waterfalls, with the town of Luang Prabang at its heart. Nestled in a Mekong river valley, this UNESCO World Heritage Site is the main center for Buddhist learning in Laos. It is a place of crumbling French architecture, impressive temples, and a connection with the natural beauty that creeps in from the surrounding jungle.

BANGKOK, THAILAND

901 **DOUBLE DOGS TEA ROOM**

This unassuming little café offers welcome respite from the physically exhausting experience of Bangkok's chaotic Chinatown. It serves a range of premium teas and Chinese cakes.

KHON KAEN, THAILAND

902 **MINDFULNESS PROJECT**

Slow down at this volunteering project in a small forest village, interweaving mindfulness, community, and sustainability, in order to better ourselves, our relationships, and our environment.

HIDDEN GEM

PHANG NGA BAY, THAILAND

903 **KOH YAO NOI**

Visit this award-winning community homestay program run by local fishermen, on an unspoiled Thai island in the country's most famous bay.

PHUKET, THAILAND

904 **KEEMALA PHUKET**

Laid-back and luxurious, Keemala's tree house villas rest like nests on a jungly hillside. This fairy kingdom-like resort is a forest-shrouded sanctuary with private pools and spacious leafy terraces overlooking the glittering sea below.

Keemala Hotel Phuket

Kamalaya Koh Samui

PHUKET, THAILAND

905 AMATARA WELLNESS RESORT

From the moment you step into the lobby and spot
the 180-ft (55-m) infinity pool that seems to drop
straight into the Andaman Sea, until the moment
you check out, you will be wowed by Amatara.
From the gold-edged pavilions to the bloom-filled
gardens and lily ponds, the understated Thai vibe
here oozes tropical luxury. Each of the sea-facing
suites in this five-star sanctuary has its own
sprawling, split-level pool, poised above the
secluded bay in stunning Cape Panwa. A team of
consultants is always on hand to offer tailored
plans for nutrition, fitness, and total destressing.

KOH SAMUI, THAILAND

906 KAMALAYA KOH SAMUI

Enjoy an authentic wellness experience at an
award-winning holistic hideaway and former
Buddhist retreat that has been designed to exist
in harmony with its natural setting.

KOH SAMUI, THAILAND

907 PANACEA RETREAT, KOH SAMUI

Named after the Greek goddess of healing, this is a
sacred sanctuary set in jungle-clad hills where your
privacy is ensured by walls of dense foliage. Each
villa includes a dining pavilion and infinity pool.

KOH RONG ISLANDS, CAMBODIA

908 SONG SAA PRIVATE ISLAND

Take an ecochic escape at this tiny resort spread across two pristine islands in the secluded Koh Rong archipelago. The villas freckle the jungle and sit on stilts, appearing to balance over the sea. Watch the sun rise from one side of your villa and then melt into the sea on the other.

PHNOM PENH, CAMBODIA

909 NATIONAL LIBRARY

Most of the books were destroyed by the Khmer Rouge when they ruled in the 1970s. After their defeat, books were donated from different sources. The colonial building has an ornate exterior with restored friezes. Inside, the high ceilings and the smell of old books recall its former splendor.

KOH THMEI, CAMBODIA

910 KOH THMEI RESORT

How many of the 150 different kinds of birds in the Ream National Park can you count from your hammock or on a long, leisurely walk around Koh Thmei island? With only seven well-placed bungalows, the resort is a world away from the larger-scale tourist development of the mainland.

Koh Rong Island

SIEM REAP, CAMBODIA

911 ANGKOR WAT

The jungle only ever seems to be in temporary abeyance from this stone-walled city of temples. Look for local yoga retreats that lead small groups to quieter spots in the complex, then roll out the mats for an awakening class followed by *pranayama* and meditation. Continue contemplation as you explore.

SIEM REAP, CAMBODIA

912 SHINTA MANI ANGKOR

A dip in the black-tiled pool set in the palm-flanked internal courtyard will help to wash away the day's exertions from touring nearby Angkor's stunning temples. The sophisticated Shinta Mani is a masterpiece of Cambodian design located in the city's French Quarter.

KEP PROVINCE, CAMBODIA

913 KEP

Once a seaside retreat for the French elite, this coastal village of Kep is now a sleepier affair offering mesmerizing sunsets and lazy hikes through the national park. Boutique hotels draw a more sophisticated crowd to its white beaches and coastal islets, or to explore the abandoned villas.

CORELLA, PHILIPPINES
914 THE TARSIER SANCTUARY

Experience near silence at this sanctuary for small nocturnal primates that are so emotionally sensitive that they can commit suicide if they become too stressed. It is run by the Philippine Tarsier Foundation.

SULU SEA, PHILIPPINES
915 BROTHER ISLAND

This tiny island, set in the Sulu Sea around the Philippines, is available to rent, providing accommodation for up to ten people in the two-story house that has been constructed in a traditional Filipino style. The island's only residents are its staff, who will take you island-hopping on a traditional outrigger boat and provide you with local food to complete your Filipino experience.

PALAWAN, PHILIPPINES
916 PALAWAN

The Philippines's most sparsely populated region is a hidden piece of paradise, where beautiful blue water mixes with emerald green and jungle-blanketed mountains, and tiny fishing villages sit on secluded shores. Island-hop around the cliffs and sinkholes of the Bacuit archipelago, dive into the depths for barracuda-filled shipwrecks, or search out the rare Philippine mouse deer on land.

Puerto-Princesa Subterranean River National Park

PALAWAN, PHILIPPINES
917 PUERTO-PRINCESA SUBTERRANEAN RIVER NATIONAL PARK

Paddle through the dark in a small boat along the world's longest navigable underground river, accompanied by the soft clicking of bats. This protected area of the Philippines forms part of the national park of the same name and is a UNESCO World Heritage Site. Limited numbers of visitors are allowed, and you need a permit, so plan ahead if it's on your to-do list.

MOUNTAIN PROVINCE, PHILIPPINES
918 SAGADA

A long bus ride takes you up above the clouds to this stunning town surrounded by caves, hiking trails, mountains, and sculpted rice terraces. Due to its remote location, Sagada's indigenous culture has been preserved. The best sunrise is at Kiltepan Viewpoint.

MANILA, PHILIPPINES
919 THIRD EYE WELLNESS

Transcending the usual manicures and massages on offer in city salons, Third Eye Wellness offers tarot reading and theta healing, and a decent cup of coffee in the calming Chakra Café.

920 GARDENS BY THE BAY

Inspired by Singapore's national flower, the orchid, Gardens by the Bay is a showcase of horticultural artistry. Ascend the fern and orchid-clad "Cloud Forest" by elevator, then gradually descend the circular mountain path, refreshed by the cool mist of the world's tallest indoor waterfall.

HIDDEN GEM

CENTRAL SINGAPORE, SINGAPORE

921 THE BOOK CAFÉ

Tucked away in a quiet spot in the city, The Book Café feels like you have stepped into someone's snug living room with plenty of inviting sofas, soft lights, and well-laden bookshelves lining the walls. The ambience here is relaxed and welcoming, and you will never feel rushed to move on.

KUALA LUMPUR, MALAYSIA

922 PURRADISE CAT CAFÉ

A pretty cat café with colorful beanbags, wood pallet furniture, and an indoor tree—and that's just for the cats. The café's furry residents are all rescue animals and are available for adoption. Order a smoothie and hang with the cats for some feline therapy.

TAIPING, MALAYSIA

923 TAIPING LAKE GARDENS

Soak in the natural beauty of the Taiping Lake Gardens. Built on top of an abandoned tin mine, the gardens feature ten lakes that are spanned by charming bridges. Take a seat on a bench by the largest lake, fringed with ancient giant rain trees, and you could easily forget that the rest of the world exists.

LANGKAWI, MALAYSIA

924 THE DATAI LANGKAWI

An outstanding spa hotel on the jungle-drenched island of Langkawi. Experience total tranquility with next to nothing to do. But then, that's rather the point of coming here. The spa villas are integrated into the surroundings for a back-to-nature experience inspired by ancient Mayan practices.

SELANGOR, MALAYSIA

925 SELANGOR RIVER

Take a sampan trip down the Selangor river on a clear night to one of the world's largest colonies of fireflies. The fairy light-like insects hang out on the Berembang trees, shining brightly to attract a suitable partner. There is nothing more peaceful than sitting on the river to enjoy the show.

The Elephant Cave, Chedi Club

BALI, INDONESIA
926 CHEDI CLUB

Lush lotus ponds and a garden of trees surround the one-bedroom poolside villas at the Chedi Club Tanah Gajah. Once the home of a respected architect and art collector, Balinese art and antiques still feature heavily throughout the resort. Ask your butler to take you trekking through the verdant rice paddies or to nearby sacred Elephant Cave to get a sense of your surroundings.

HIDDEN GEM

BALI, INDONESIA
927 SWING IN THE JUNGLE

Skip the busy officially operated jungle swing and head instead to the private swing at Zen Hideaway. You won't have to queue for long, in order to fly high above a dense canopy of palms and see the jungle from a totally new perspective.

BALI, INDONESIA
928 COMO SHAMBHALA ESTATE

Treat yourself to a treetop massage in the Ojas spa from where you can take a new perspective on life. Afterwards, plunge into your private infinity swimming pool to cool off. The stunning retreat is located just 15 minutes' drive from Ubud but you could be a million miles from anywhere once you have checked into your private thatched pavilion.

JAKARTA, INDONESIA
929 AWAN LOUNGE

The rooftop lounge on the eighth floor of the
Kosenda Hotel offers sweeping city views
surrounded by lush green gardens. Aim to arrive as
the sun is setting: this is when the city lights start
twinkling and you will smell the delightful aroma of
Asian cuisine coming from the small gourmet
kitchen in the corner. The food served here is the
perfect partner for an exotic cocktail or two.

JAKARTA, INDONESIA
930 PANTJORAN TEAHOUSE

Many types of premium tea are on offer at this
recently revitalized 1920s teahouse. Flourishing
with antique architectural charm and old-time
atmosphere, the importance of tea is as relevant
here today as it was in years gone by. The tables
by the window on the second floor are prime
people-watching real estate; take a seat and
watch the city go about its business.

EAST JAVA, INDONESIA
931 BROMO TENGGER SEMERU NATIONAL PARK

Take a horseback ride at dawn across the
deserted Tengger Caldera, to the edge of
Mount Bromo, to watch the sunrise in
spectacular fashion from the summit.

BALI, INDONESIA
932 **ANTIGRAVITY YOGA**

Take part in this highly therapeutic form of yoga that is held at the exclusive Four Seasons Bali. Classes run in the lotus petal-inspired Dharma Shanti yoga studio above the Ayung River basin. Beginners and advanced practitioners are welcome to join, as the technique is easy to grasp.

BALI, INDONESIA
933 **NYEPI**

The Balinese Day of Silence is held each year in early spring. Join locals and maintain silence from sunrise to sunset for a day of fasting and meditation.

Antigravity yoga

BALI, INDONESIA
934 **TI AMO BALI**

A spa hotel in the middle of the rice fields that is so completely quiet that you will begin to wonder if there is anyone else left on Earth. This is how the real Bali ticks.

RIAU ISLANDS, INDONESIA
935 **CEMPEDAK ISLAND**

Silver-leaf monkeys, sea otters, and endangered Pangolin are some of the only inhabitants across the forty-two acres of virgin rain forest that is surrounded by secluded shell-strewn beaches.

BALI, INDONESIA
936 CANGGU

Not long ago, Canggu was a sleepy little fishing village with just a smattering of cafés and local homestays dotted across the natural landscape. However, now it is one of Bali's coolest corners, its laid-back surf-shack vibe attracting an arty crowd. The scent of frangipani is in the air while turmeric lattes and buckwheat pancakes are on the menu. However, despite the sharply designed yoga studios and the thriving coffee scene, there is still a strong presence of old Bali culture and community here, and the village is still surrounded by rice paddies. For something to eat, or just to kick back and relax, try The Shady Shack, a pretty whitewashed wooden café serving fresh vegetarian fare and featuring a shady veranda (hence the name) that overlooks the rice fields beyond.

The Shady Shack, Canggu

GILI ISLANDS, INDONESIA
937 GILI MENO

The lure of total escapism draws people to Gili Meno, the smallest and by far the most peaceful of the Gili Islands. Play chess with friendly locals or take long, leisurely strolls on the largely empty beaches.

BANDUNG, INDONESIA
938 KAMPUNG DAUN

Individual dining gazebos scattered in a lush bamboo forest ensure an intimate experience amongst nature.

SUMATRA, INDONESIA
939 KERINCI SEBLAT NATIONAL PARK

Take the two-day trek through swamps and rain forest to the summit of Mount Kerinci. Keep an eye out for tigers.

940 FREE DIVING IN KOMODO NATIONAL PARK

Think Komodo Island and it is probably the giant carnivorous lizards that bask upon its shores that come to mind. However, the waters around the national park are also a premier dive destination and have recently become popular with those who practice the sport of free diving.

Also known as breath-hold diving, free diving is a form of underwater diving that relies on the diver's ability to hold their breath, rather than using scuba gear. Unencumbered by the breathing apparatus, and using only fins and an impressive amount of willpower, free divers are liberated to explore a more intimate connection with the ocean and their own limits. The key to successful free diving is a subtle defocusing of the mind to attain something akin to a Zen-like state of meditation; to not try too hard, not think too much, and relax into a state of serenity as you dive deeper. Preparations for a dive often include breathing exercises and yoga asanas, so the two activities are closely linked.

The waters around the national park are positively riotous with marine life. Early morning at Crystal Rock, the visibility is impressive, and you can spot baby bluefin tuna, poisonous lionfish, colorful coral cod, shoals of bluestreak fusiliers, and white-tip reef sharks on the hunt for breakfast. At Batu Bolong, a rock juts out into the ocean, creating a steep underwater wall that descends more than 66 ft (20 m) to the seabed and is busy with reef life. The highlight of a dive at Manta Point is its eponymous manta rays that glide gracefully through the still water.

Small tour companies offer week-long free-diving cruises on live-aboard boats. These allow you to avoid large groups and leave you free to dive the best sites day and night. You will fall asleep under a blanket of stars to the gentle rocking of the boat, and wake up moored at the best sites to catch the early morning marine life. You will literally be left breathless as you explore the magnificent underwater world.

To take part in the tours, you will need a level 2 AIDA free-diving certificate. If you don't have one, local companies and resorts offer the course, which can be taken over three days prior to your trip. If you don't want to spend all your time at sea, the Komodo Resort has beachside bungalows from which you can breathe deeply between dives.

Coogee Pavilion Rooftop

SYDNEY, AUSTRALIA

941 THE ROYAL BOTANIC GARDEN SYDNEY

A bench in the gardens by the iconic Sydney Opera House is the ideal place to pass the day with a long, lazy read. The park—which sits on the site of the colony's first vegetable patch—covers seventy-five acres, so there are plenty of spots to be alone with only the ibis for company. The garden also plays host to talks, events, and an annual open-air movie season, and holds horticultural excursions with expert guides.

SYDNEY, AUSTRALIA

942 THE ROCKS

Step away from the modern sheen of downtown Sydney onto the cobbled streets and colonial-style buildings of the historic Rocks district. Once home to a motley mix of pirates, prostitutes, and con men, you will now find a plethora of galleries, arty boutiques, and cute restaurants. The Susannah Place Museum is a time capsule of nineteenth-century cottages that takes you on a journey back through history.

Wendy's Secret Garden

Camperdown Commons

943 COOGEE PAVILION ROOFTOP

Top-notch beachside pub that is located a short bus ride from the city. Sit and enjoy knockout views that let the sea breeze tickle the love seats and sofas.

944 MILK BEACH

Small, isolated beach at the base of Hermit Bay surrounded by the historic Strickland House, a well-kept secret in one of Sydney's easternmost suburbs.

945 CAMPERDOWN COMMONS

Pocket City Farms has transformed a disused space into a sustainable farm in the center of the city. Camperdown Commons occupies the space, which is located on a former bowling club. Featuring an onsite restaurant with local produce on the menu, this relaxed urban retreat is the perfect place for getting away from it all. If you want to muck in, volunteers are welcome.

946 WENDY'S SECRET GARDEN

Wendy's is a homage to a lost love: this secret space sees a derelict train yard transformed into a peaceful landscape of native and exotic plants.

QUEENSLAND, AUSTRALIA
947 ST. STEPHEN'S CHAPEL

Tucked beside the shining skyscrapers of central Brisbane is this tiny nineteenth-century stone church. Built in the Gothic revivalist style, with a magnificent stained-glass window, the peaceful chapel is used for meditation and spiritual talks, as well as musical performances. You can join tours of the site during the week.

QUEENSLAND, AUSTRALIA
948 PREMA SHANTI YOGA & MEDITATION RETREAT

Your call to meditation is the song of the tropical birds that live in the Daintree Rainforest. Spend the day with your toes sunk in the sand of secluded beaches surrounded by the Great Barrier Reef. Yoga is practiced in the timber-floored temple each evening, so your day ends on a peaceful note.

QUEENSLAND, AUSTRALIA
949 WHITSUNDAYS

These are made up of seventy-four wonderfully tropical islands dotted with secluded beaches and friendly towns. Camp out by the beach and go self-sufficient, or explore the islands on a fully staffed boat. The coastlines are dotted with small campsites, and it's possible to have the whole place to yourself if sailing tours have docked elsewhere.

Blue Mountains National Park

QUEENSLAND, AUSTRALIA
950 MAKEPEACE ISLAND

Known as multimillionaire Richard Branson's "other" island, Makepeace is a sanctuary of seclusion that can accommodate up to twenty castaways in a fusion of luxury and wilderness. Located in the Noosa river, the island is naturally heart-shaped, which makes it a popular choice for honeymoons and other romantic getaways.

NEW SOUTH WALES, AUSTRALIA
951 BLUE MOUNTAINS NATIONAL PARK

Tiny hamlets and laid-back villages dot the dramatic forests and sandstone cliffs of this rugged region. Locals run guesthouses and offer invaluable information about the best trails to follow, and the viewpoints from which to see the natural blue haze, created by vast eucalyptus forests, that give the park its name.

Flinders Street Station Ballroom

TASMANIA, AUSTRALIA
952 McHENRY DISTILLERY

Australia's most southern distillery may also be its most beautiful, resting on the side of Mount Arthur and overlooking the deep harbor of historical Port Arthur and out across to Hobart. Natural springs provide the distillery with pure water, and Tasmanian art is exhibited on the walls.

TASMANIA, AUSTRALIA
953 PUMPHOUSE POINT

New life has been breathed into a former pump house in the middle of Lake St. Clair, bringing industrial chic into wildest Tasmania. This surreal building in the middle of a majestic landscape has twelve bedrooms, each one enjoying epic views through soaring windows.

TASMANIA, AUSTRALIA
954 BAY OF FIRES

The Tasmanian Walking Company offers incredible multiday walks. The Bay of Fires walk is on the wonderfully remote coastal heaven of Tasmania's east coast. With miles of sugar-white sandy beaches, you will feel like the only person to have ever set foot here.

HIDDEN GEM

VICTORIA, AUSTRALIA
955 SQUEAKY BEACH

This secret beach in Wilsons Promontory National Park gets its name from the rounded grains of quartz that make a squeaking sound when you walk on them.

MELBOURNE, AUSTRALIA
956 FLINDERS STREET STATION BALLROOM

This abandoned ballroom can be found on the top floor of one of Australia's busiest rail stations. The decaying beauty recalls the railroad romance of yesteryear. The ballroom occasionally opens its doors for guided tours but numbers are limited and timings vary so check regularly for more details.

MELBOURNE, AUSTRALIA
957 LA TROBE READING ROOM

The highlight of the landmark State Library Victoria is the magnificent octagonal La Trobe Reading Room, with its majestic glass domed ceiling and heritage desks bathed in glorious light from above. The sixth-floor viewing platform offers a fabulous view of the huge dome and the reading room below.

Kati Thanda–Lake Eyre

HIDDEN GEM

SOUTH AUSTRALIA, AUSTRALIA

958 KANGAROO ISLAND

Make the five-day trek through an unimaginably beautiful area on the Kangaroo Island Wilderness Trail. You will follow the roaring sound of the Rocky River to the remote and spectacular coastline of the Southern Ocean at the edge of the world. The hike continues through storm-blasted coastal scrub, along towering cliffs of limestone and magma, where ships wrecked on the wild coastline are still visible. The curves of bone-white beach give you a chance to sit in stillness as you spot seals off the shoreline, before heading inland through dense eucalyptus woodland to the trail's end at the Kelly Hill Caves.

SOUTH AUSTRALIA, AUSTRALIA
959 KATI THANDA–LAKE EYRE

One of Australia's little-known wonders, this vast heart-shaped salt lake, surrounded at its far edges by low red desert dunes, exemplifies the remoteness and wilderness of the Outback. When you stand on the edge of the dry lake, endless white stretching to the horizon, the sense of isolation is immense, and you will enjoy an overwhelming feeling of inner peace.

INDIAN OCEAN, AUSTRALIA
960 CHRISTMAS ISLAND

The remote Australian territory rises from the tropical depths of the vast Indian Ocean. The tiny dog-shape island is surrounded by azure waters and is famous for the annual migration of forty to fifty million red land crabs. It is a lush off-the-beaten-path destination.

WESTERN AUSTRALIA
961 KOOLJAMAN AT CAPE LEVEQUE

Part remote wilderness camp, part luxury resort, Kooljaman at Cape Leveque is owned and run on native land by two indigenous Bardi Jawi communities. In an area famous for its beaches, you will be unlikely to see another footprint in the sand beside yours at this resort, one of the most isolated in the world.

WESTERN AUSTRALIA, AUSTRALIA
962 WITTENOOM GHOST TOWN

Wittenoom was officially removed from the map in 2007 after the dangers of mining asbestos became apparent. The residents were relocated, shops boarded, and schools closed. The deserted streets are accessible to visitors, but those who ignore the warning signs around town do so at their own risk.

WESTERN AUSTRALIA, AUSTRALIA
963 INDIAN PACIFIC RAILWAY

Cross the vast continent from Perth to Sydney on an elegantly luxurious train with modern suites and panoramic windows, with opportunities to alight along the way. If you don't have time in your itinerary for the full three-day, four-night journey, you can board or alight in Adelaide.

CAPE RANGE NATIONAL PARK, AUSTRALIA
964 SAL SALIS NINGALOO REEF

Drop out of modern life for a few days and fully embrace barefoot wild bush luxury in the coastal dunes of the Cape Range National Park at ecocamp Sal Salis Ningaloo Reef. Here, the warm waters of the Indian Ocean lap the shores of the beachside bush camp, which is completely off the grid for cell phones, electricity, and Wi-Fi.

Sal Salis Ningaloo Reef redefines remote, offering only a scattering of spacious safari-chic tents pitched on elevated wooden platforms to ensure minimal contact with the ground below. Each has a private deck overlooking the ocean, with an en-suite bathroom at the back, complete with ecofriendly products and a composting toilet. The tents themselves have been well appointed with fine furnishings, the handmade jarrah beds fitted with quality cotton sheets. The whole camp has been designed to blend in with the surroundings and to expose you to the nature around you. At the end of a boardwalk at the edge of camp, the honeymoon tent has more space and privacy.

After a leisurely breakfast on the beach, you might choose to borrow some snorkeling gear and spend the afternoon in an underwater wonderland at Ningaloo Reef, just a few feet off shore, where more than 500 species of fish and 250 species of coral thrive. The reef teems with shoals of rainbow-colored fish, while beyond the reef you can frolic with turtles cruising the coastal currents. This is also one of the best places in the world to swim with whale sharks, since these gentle giants migrate here every year. If you want to explore on shore, camp guides will lead you through the Cape Range National Park to discover the unique flora and fauna of Australia. Watch out for wallabies, goanna, echidnas, and the many jewel-colored varieties of birds. On return to camp, you might even find a kangaroo snoozing in the shade of your deck.

In the evening borrow a book from the library and swing in the hammock, perhaps catching the spectacle of breaching whales on the horizon. Then dine outdoors on the best Australian bush cuisine and finest Australian wine. By the light of oil lamps beneath a canopy of stars, you are always within earshot of the ocean. Sal Salis Ningaloo Reef is a luxury destination, but the real luxury is being almost alone in such a beautiful place, immersed in nature and totally disconnected.

NORTH ISLAND, NEW ZEALAND
965 CATHEDRAL COVE

From the northern end of the beautiful and remote Hahei Beach, the track to Cathedral Cove hugs the coastline of the spectacular Coromandel Peninsula. It eventually leads to the dramatic cliffs and iconic rock archway of one of New Zealand's most picturesque beaches.

NORTH ISLAND, NEW ZEALAND
966 TARANAKI

Only 2 percent of international travelers to this region visit this area, with its black-sand beaches, rugged wild coastline, rolling farmland, and easygoing villages presided over by the volcanic cone of Mount Taranaki. Visit Cape Egmont, one of the last working lighthouses in New Zealand.

NORTH ISLAND, NEW ZEALAND
967 WAITOMO CAVES

Jump on an inner tube and float peacefully through the labyrinth of pitch-black rivers under the green hills of Waitomo. Above you, a galaxy of tiny living lights illuminates the cave as thousands of glow worms emit their phosphorescent glow like a spectacularly starry night.

NORTH ISLAND, NEW ZEALAND
968 LAKE TAUPO

Lake Taupo is New Zealand's largest lake in the crater of a volcano. Its deep blue waters are ideal for sailing, and you charter boats to explore the lake at your leisure. Once back on land, stay in the town of Turangi, at the southern end of the lake, which is a good base for fly-fishing, mountain biking, and bush walking.

NORTH ISLAND, NEW ZEALAND
969 BAY OF ISLANDS

Charter a yacht to explore this region that encompasses almost 150 predominantly undeveloped islands. Well known as a destination for big-game fishing, it also has a fascinating colonial history. If your budget won't stretch to include a yacht, you can rent a kayak and take your time to explore the small golden beaches and scenic outlooks of the coastline. Little light pollution makes for some of the best stargazing in the north of New Zealand.

NORTH ISLAND, NEW ZEALAND

970 TONGARIRO ALPINE CROSSING

Go tramping in New Zealand's oldest national park. The
Tongariro Alpine Crossing is a world-renowned 12-mi (19-km)
trek across a volcanic alpine landscape. It is a challenging but
popular day hike that climbs the active Tongariro volcano and
the saddle across to Mount Ngauruhoe. There are plenty of
pretty spots to stop along the way for a moment's pause.

Moeraki Boulders

AUCKLAND, NEW ZEALAND

971 KAREKARE BEACH

Karekare Beach on the wild west coast is all rugged, dramatic beauty and pounding waves. Part of the Waitakere Ranges National Park, Karekare is magnificent in its isolation, which draws artists, writers, and photographers to its shore. The black-sand beach was made internationally famous by Jane Campion's Oscar-winning movie *The Piano*.

SOUTH ISLAND, NEW ZEALAND

972 MOERAKI BOULDERS

Visit this group of large, spherical stones on Koekohe Beach on the Otago coast. Maori legend tells that the boulders are the remains of things that washed ashore after a mystical canoe was wrecked. The stones offer perfect photographic opportunities in the early morning.

AUCKLAND, NEW ZEALAND

973 56 WAKEFIELD STREET

Head up to the seventeenth floor at 56 Wakefield Street to find a secret rooftop garden that is perfect for a bit of sunbathing.

Devonport

AUCKLAND, NEW ZEALAND
974 DEVONPORT

A short 12-minute ferry ride from the city transports you to the pretty village of Devonport; perched on a picturesque peninsula with wonderful sea views, chilled-out beaches, and a relaxed seaside ambience. Hike to the top of Mount Victoria, the north shore's highest volcano cone, for incredible views of the Auckland cityscape and its stunning harbor.

AUCKLAND, NEW ZEALAND
975 MONDAYS WHOLEFOODS

A bright wholefood café and yoga studio that is draped from head to toe in green vines and splattered with colorful flowers, tucked down an unassuming driveway in Kingsland.

SOUTH ISLAND, NEW ZEALAND
976 ARO HĀ

Aro Hā creates "wellness adventures" from its base in the southern Alps. Focused on optimal living, Aro Hā offers physically stimulating programs of hiking, yoga, and dynamic movement combined with vegetarian cuisine, mindfulness, and healing bodywork. Accommodation is in Zen-inspired luxury lodges.

SOUTH ISLAND, NEW ZEALAND
977 FOX GLACIER

The awe-inspiring sense of silence hits you as soon as the helicopter turns its engine off. High up on the surface of Fox Glacier, you are left standing amid the towering pinnacles and brilliant blue ice, ready to explore. Experienced guides will lead you across the glacier, where you will experience otherworldly landscapes.

SOUTH ISLAND, NEW ZEALAND
978 MOUNT JOHN OBSERVATORY

Spend the evening exploring the southern night skies through the powerful telescopes of the Mount John Observatory, set within the Aoraki Mackenzie International Dark Sky Reserve, the largest in the world and the only reserve in the Southern Hemisphere. Tours are run by Earth & Sky.

SOUTH ISLAND, NEW ZEALAND
979 DOUBTFUL SOUND

Sometimes called "the Sound of Silence," this deep fjord basks in a cloistered sense of serenity surrounded by rugged peaks and rich rain forests. An overnight cruise will take you down its twisting arms, past hidden inlets and islets where, if you're lucky, you may spot the rare Fiordland crested penguin.

SOUTH ISLAND, NEW ZEALAND
980 WHARE KEA LODGE AND CHALET

Seeming to float upon the tranquil waters of Lake Wanaka, Whare Kea's luxury lodge is an intimate alpine retreat. A private helicopter is on hand to take you to the exclusive mountaintop chalet, where you can watch the stars come out with a glass of champagne in hand.

WELLINGTON, NEW ZEALAND
981 WRIGHT'S HILL LOOKOUT

This high hill with panoramic views of the city and walking tracks is home to a 1940s circular fortress and artillery embankment. The fort is open only for a few days each year, when you can explore the extensive network of underground tunnels.

Yellow-eyed penguin, Stewart island

Male New Zealand fur seal, Kaikoura

SOUTH ISLAND, NEW ZEALAND
982 STEWART ISLAND

New Zealand's third island offers a simpler, slower lifestyle in rhythm with the sea. The closest point in the country to Antarctica also offers penguins.

SOUTH ISLAND, NEW ZEALAND
983 LOCHY RIVER

The mouth of the Lochy River, where it meets Lake Wakatipu, is a peaceful spot, abundant in brown and rainbow trout, along with salmon.

SOUTH ISLAND, NEW ZEALAND
984 COASTAL PACIFIC TRAIN

The long-distance route between Picton and Christchurch runs along the Pacific coast, with blue waters on one side, and mountains on the other.

Christchurch Gondola

985 CHRISTCHURCH GONDOLA

Drift over the dramatic hills of Banks Peninsula, the vast Canterbury Plains, and sprawling cityscape of Christchurch in your own peaceful little pod.

986 NUGGET POINT LIGHTHOUSE

A five-minute walk along the steep headland takes you to Nugget Point Lighthouse. Look down to see fur seals stretching out on the rocks below.

Negget Point Lighthouse

HIDDEN GEM
SOUTH ISLAND, NEW ZEALAND
987 KAIKOURA

If you want to learn more about Maori people and their culture, the laid-back coastal town of Kaikoura is a great place to go. Maori Tours Kaikoura offers tours lasting from half a day to three days, exploring the traditions and history of the Ngāti Kuri subtribe who have an eight-hundred-year history in the area. The tours are run by a descendant of the Ngāti Kuri, who invites you to experience the hospitality of the Maori people in a natural and personal setting, learning through storytelling and hands-on activities. Kaikoura is a small town lodged between high mountains and the rich ocean.

The Tuamotus

THE TUAMOTUS,
FRENCH POLYNESIA
988 **THE TUAMOTUS**

Seventy-seven ring-shape islands encircle turquoise lagoons thrown across the deep blue sea. Come here for starry skies and silence, coral beaches, and a languid pace of life. Spend a week on a live-aboard dive safari, enjoying unrivaled visibility as you get up close to the marine life that makes its home around the atolls.

SOCIETY ISLANDS,
FRENCH POLYNESIA
989 **MAUPITI**

The beauty of Bora Bora's shy little sister hits you as the plane circles above the lagoon's shimmering layers of turquoise and blue, a towering mountain rising from the island's heart. There is only one road circling the island. No cars drive upon it, no big resorts line it, and local pensions and homestays are the only accommodation.

AUSTRAL ISLANDS,
FRENCH POLYNESIA
990 **RURUTU**

Not many tourists make it to Rurutu. There are no overwater bungalows, no beachfront restaurants, or spa pavilions. Here is a wilder beauty than other pristine palm-fringed Polynesian islands. Those who come, do so for the chance to swim with the humpback whales that bring their newborn calves here between June and October.

The Belvedere Lookout

MOOREA, FRENCH POLYNESIA
991 BELVEDERE LOOKOUT
The journey is as divine as the destination on the way to the Belvedere Lookout, where the panorama takes in the island and its coastline.

RANGIROA, FRENCH POLYNESIA
992 KIA ORA SAUVAGE
Five thatched one-room bungalows on a remote atoll offer pared-down luxury on a spotless beach. At just one hour from the main island, the journey is repaid with peace.

TETIAROA, FRENCH POLYNESIA
993 THE BRANDO
Marlon Brando's private island retreat fulfilled his dream before his death of creating a sustainable ecological habitat. The resort is almost 100 percent energy independent.

FIJI, MELANESIA

994 GARDEN ISLAND RESORT

A premier dive resort set within gorgeous lush tropical surroundings. Be lulled to sleep by the sound of the waves lapping on the shore of Taveuni, which is the "Garden Island of Fiji." Only ten minutes by boat from the renowned Rainbow Reef, which is arguably Fiji's best dive destination.

BORNEO, MELANESIA

995 TANJUNG PUTING NATIONAL PARK

Borneo has several high-profile orangutan reserves, but catching sight of them in the wild is a trickier task. Head for the riverbanks of Tanjung Puting National Park, hop aboard a traditional houseboat, and float down the Sungai Sekonyer river for a few days' wildlife watching—you might be lucky.

BORNEO, MELANESIA

996 MALIAU BASIN

One of the last areas of untouched jungle left in Malaysian Borneo has been nicknamed "Borneo's Lost World." Basic camps in the jungled interior offer little more than hammocks and camping stoves but this back-to-basics accommodation has the upside of allowing you to explore an area few people will ever see.

SAMOA, POLYNESIA

997 TO SUA OCEAN TRENCH

Make the daredevil jump from the mossy rim or descend the narrow ladder to the sparkling emerald green waters of this natural swimming hole. The pool is fed through an underwater cave by the ocean, which can be heard pounding through the cliff wall. After your swim, relax in the surrounding gardens.

SAMOA, POLYNESIA

998 JOELAN BEACH FALES

Fales are open-sided Samoan cabins with thatched roofs. On Lano Beach they are so close to the water's edge that the sea laps at the door when the tide is high. All meals are traditional home-cooked Samoan fare, and you dine together with the friendly family who runs the fales.

HIDDEN GEM

POHNPEI, MICRONESIA

999 NAN MADOL

The abandoned ruins of a once-great South Pacific island city dating back more than 2,000 years are now mostly covered in jungle. Built on a series of artificial stone islands in the shallow water off the coast of Pohnpei, Nan Madol receives fewer than 1,000 visitors per year, so you are guaranteed space to move freely.

To Sua Ocean Trench

1000 AMÉDÉE LIGHTHOUSE

Wrapped in the protective waters of the largest lagoon in the world, and encircled by 1,000 miles of pristine coral reef, New Caledonia is a cluster of islands where nothing happens at a fast pace. The iridescent blues of the sea and sky are ever present, and the French influence on this Polynesian paradise is everywhere, from the language to the croissants served at breakfast. A short thirty-five-minute boat ride from the capital, Nouméa, across the stunning blue waters of the lagoon, one of the world's tallest metal lighthouses stands proudly on its deserted coral island base. At 184 ft (56 m) tall, the bright white tower gleams in the South Pacific sunshine, surrounded by fantastic stretches of equally white sandy beach.

Amédée Lighthouse was France's first metal lighthouse. It was commissioned in 1862 to prevent the ships that carried prisoners to the island's penal colony from being wrecked upon entering the lagoon. The lighthouse was designed and built in Paris, where it towered above the city for several years, garnering praise and admiration before being divided up into 1,265 pieces and transported to New Caledonia to mark out the entrance of the Nouméa port through the Boulari channel.

Those day-trippers to Amédée Island, who make the effort to rouse themselves from their loungers on the beach, can climb the 247 cast-iron spiral steps to the top of the lighthouse. There, they will be rewarded with a breathtaking panorama over the beautiful turquoise water of the lagoon, the large reef, and the mountains of Grande Terre, the largest island of New Caledonia. The passage through the reef is also visible, as is the rusty red wreck of L'Ever Prosperity, which ground into the reef in 1970.

The rich and colorful reef system around the island is one of the most extensive in the world, and an ideal place to snorkel. Turtles are everywhere, and the third-largest population of dugongs makes these waters their home. Life is laid-back and peaceful in the undersea garden, designated a UNESCO World Heritage Site to protect the dramatic displays of coral diversity below the surface. The waters here are so clear that you can rent a stand-up paddleboard and see the turtles, fish, and coral without getting your hair wet. With the lighthouse standing guard silently from the shoreline, you can sit on your board in blissful quiet, letting the gentle waves carry you and your thoughts away.

INDEX

ABOUT THE AUTHOR

Victoria Ward is a writer and a Cognitive Hypnotherapist. She teaches mindfulness techniques and generally helps people to live happier lives.

Prior to establishing her practice in London's Harley Street, Victoria made her living as a journalist and magazine editor focusing on food and travel publications. Wanderlust called, and she left London to travel solo through South America, contributing articles to national newspapers and blogging as she traveled. It was a commission from a leading newspaper that led to her living for two years in one of the world's most remote places—Easter Island.

Victoria is an avid explorer and adventure-seeker whose travels have seen her whitewater raft down the Apurimac in Peru, bungee jump into the Mediterranean Sea, hitch-hike from the east to the west coast of America for charity, and throw herself out of a plane over Stonehenge.

Despite the thrill-seeking, Victoria is a self-confessed introvert and likes nothing more than finding a place of solitude to read and write.

IMAGE CREDITS

t = top, b = bottom, l = left, r = right, m = middle

Alamy: Danita Delimont 15; Michael Ventura 47; Patti McConville 58–59; Andrew Titmus 87; Michael Wheatley 91; Vast Photography 94; Michelle Valberg 98–99; Stefano Paterna 118t; James White / DanitaDelimont.com 122; J.W.Alker 123; Lee Dalton 137; Carlos Mora 139; Sergii Broshevan 142; Adwo 170; Jeremy Hoare 176; Design Pics Inc 183; Konrad Zelazowski 211; Hänel, Gerald 213; MAISANT Ludovic / hemis.fr 223; Paul Sampson / Travel 232; BARRERE Jean-Marc / hemis.fr 239; picturelibrary 241l; Pedro Ferrão Patricio 246–247; Neil Setchfield 248; B.O'Kane 255t; PHOTOMAX 255lb; Selbach, Arthur F. 282; GRANT ROONEY PREMIUM 292; Sjvaughts/Stockimo 294–295; Kymri Wilt 300; Hauke Dressler 320l; Kevpix/ 330; Robert Preston 342–343; Jeremy Woodhouse 348; Thomas Roetting 354; BOISVIEUX Christophe/ Hemis.fr 361l; Travel Asia 363; John Steele 364t; Ben Perry 378; graham jepson 384; Nazman Mizan 401b; Douglas Peebles 403; LOOK Die Bildagentur der Fotografen GmbH 404

Getty: National Geographic Magazines 2–3, 175, 372–373; Jordan Siemens 13; Jason Jaacks 21t; Pete Ark 25; www.sand3r.com 8, 33; CampPhoto 36–37; Pete Saloutos 38; Matt Anderson Photography 39; chapin31 40; Andrew Kornylak 46r; Glowimages 48; larrybraunphotography.com 50t; Sam Spicer 74; B. E. Butler 75; Julie Thurston 82–83; James + Courtney Forte 86t; Jad Davenport 129; Elizabeth Fernandez 134; Luiz Felipe Sahd 154–155; Pulsar Imagens 158–159; National Geographic Magazines Doug Chinnery 180; Oscar Wong 182l; Andrew Johns / EyeEm 192; Michael Betts 196; Caiaimage/Anna Wiewiora 199; Maskot 205; Richard Hylerstedt / EyeEm 208; Stanley Chen Xi, landscape and architecture photographer 234; Manuel Sulzer 252t; xavierarnau 256; Buena Vista Images 258; PATSTOCK 262; Andrea Ricordi 264–265; Witold Skrypczak 266; Marius Roman 268–269; Yunhao Liang / EyeEm 272–273; Philipp Chistyakov 274–275; Johnny Haglund 276; Getty 280, 303; Andrew Gunners 287; Vicki Jauron, Babylon and Beyond Photography 296; John Seaton Callahan 298; Bruno De Hogues 301; Ascent/PKS Media Inc. 324–325; Zephyr18 326b; xavierarnau 338; GCShutter 339; Maremagnum 355; Topic Images Inc. 359; Bloomberg 364b, 365; Michael Runkel/robertharding 375; S3studio 376; Education Images 379; Boy_Anupong 388; Givenworks 390; swissmediavision 396

iStock: SeppFriedhuber 4, 174t; Twphotos 12; Narvikk 21b; Traveler1116 77; Felixairphoto 84–85; Vladone 100; Tane-mahuta 131; Flavio Vallenari 132; ChandraDhas 140–141; Mlenny 164–165; DC_Colombia 172;; Martin-dm 210; RolfSt 252b; Martchan 278–279, 293; Gim42 284, 286; LordRunar 328; Paylessimages 361r; SeanPavonePhoto 366; Sean3810 367; Olga Kashubin 387; Global_Pics 402

Picfair Chris Dale 189; Jess Kraft 171

Shutterstock: Levent Konuk 22; Kushal Bose 43; Orhan Cam 72–73; Jean-Claude Caprara 96l; Nick Goetz 96r–97; BondRocketImages 108; RODRIGOBARRETO 151; Christian Vinces 153; canyalcin 162–163; Julietphotography 187; Rob Wilson 229; iascic 263; Pavel Baturin 277; Ekix 289; Mihai Speteanu 312; Philip Lange 329; Ryszard Stelmachowicz 350–351; YMZK-Photo 360; TY Lim 385t; Stanislav Fosenbauer 400l; ChameleonsEye 401t

Stocksy: BO BO 14; Molly Steele 20; Alicia Magnuson Photography 24t; L & S Studios 62; Raymond Forbes LLC 67t; Léa Jones 67rt; Alison Borrelli 67rb; RZ CREATIVE 78; Jake Elko 86b; Kristen Curette Hines 93t; ACALU Studio 112; Daniel Kim Photography 124;

Lucas Brentano 114–115, 166; Helen Sotiriadis 182r; Andy Lee 190–191; Kevin Faignaert 202; Leander Nardin 216; Christian Richter 228; Leander Nardin 229; Juri Pozzi 242; Luca Pierro 250; Good Vibrations Images 255r; Maja Topcagic 267; Gavin Hellier 281; Micky Wiswede 319;Holly Clark 346; Manuel Chillagano 362; Jaydene Chapman 374; Felix Hug 380; Joaquim Bel 386; Andrey Pavlov 395; Andrey Pavlov 397; Dominique Chapman 400r

Also: @wanderingjohnnn 30; Peter Stewart 7, 368–369; www.localkin. com 10; Lainey Morse/Founder of The Original Goat Yoga 16; www. wanderlusttours.com; Hanna Lysenko 18t; Carl Rice 18b; www.autocamp. com 19; www.brushcreekranch.com 26; Solitude Mountain Resort 28l; Hill & Dean PR 28r–29; Jimmy Warsham 32; duntonhotsprings.com 34; Hotel Emma 42; Zachary Hargrove 44–45; Leighanne's Photographs 46l; Jacqueline Oshiro www.underwaterclouds.com 51; Caters News Agency 53; NYPL/Jonathan Blanc 54; Nicholas Knight 55; Julie Turkewitz for Housing Works 56; Courtesy of Wave Hill. Credit: Joshua Bright 60–61; Antoine Buchet 64–65; Sophie Roux 67l; Roderick Aichinger 68; Christopher Little, courtesy of the Western Pennsylvania Conservancy 70; Longwood Gardens 70t&b; Gonca Tabanli Karns 80; Kelly Vo 81; Bryan Stockton Photography 88–89; Reuben Krabbe 90; Victoria Haack 93b; Gabrielle Milin 99l,r; @mr_ gardy 101; James Brittain 102–103; Melanie Coates 104–105; www. grupoencuentro.com.mx, photo by Edgar Lima 106–107; @SethAYates 110t; Yaan Wellness Energy Spa 110b; Kelsey Beriasch 111; kickthegrind 113; Steven W. Likens 116; @smileyouretraveling 117; Surfing Turtle Lodge 118; Marianne Jamadi 119; Gloriana Fernandez 120–121; @kellyharperphotography 126; Jumby Bay Island 127; Mandalay 128; Pamela Duffield 130; Madison Dorman 133; Ilse Geyskens 138; Mashpi Lodge 144–145; GalaPacific SA 146–147; Bianca Ledur 148; www. mondeando.com 149; Miguel Poyet 152; Kay Fochtmann 156; Uxua Casa Hotel & Spa/The Massey Partnership 157; Hotel Villa Bahia 160; Tuca Rëines 161; Hotel Hacienda Vira Vira 167; European Organisation for Astronomical Research in the Southern Hemisphere 168–169; Stefan Mahlknecht 178–179, 198, 255lt; Elaine O'Reilly 184; Kate Cameron, @crossbowphotography 186, 241t 241r, 290–291, 340–341, 347, 353; Max Colson 195; The Ivy Collection 197; Paul Edmundson 200; Peter Lundstrom 204; Luca Russo 206, 207b; Mara Robles Manahan 207t; Madal Cafe, Peter Repka 212; René Volfík, Dox Center for Contemporary Art 214; Gregor Lechner 218; Tourismus Salzburg GMBH 219; Hotel Honegg AG 220–221; Jack Harding 222; Lars Hauck 224; Sandy Tai 228; @makethisonecount 231; Paul K Porter 236; NELSON GARRIDO 244–245; Maurice Moeliker 249; Nebotcnick Skyscraper 260; Luke Bowles 261; Alice Inn Athens 270; Claire Christie 271t; Serendipity Villas 271b; Tongabezi 304; Francis Moult, for Mumbo Island www.kayakafrica.com 305; Sandibe EcoLodge 307; Mindy Roberts 308; Nicolas Leurident 309; Antoine Buchet 310; Richard Laburn 314; Tswalu Kalahari 317; Saxon Hotel 318l; Nirox Foundation Trust 318tr; The Living Roomn Pty Ltd 318br; Stuart Carter 320r; Six Senses Zil Pasyon 321; Reuben Krabbe 322; Feynan Eco-Lodge 326t; Antoine Buchet 331; Victoria Benz 332; Rafaela G. Vidal Amouin 333; Keemala Phuket 334–335, 370; www.bruisedpassports.com 336; Myla Alpaz 344; Mena Gobran 345; Christoph Theisinger 349; Casey Hamilton 356–357; Kamalaya Wellness Sanctuary & Holistic Spa 371; @littlemissbali 381; kickthegrind 383; Tracey Novak 385b; Sally Cranswick 393; Aro Ha Wellness Retreat 398–399; amélie gaschet 406

While every effort has been made to credit photographers, The Bright Press would like to apologize should there have been any omissions or errors, and would be pleased to make the appropriate correction for future editions of the book.